RETHINKING EARLY MODERN INDIA

Rethinking Early Modern India

edited by

RICHARD B. BARNETT

MANOHAR
2002

First published 2002

ISBN 81-7304-308-6

Published by
Ajay Kumar Jain for
Manohar Publishers & Distributors
4753/23 Ansari Road, Daryaganj
New Delhi 110002

Typeset by
A J Software Publishing Co. Pvt. Ltd.
New Delhi 110005

Printed at
Lordson Publishers Pvt. Ltd.
Delhi 110007

Contents

Illustrations

Maharaja Krisnacandra, Hinduism, and Kingship in the Contact Zone of Bengal by DAVID L. CURLEY

Symbolic Structural Constraints on the Adoption of European-style Military Technologies in the Eighteenth Century by STEWART N. GORDON

'Passionate Delineation and the Mainstream of Indian Painting': The Mughal Style and the Schools of Rajasthan by DANIEL J. EHNBOM

Piety, Religion and the Old Social Order in the Architecture of the Later Mughals and their Contemporaries by CATHERINE B. ASHER

Acknowledgements

OVER THE COURSE of putting this project together, the assistance of several important people and offices proved indispensable, and we are deeply grateful for their generosity. The conference at the University of Virginia was sponsored jointly by the Dean of the Faculty of Arts and Sciences, the Center for South Asian Studies, the Office of International Studies, and the Bhatta Urdu Studies Fund. Publication was underwritten by two generous anonymous donors, plus the Bhatta Urdu Studies Fund.

I thank the contributors for their patience while I sought to assist potential and actual chapter authors and address the production values of five disciplines. I am grateful to Shireen Moosvi, the then director of the Centre for Advanced Study in History at Aligarh Muslim University, and her colleagues for their hospitality during the time that the book was being edited. The Sesquicentennial Associateship Program at Virginia helped underwrite the final stages of the project, during which I spent a very pleasant term as Jefferson Visiting Professor at Downing College, Cambridge. Thanks go also to colleagues in the History Department of Jawaharlal Nehru University for their helpful comments on the project. Ramesh Jain, Ajay Jain, and B.N. Varma of Manohar Publishers & Distributors were available and gracious as the volume matured.

The authors of these chapters were joined at the conference by colleagues from around the world, whose commentaries and helpful criticisms aided the project: Kumkum Chatterjee, John Echeverri-Gent, David Gilmartin, Kathryn Hansen, Eugene F. Irschick, Aftab A. Kazi, John F. Richards, Rupa Roy, Moazzam Siddiqi, Peter Schmithenner, Pillarisetti Sudhir, David L. White, and especially Walter Hauser. Ruhi Grover ably mastered the conference logistics.

On behalf of all contributors and participants, I dedicate this volume to the memory of two good friends: Fritz Lehmann, one of the earliest revisionist historians of eighteenth-century India, and M. Athar Ali, who taught us, among many other things, that tenacity and collegiality are not mutually exclusive.

Charlottesville
June 2001

RICH BARNETT

Introduction

RICHARD B. BARNETT

THIS BOOK GREW OUT of a conference at the University of Virginia. Twenty years had passed since a similar workshop at Duke University, and nine since one at Warwick University. Looking at these two decades, it can safely be said that this era of India's history—its themes, boundaries, and debates—has effectively been rewritten and redefined. It was thus time for a modest reassessment of our progress. Whereas the Duke and Warwick meetings involved mainly historians, we planned the Virginia workshop to have an interdisciplinary flavor, inviting colleagues with diverse theoretical points of view, spanning three generations from South Asia, the U.K. and the U.S. The gathering in Charlottesville also showed that more scholars than ever study this period, treating issues that are accordingly in sharper focus. Students of the eighteenth century will not necessarily have smooth sailing from now on—alas, some have been lost overboard—but at least the choppy waters are no longer making us seasick. We were reminded during three glorious October days in the Piedmont that the disciplines of history, art history, architecture, political science, drama, and literature have much to teach each other.

Studying Eighteenth-Century India: Reckoning with Mughal Immortality

The eighteenth century has long been depicted as a major formative era for South Asian civilization. What has emerged in the last two decades is mainly a contextualizing de-emphasis on the role of European agency and a correspondingly greater focus on what Indians were thinking and doing. There is now general agreement that a radically different research agenda has been articulated for this era. Virtually all recent scholarly treatments of the period 1724-1835, plus a few foundational works before that,[1] characterize it as one of economic growth or continuity, robust cultural activity, political and environmental pragmatism, and a surprising amount of resistance to European interference.[2] The major exception to this consists of works on political events in Bengal, but as revisionists point out, Bengal is a special case and cannot typify all of India.[3]

Such a phalanx of revisionist views, although varied—a few by now even somewhat long in the tooth—challenge a conventional typology, or stereotype. This older and surprisingly persistent point of view stigmatizes the century as rife with abrupt discontinuities, brittle in political loyalties and structures, exploitative of a suffering and silent peasantry, rapacious in both war and peace, hedonistic in urban lifestyle and conspicuous consumption, and decadent in artistic and literary expression—a tradition echoing Georgian and Victorian imperial historians, but shared by most nationalist scholars of the period and, for different reasons, espoused by some present-day Marxists. Let us try to untangle these diverse strains of historical thought, which to a very large degree, determine the way that most educated South Asians view the period even today.

First, we need to define and delimit the eighteenth century. The period 1724-1835 was admittedly an era of transition between the Mughal and the British empires. Many would now say, however, that it was much more than merely that. The former date, as we will recall, was when Nizam ul-Mulk, after a surprisingly long time trying, including lecturing Emperor Mohammad Shah 'Rangila' (the Dandy) to his face, finally gave up on reforming or reconstituting the political black hole that Delhi had become. Abandoning Delhi, he sought his fortunes in the Deccan, founding the greatest and longest-lasting Mughal successor state, Hyderabad. And the latter date more generally marks the ideological ratification of the British military domination that had been acknowledged a generation earlier. Moreover, Indian producers and consumers were feeling the harsh effects of the world economy, Ranjit Singh was declaring dolefully in Lahore that the map of India would become completely red (i.e. British), colonial elites were staking out visible professional terrain in the Presidency cities, Macaulay's Minute on Education asserted European intellectual hegemony, and Indian arms could no longer resist the assertions of Company rule within the remaining pieces of the empire that Bentinck and Council targeted for benign inclusion in the grand scheme. The major objection to this periodization is that the century of transition was experienced in different ways in different parts of the subcontinent. Most revisionists grant that the realms of Bengal and Bahawalpur, of Arcot and Ajmer, and of Patna and Panjab are indeed dynamically and temporally different. The processes of segmentalization and reconstitution, of intellectual redefinition, of literary advancement, of social and religious self-statement and reform, and of military and commercial realignment, do however form common patterns between these dates.

The prevailing, indeed entrenched view of this era has for two centuries been harshly negative for several reasons, the two most important being imperial justifications for the Raj (the British rescued India from chaos, sloth, ignorance, and decadence), and Indian nationalist explanations for the loss of sovereignty (post-Mughal rulers and elites were lazy, selfish, confused, and divided, allowing the British to take over). A variant on both is the Marxist conception that the British Raj was the vehicle for replacing feudalism with capitalism, an inevitable and even temporarily welcome stage in the Hegelian development of human progress in the wider world. These are but a few of the historiographical issues embedded in such treatments, mostly products of the rhetorics that come from a hegemonic British social, scholarly, and political presence. It might help our understanding of what the revisionists have been up against if we delve briefly into the pedigree of this older view of the era.

The foundational text of what I will call the dismissive approach to the century is Charles Grant's 1792 Evangelical broadside, 'Observations on the State of Society Among the Asiatic Subjects of Great Britain, Especially with respect to Morals, and on the Means of Improving It'. One of its fundamental axioms is that Indian society was 'decadent'. This label, with its many synonyms and glosses, was indiscriminately applied to all of Indian society by Alexander Dow and James Mill as well as Charles Grant, reflecting the growing social power differential arising in the new colonial situation, and giving ideological justification to the British takeover of some Indian regions by that time. Europe, seen as technically but also morally superior, was being credited for rescuing an effete, chaotic, morally bankrupt, and self-destructive civilization from itself and leading it down the path to modernity and enlightenment.[4] This tract, reprinted decennially in the *Parliamentary Papers* each time the East India Company charter came up for renewal, is widely acknowledged as the most vicious and demeaning attack by a representative of one citied civilization on all the members of another. Marx and his followers eagerly accepted this teleology, following James Mill, from whom he learned much of his misinformation about India. Marx saluted European capital as the 'progressive impetus' that would 'liberate' India and escort it 'into History'.[5]

The imperialist historians were, and to an extent are, trying to justify the British Empire in India by contrasting it favorably with what allegedly went before, a project that involved certain exaggerations, emphases, and blind spots. A revealing example of this is W.W. Hunter's article on Indian history in the 1881 edition of the *Encyclopaedia Britannica*, which portrays early modern India as despotic, decadent, and divided, hardly mentions any features of Indian life except the dryly political, and lovingly traces how it was emancipated by British conquest.[6] Versions of the imperialist view are still widely found, especially in textbooks, including, in diluted form, Wolpert's *A New History of India*.[7] Much of Percival Spear's highly influential writing targets the century as one of chaos and darkness, from which the united, logical, disciplined and peacemaking British rescued India.[8]

C.A. Bayly and others of the so-called Cambridge School, who are anything but imperialist historians (although most regard empire as a useful field of discourse), have been criticized for portraying the century through the lives, experiences, and motivations of middle-level commercial, agricultural, and service gentries—not only reminding us of their importance, but asserting that the influence, at those levels, of both the Raj and the Mughal Empire before it, has been vastly overstated. Critics of this approach, mainly in India, seem to be agitated about it for three interrelated reasons: first, many have devoted their lives to the study of the Mughals, and resent the implied peripheralization of that great empire and its elites; second, Baniyas and pen-pushers were often mendacious and uncultured and should not be taken to typify any era of Indian history; third, the Cambridge writers seem almost to be saying that the trading, banking, and scribal classes invited or even helped the British to come in and rule—a grossly unacceptible proposition.

Some pre-independence Indian professional historians—conventionally called 'nationalist' historians—could not stomach the Georgian/Victorian imperialist view of the period, so accordingly made a more palatable set of assertions. Yes, they said, of course there was weakness and egotism, anarchy and self-indulgence in this century, but it was a momentary lapse in an otherwise vigilant, patriotic, centralized, ordered Indian polity, which allowed the expansionist British access to its raw materials, markets, manpower and treasure, the outward flow of which drained India in order to sustain the British Empire for one and a half centuries. This is, to an extent, a 'Mughal-centric' view of the period, although it produced numerous laudatory works on regional rulers such as Nizam ul-Mulk, Shuja ud-Daulah, and Tipu Sultan. The product of five generations of South Asian scholars trained in the historiography of imperialism, if not Orientalism, it survives in the best universities of India , Pakistan and elsewhere, and is widely accepted as an unchallenged paradigm by the educated South Asian public.

One difference between those who see discontinuity and decadence, and those who see signs of vitality and adaptation beneath the imperial veneer, is generational. The leading scholar of the Mughals, whose influence has been profound during a career under seige by reactionary forces, has yet to amend his view that the eighteenth century was a period of 'reckless rapine, anarchy and foreign conquest'.[9] Our late friend and colleague M. Athar Ali, long a fixture at Aligarh, echoed this view, dismissing portrayals by Perlin, Bayly, Wink, and Muzaffar Alam of the continuities which undermine the assumptions of imperialist and nationalist historians alike. He concluded one of several articles on this issue as follows: '. . . the conventional bifurcation, as presented in old textbooks [of the 1757 Battle of Plassey abruptly proving British hegemony, is] far closer to the realities of social and economic history of India than the many recent theories endeavoring to present us with vistas of continuity and progress in that troubled century'.[10] Dozens of South Asian textbooks still reinforce this typology, rehearsing the viewpoint taken long ago by such as Ishwari Prasad's *India in the Eighteenth Century.*[11]

The counterview, launched in the late 1970s, is slowly being accepted, even among some Indian Marxists. Among other things, it seeks out and interprets more indigenous narratives, issues, and categories of historicization, especially in Indian-language sources, seeking a wider perspective than those allowed by Mughal and imperial viewpoints. It also assesses the relevance of the global context—economic, political, and technological forces that impinged upon, and that were often transformed by post-Mughal South Asian regimes and social groups.

I must make it clear that this counterview poses radically different agendas from that held by those who demean, stigmatize, or dismiss the eighteenth century. Singing different verses from the same song, imperialist and nationalist writers were, and are, trying to locate the causes of imperial decline, and by implication follow a problematic that, by explaining 'what went wrong', echoes the agonized distress calls of a dispossessed Mughal aristocracy that was witnessing the collapse of a stunningly grand military, administrative, cultural, and ethical success story. The old paradigm looks back in nostalgic sadness, if not anger; it continues to rehearse and lament a grand tragedy. In its vicarious helplessness at the alleged *Gotterdammerung* of an entire civilization, it seems ruefully and even pathetically to wish it everlasting life. This conservative longing for permanence recalls Milan Kundera's famous observation, 'Man reckons with immortality, and forgets to reckon with death'.[12]

Beyond the Gloomy Paradigm of Decline

Several older explanations for this decline, tautologically reinforcing the negative view of the period, have had their turns on center stage, going back two centuries. They involve theories that have long since been discarded by academics, but are still embraced by the educated public in South Asia, such as Oriental Despotism (the personal traits and morals of a despot determine the success of state and society); the alleged communalism of Aurangzeb (non-Muslims became alienated, bringing down the empire); the militant nativism of the Maratha Hindu Padpadshahi (true Indians brought foreign Mughal rule to its knees); and the failure of Mughal pacification strategies and tactics in the Deccan (the cumbersome Mughal army was helpless against guerrilla tactics).

These theories of 'decline', with their implied essentialisms about Indian civilization and its resulting vulnerability to a rescuing and revivifying West, constitute Round One in the debate on the eighteenth century. This lasted from 1790 to about 1960, and was dominated by both amateur and professional scholars looking mainly at sources produced by a distressed, desperate, and doomed Mughal aristocracy and its literary clientage.

Round Two in the debate, *c.* 1960-80, although based on a wider cross-section of original sources and therefore correspondingly more sophisticated, was however also preoccupied with 'decline', and produced the following three arguments that retain enormous influence on this subfield:

First, according to Irfan Habib, the three-way contradictions of exploitation and contestation—between and among ruling class, hereditary landholding classes, and cultivators—produced chronic endemic distress, which exhausted over time the ability of the system's participants to contain it. Revolts, migrations, administrative breakdowns, elite flight, fiscal laxity, and economic disruption ensued. In other words, the system dug its own grave because structurally it was unworkable in the long run.[13]

Second, Satish Chandra presents the view that after Aurangzeb died in 1707, a divided and factionally frenzied nobility failed to keep the system working in a destructive pursuit of power at the centre, while the provinces were breaking away under the leadership of those fed up with mendacity and short-sightedness in Delhi. Even crown lands were exhausted in the rush for preferment and temporary advantage. In other words, the greedy, panicked manoeuvering of the nobility in the early part of the century produced fatal strains in an otherwise workable system.[14]

Third, throughout the four major 'gunpowder' empires—Mughal, Safavid, Ottoman, and Uzbek—roughly the same thing was happening. Thus the historian needs to look at changes in trade, maritime dominance, the influx of precious metals from the New World, and inflation, to determine common patterns if any there are. For young scholars who might wish to address this, there is the immense problem of language control; at least nine research languages are involved in such a broad sweep of comparative history.[15] One important attempt at explaining the eighteenth century throughout these empires and beyond, one largely neglected outside the realm of Middle East studies, is Marshall G.S. Hodgson's *The Venture of Islam*, vol. 3, *The Gunpowder Empires and Modern Times*.[16] To summarize his sweeping world-historical argument in one sentence: owing to the ability of northern Europe to remain relatively isolated from invasions and severe weather, to borrow Asian ideas and commercial networks, and to wrench precious metals from the New World, it had developed by 1700 a morally neutral culture of standardization, precision, and information sharing that enabled both the Industrial Revolution and imperialism to occur, and accordingly produced chronic differentials in social power between it and the rest of the world, which could not be matched, because of the despoiling effects of colonialism until after European empires receded.

These major statements are not mutually exclusive, and although they have been added to and refined, they have been only incidentally undermined by the revisionists. There seems to be a consensus within Round Two of late, focusing on what is called the Crisis of the Jagir System. This has several variants, including the arguments that the Mughals ran out of land to assign in jagirs, that the empire had enough land but could not allot it efficiently enough in newly-annexed Golkonda to all claimants, and that the amounts of jagirs thought to be needed to satisfy the demands of the nobility mounted too swifly for the administration to handle them (the '*yak aanaar, sad bimaar*' argument).[17] One is reminded here of Peter Hardy's insightful observation, that the aristocracy were suffering from 'status inflation', and needed more and more resources to keep them satisfied with their elite station in life.[18]

Round Three in the debate—1980 to the present—challenges all of the above, and was neatly summed up by the late Burton Stein:

> Most writers who have contributed to this revision of early modern Indian history [M. Alam, R. Barnett, C. Bayly, S. Bayly, S. Bhattacharya, S. Gordon, D. Ludden, F. Perlin, S. Subrahmanyam, D. Washbrook, A. Wink, and himself] agree that the rural economy over most of 18th-century India enjoyed substantial, if uneven, growth notwithstanding both the destructive wars culminating in those which won the subcontinent for the British, and the supposed political disorder in many areas. It is claimed that new, smaller states with efficient tax-gathering procedures replaced the Mughal military imperial order, that market networks proliferated and became to a degree interlinked, that a more prosperous agriculture came into being with increased commodity production as a result of rural investments by the revenue farmers of the time, that all of this was buoyed up by an ever-increasing level of international trade in which Indian artisans, merchants and especially bankers played key and lucrative roles, and that this phase of political economy obtained until the first quarter of the 19th century. Such a view clashes with the assumptions of nationalist historians, who take it that the imposition of British rule in the middle of the 18th century was a determining economic as well as a political disjuncture.[19]

Round Three, in other words, is only marginally concerned with why the empire fragmented, which may never be agreed upon, and more with what actually happened during and after imperial segmentation, and with the nature of state and society in those important regional and smaller local state systems that not only survived it but flourished for many generations. It can thus be called, in contrast to the dismissive view, the pragmatic approach to the historical problems of the century.[20]

What the revisionists have been saying is that a different way of looking at the period might be more fruitful as well as more faithful to a wider cross-section of Indian sources. Victorian dogmatic presumptions about history, humankind, or Indian essentialism or particularism, are to be noted and bypassed. Should we not follow our own advice to our students, and simply let all evidence that passes rigorous tests speak for itself? Moreover, why not ask unusual or even outrageous questions, such as: Does the fact that we talk of the century mostly in terms of imperial 'decline' itself determine the results of our enquiry? Are we victims, epistemologically speaking, of our own rhetoric or labels?[21] Was there really a systemic civilizational failure, or simply the conclusion to a great era of imperial success? The Mughal Empire had been maintained successfully as an agrarian-based military despotism, with a patrimonial-bureaucratic administrative structure, with no military defeats in open battle, and with a splendid legacy of material and intellectual creativity. Is it reasonable to presume that such a success be sustained forever? Mughals stayed with the familiar because it had succeeded so well, refusing to adapt to new conditions of massive fiscal, scientific, and managerial innovation the world was thrusting on them. This refusal cannot be interpreted as stupid, weak, morally bankrupt, or treasonous; it thus was not a 'failure' but an almost inevitable conclusion to a lasting, dazzling civilizational achievement. This conclusion was accompanied, no doubt, by the usual regional and local readjustments that had characterized all previous post-imperial eras. We must free ourselves from the late Mughal elite view of imperial segmentation, which was naturally one of lamentation, as the *ancien régime* gave way to forces beyond its control. One major expression of this elite view is the *s̄hahr-i aashob* genre of Urdu poetry; composed by exiles from Delhi, who had lost their patronage during this period, it was naturally full of foreboding, terror, and doomsaying.[22]

The late Professor Athar Ali, addressing yet another explanation for 'decline', argued that imperial and eighteenth-century Islamic society had no use for science or technology beyond that needed to collect surplus agrarian and commercial wealth.[23] This is no doubt true for science as such. But the elites in the new post-Mughal regimes had attitudes to technology and rationalism just as robust as those of the old. Recent research by one of our contributors, also at Aligarh, indicates that the technicalistic [or reason-based, *falsafi*] content of elite education was reinforced under the revised *Dars-i Nizamiyya* of Mulla Nizamuddin Sahalvi and his colleagues in the seventeenth to nineteenth-centuries Firangi Mahal in Lucknow, and then was widely adopted across north India.[24] Thus the courtiers of Mohammad Shah 'Rangila' (r.1719-48 CE)—and those of the regional courts—were no less well versed in metallurgy, chemistry, agrarian management, cost-accounting, maths, astronomy, craft-related sciences, and hydrology than were those of the high Mughal period, who also were keenly interested in technology, if not science. So labelling the century a 'cultural failure of the Islamic world'[25] is a prefiguring of modernity, judging the actions of historical societies by the standards of our own, and finding them wanting by comparison. It also is what the British wanted us to think about the precolonial period: after all, they had to have some 'improving' ideology to justify their colonial exploitation. We should, to echo a platitude long current in our discipline, be wary of the Whig interpretation of history.

Eighteenth-century South Asian studies have, in sum, matured enormously. Most active scholars now consider it a foundational era in the formation of South Asian civilization, especially in areas such as scholarly preservation, environmental awareness and engineering, social and religious reform, political roles for women, religious and communal accommodation, commercial institution-building, and the development of regional and local political identities. Britain's seniormost eighteenth-century historian, now Emeritus at the University of London, deftly and delightedly highlights the more recent additions to the revisionist view of the era.[26]

Thus early modern India's revisionists are not laying out a theory of Mughal decline at all. They are responding to growing evidence of continuity rather than discontinuity, of local and regional economic growth, of ecological pragmatism and political realism on the part of one regime after another, of entrepreneurial activity indigenous to India and not imported from outside. The new impetus of eighteenth- and early nineteenth-century research is free from Eurocentric, dogmatic, prefiguring, Mughal-centric, and essentialist viewpoints, and increasingly concerned with actual indigenous Indian pragmatism and realism from the ground up—a heterogeneous vision with multiple discourses and much tolerance of ambiguity. We revisionists are not reckoning exclusively with immortality; we acknowledge the immortality of Mughal accomplishments, but instead of obsessing about the loss of empire, we seek to appreciate the emergence of a rich variety of highly pragmatic social and political formations that could, by the 1720s, emerge as young plants where before grew only the mammoth imperial banyan tree.

The first section of papers boldly addresses several related issues within the realm of hardboiled political action, or what regimes decided to do with their material and symbolic resources in post-imperial situations of functional autonomy. All four authors focus on how relatively small groups of people, whether rulers, regional elites, minor land controllers, or foreign and Indian merchants—all 'below' the level of later Mughal nobility—conducted themselves in competition, collaboration, and accommodation. The reader is invited to ask, do these complicated transactions portray either brittleness, despondency, panic or paralysis as imperial structures were replaced by regional and local initiatives? What degree of newness, novelty, or innovation did these actors accomplish? Do we see unique eighteenth-century political idioms developing, business as usual, or a combination of both?

Edward Haynes shows the indispensability of lineage identity in the building of the Kachhawaha polity and its aware usage within the ideology of rightful rulership, accompanied by the sharing of material resouces and status, and the judicious use of coercion. Demographically only 1.4 per cent of the region's population, this clan carefully mapped the kinship networks within which Rajasthan's centuries-old conflict and co-optation took place. By asserting and investing its genetic code and building its family reputation, the clan established its legitimacy with impressive efficiency.

A different population mix may have determined equally regional values for lineage identity within Krisnacandra's rule of Nadia in Bengal, and David Curley argues that this regime aimed for both inclusivity and competitiveness as it asserted new modes of identity while withdrawing from virtually all military pursuits. Court poets developed imaginary theological and ethical debates between Muslim luminaries and local pandits, remarkably informed and often appreciative points being made by both sides. Court architects designed popular temple structures—which Curley illustrates with his own photographs—incorporating Islamic elements early in the reign, and European elements by 1762, while the raja launched a revival of Vedic ritual observance. Not only was this a more unitary and welcoming set of meanings for Hinduism, adeptly tailored to compete with his Vaiṣṇava neighbours, but on the strength of the raja's 'ability to re-imagine the sacred basis of his authority', enabled him to stand up first to Nawab Mir Jafar at the time of Plassey (1757), and then to the East India Company and their puppet, Mir Qasim, during Bengal's rapacious dual government.

Iqbal Husain then offers up a microstudy of agrarian rights and administration in two districts of what is now western Uttar Pradesh. Imperial appointments to revenue-collection rights evaporated in the second quarter of the century but were not abruptly withdrawn. Landed families, plus a few enterprising newcomers, managed through various devices to weave a safety net for themselves by acquiring local rights as hereditary magnates in the absence of imperial appointments. These devices included outright purchase of such rights, obtaining written confirmation of continued rights from superior authority upon the death of a landholder (especially interesting in the case of Aizaz Khan's widows, who approached Asaf ud-Daulah for such in 1796), and occasionally the threat of violence. Noteworthy in the process is the implicit recognition of the landed family's former service to a now-defunct regime *v.* the regional rulers' concern for the potential added security of the new regime, balanced further against the need to maximize productivity and state income.

The last chapter in this section is a persuasive regional corrective to notions of eighteenth-century continuity, whether economic or political, focusing on Bengal's trade and the machinations of private British merchants leading up to the conquest of the province in 1757. In it, Sushil Chaudhury aims a wrecking ball at the so-called Cambridge School, insisting that private trading interests and competition with the French and the Dutch, not implicit overtures from Indian collaborators, brought the East India Company to confront Bengal's ruling elites. Measuring the health of the economy through a populist lens (prices of more heavily traded 'wage-goods', i.e. coarse rice, not the varieties found in wealthy kitchens; *khasa* and *malmal* textiles rather than the finer weaves), he pulls the rug out from under the view that economic distress had so undermined the regime that Bengal was ripe for a radical change. In other words, Bengal was not conquered commercially through the hearts and minds of those itching to be rid of the old order, but militarily and for (largely private) commercial reasons.

The next three chapters, enriched by illusti ations, remind us that artistic and architectural sensibilities can profoundly broaden our understandings of important changes and tendencies. Stewart Gordon, in a revised and expanded version of an article that appeared after the Virginia conference in *The Indian and Social History Review,* XXXV: 3 (July-Sept. 1998), traces the dynamics and socio-economic consequences in Indian states that borrowed European military managerial technology, specifically infantry and light artillery, which ousted the land-based and honour-saturated 'ethos of horse service', or indigenous cavalry. Those regimes adapting the new did not always succeed, but the process of adjustment gradually altered the age-old relationship between military duty and control of ancestral real estate.

Daniel Ehnbom gives us a critical magnifier for a detailed look at the relationship between Mughal and Rajput artistic creativity, gently deconstructing received wisdom that has somewhat rigidly tended to separate these painting styles and modes of production. Not only the archival evidence from the atelier, but more importantly the substance of the works themselves, is brought to bear to analyse mutual influence, continuity, and appreciative imitation. His theme is further substantiated by fellow art historian Catherine Asher, whose multiregional study of eighteenth- and early nineteenth-century architectural investment reveals a surprising degree of syncretic purpose. Most of the buildings of this era, especially Hindu temples and residences, were privately designed and built, not state sponsored. As we can see from her photographic archive, they show a consistent tendency to innovate in the direction of cosmopolitan, composite Indo-Islamic styles, clearly stating a populist preference for a comfortably Indian built environment. These two papers deepen and enrich Hermann Goetz's well-known celebration in the 1930s of a post-Mughal sensibility that was cheerfully immune to twentieth-century communalisms.

The final section traces three related contributions of early modern India to the present day, namely the development of a mature literary tradition in Urdu, the use of technology, and the rise of a pan-Indian genre of dramatic performance. Carla Petievich gives us a close look at the de-feminization, or at least re-genderization, of Urdu usages, from *rekhti* and Dakani to a Persianized, masculine, neo-Islamic and therefore 'non-decadent' vehicle. Iqbal Ghani Khan looks closely at the way Afghan adventurers in Rohilkhand conceptualized and incorporated technical innovations in military, agrarian, and craft sectors, based on their mastery of Mughal precedent and a flexible, pragmatic view of local application. And finally, Afroz Taj celebrates the conceptualization, production, critical success, and later impact of Awadh's most famous work of dramatic creativity, the *Indar Sabha.* In inspiration, thematic construction, diction and subsequent revival, this major drama revealed and strengthened a legacy of harmony and accommodation among north India's communities that can perhaps typify the best that this era achieved.

Styles of annotation and source referencing specific to each writer's discipline have been followed in this anthology, for authenticity as well as convenience.

NOTES

1. I refer to those stalwarts Hermann Goetz, *The Crisis of Indian Civilization in the 18th and early 19th Century* (Calcutta: Calcutta University, 1938); B.S. Cohn, 'Political Systems in Eighteenth-Century India: The Banaras Region', *Journal of the American Oriental Society*, 82: 3 (Sept. 1962): 312-19, reprinted as a chapter in his *An Anthropologist Among the Historians*; Satish Chandra, *Parties and Politics at the Mughal Court, 1700-1740* (Aligarh: AMU, Department of History, 1959); Zahir Uddin Malik, 'Some Aspects of Mughal Culture during the First Half of the 18th Century', *Studies in Islam* (Jan. 1965): 17-44; and Ian J. Catenach, 'Some Continuities in Indian History in the Eighteenth and Early Nineteenth Centuries', *New Zealand Journal of History*, 3: 1 (1969): 1-13.
2. Burton Stein, 'A Decade of Historical Efflorescence', *South Asia Research* 10: 2 (Nov. 1990): 125-38, focusing almost entirely on eighteenth-century issues, assesses the early portion of this scholarship. The main works in this early revisionist effort are R.B. Barnett, *North India Between Empires: Awadh, the Mughals, and the British, 1720-1801* (Berkeley: University of California Press, 1980; rpt. edn., Delhi: Manohar, 1987; rpt. edn., Lahore: Vanguard, 1988); Frank Perlin, 'Proto-industrialization and Pre-colonial South Asia', *Past and Present*, 98 (1983); and C.A. Bayly, *Rulers, Townsmen, and Bazaars: North Indian Society in the Age of British Expansion* (Cambridge: CUP, 1983).

   Also see C.A. Bayly, *Indian Society and the Making of the British Empire* (The New Cambridge History of India, II, 1) (Cambridge: CUP, 1988); Stewart N. Gordon, *The Marathas, 1600-1818.* The New Cambridge History of India, II, 3 (Cambridge: CUP, 1993); Satish Chandra, 'The 18th Century in India: Its Economy and the Role of the Marathas, the Jats, the Sikhs and the Afgthans', S.G. Desukar Lecture, 1982, Centre for Social Studies, Calcutta, 1986; André Wink, *Land and Sovereignty in the Maratha Svarajya* (Cambridge: CUP, 1986); Sunil Chander, 'From a Pre-Colonial Order to a Princely State: Hyderabad in Transition, c. 1748-1865', Ph.D. thesis, Cambridge University, 1987; Burton Stein, 'Arrested Development: But When and Where?', in Clive Dewey, ed., *Arrested Development in India: the Historical Dimension* (Riverdale, Md.: Riverdale, 1988); and Muzaffar Alam, *The Crisis of Empire in Mughal North India: Awadh and the Punjab, 1707-1748* (Delhi: OUP, 1986).

   More recent works accelerating this revision are Jos Gommans, *The Rise of the Indo-Afghan Empire, c. 1710-1780* (Leiden: Brill, 1995); Veena Sachdeva, *Polity and Economy in the Punjab during the Eighteenth Century* (Delhi: Manohar, 1993); Peter Hardy, 'Approaches to pre-modern Indo-Muslim historical writing: some reconsiderations in 1990-91', in Peter Robb, ed., *Society and Ideology: Essays in South Asian History Presented to Professor K.A. Ballhatchet* (Delhi: OUP, 1993), 49-72; Kumkum Chatterjee,

Merchants, Politics and Society in Early Modern India: Bihar, 1733-1820 (Leiden: Brill, 1996); Iqbal Husain, *The Rise and Decline of the Rohilla Chieftaincies in 18th-Century India* (Delhi: OUP, 1994); Kate Brittlebank, *Tipu Sultan's Search for Legitimacy: Islam and Kingship in a Hindu Domain* (Delhi: OUP, 1997); Muhammad Umar, *Islam in Northern India During the Eighteenth Century* (Delhi: OUP, 1993); Richard M. Eaton, *The Rise of Islam and the Bengal Frontier, 1204-1760* (Berkeley: University of California Press, 1993); and Iqbal Ghani Khan, *Agriculture, Warfare and the Crafts: Technical Knowledge and the Elites in 18th-Century North India* (Delhi: Manohar, forthcoming).

3. For a reminder that Bengal is not India, and that no region of eighteenth-century South Asia may safely be ignored, see Barun De, 'Problems of the Study of Indian History: with Particular Reference to Interpretations of the 18th Century', Occasional Paper 116, Centre for Studies in Social Sciences, University of Calcutta, 1989; revised and expanded in his General Presidential Address, *Proceedings, Indian History Congress*, Karnatak University, Dharwar Session, 1989 (Delhi: Indian History Congress, 1989), pp. 1-56.

   Recent arguments for discontinuity are Sushil Chaudhury, *From Prosperity to Decline: Eighteenth Century Bengal* (Delhi: Manohar, 1995), especially his Chapter 11 and conclusion; and John McLane, *Land and Kingship in 18th-century Bengal* (Delhi: OUP, 1993). For a counter-view, based on an all-India focus, see Lakshmi Subramanian and Rajat K. Ray, 'Merchants and Politics: from the Great Mughals to the East India Company', in Dwijendra Tripathi, ed., *Business and Politics in India: a Historical Perspective* (Delhi: OUP, 1991), pp. 19-85.

   Occupying a middle ground, by arguing that even in Bengal and the lower Gangetic Valley, the British succeeded largely by adapting to, rather than overthrowing, Indian economic and political conditions, are Peter J. Marshall, *East Indian Fortunes: the British in Bengal in the Eighteenth Century* (Oxford: OUP, 1976), and Sudipta Sen, *Empire of Free Trade: the East India Company and the Making of the Colonial Marketplace* (Philadelphia: University of Pennsylvania Press, 1998).

4. For the definitive treatment of Grant's career, including the emotional and mental upheaval leading up to his writing the tract, see Ainslee T. Embree, *Charles Grant and British Rule in India* (New York: Columbia University Press, 1962).

5. Quoted in Burton Stein and David Washbrook, 'Eighteenth-century India: Historiography, Perspectives and Propositions', a working paper for the University of Warwick conference on eighteenth-century South Asia, August 1985. For an accessible overview of Marx's assessment, see S. Naqvi, 'Marx on Pre-British Indian Society and Economy', *Indian Economic and Social History Review*, IX: 4 (Dec. 1972): 380-412.

6. *Encyclopaedia Britannica,* 9th edn. (Edinburgh: Adam and Charles Black, 1881).
7. Stanley Wolpert, *A New History of India* (New York, Delhi: OUP, 1977 and several reprints). Wolpert is not an apologist for the Raj by any means, but his treatment of the early modern period clearly echoes some of the assumptions of Dow, Grant, and Mill.
8. Percival Spear, *A History of India,* vol. 2 (London, Baltimore: Penguin, 1965); *The Oxford History of Modern India* (Oxford: OUP, 1966); *Master of Bengal: Clive and his India* (London: Thames and Hudson, 1975); *Twilight of the Mughals* (Oxford: OUP, 1962).
9. Irfan Habib, *The Agrarian System of Mughal India* (Bombay: Asia Publishing House, 1963), p. 351.
10. M. Athar Ali, 'Recent Theories of Eighteenth Century India', *Indian Economic and Social History Review,* XIII: 1-2 (1989).
11. (Allahabad: Chugh, 1973).
12. *Immortality,* transl. from the Czech by Peter Kussi (New York: Grove, 1991; rpt. edn., New York: Harper, 1992), p. 74.
13. *The Agrarian System of Mughal India.*
14. *Parties and Politics at the Mughal Court.*
15. Dutch, Portuguese, French, German, Persian, Ottoman Turkish, Arabic, Urdu and Russian at the minimum.
16. (Chicago, 1974 and 1977), vol. 3, pp. 134-222. Cf. M. Athar Ali, 'The Passing of Empire: The Mughal Case', *Modern Asian Studies,* 9: 3 (1975): 385-96.
17. 'There is only one pomegranate to heal a hundred sick men'. Khafi Khan, *Muntakhab al-lubaab, c.* 1733 CE.
18. Peter Hardy, 'Comment', in response to Michael N. Pearson, 'Shivaji and the Decline of the Mughal Empire', and John F. Richards, 'The Imperial Crisis in the Deccan', in 'Symposium: Decline of the Mughal Empire', *Journal of Asian Studies,* 35: 1 (Feb. 1976): 221-64.
19. Burton Stein, 'A Decade of Historical Efflorescence', pp. 132-3.
20. The contrast between the old and new paradigms is neatly drawn out by Andrea Hintze in *The Mughal Empire and its Decline: An Interpretation of the Sources of Social Power* (Aldershot: Ashgate, 1997), the most comprehensive and insightful treatment to date of the historiography of eighteenth-century South Asia. See especially her Chapters I, II, VII and XI.

    The most welcome and pragmatic treatment of the period by textbook writers to date is Sugata Bose and Ayesha Jalal, *Modern South Asia: History, Culture, Political Economy* (London: Routledge, 1998; rpt. edn., Lahore: Sang-e-Meel, 1998).
21. For a recent treatment of how a prefiguring notion of decline still resonates and persists in several distinct strands of modern Western

thought, see Arthur Herman, *The Idea of Decline in Western History* (New York: Free Press, 1997), which shows how a long-standing linguistic pattern can influence rhetorics from writers as diverse as de Gobineau and Du Bois.

22. For this genre, see Carla R. Petievich, 'Poetry of the Declining Mughals: the Shahr Ashob', *Journal of South Asian Literature*, 25, no. 1 (1990): 99-110; Kumkum Chatterjee, *Merchants, Politics, and Society in Early Modern India: Bihar, 1733-1820* (Leiden: E. J. Brill, 1996), Chap. 9; Fritz Lehmann, 'The Eighteenth-Century Transition in India: Responses of Some Bihar Intellectuals', Ph.D. thesis, University of Wisconsin, 1967; Fritz Lehmann, 'Shah Ayat Allah "Jauhri" and his Shahr Ashob', *Abdul Karim Sahitya-Visarad Commemoration Volume* (Dhaka: Asiatic Society of Bangladesh, 1971), pp. 73-82; Ralph Russell and Khurshidul Islam, *Three Mughal Poets* (Cambridge, Mass.: Harvard University Press, 1968).
23. M. Athar Ali, 'Passing of Empire'.
24. I.G. Khan, *Agriculture, Warfare and the Crafts: Technical Knowledge and the Elites in Eighteenth-Century North India* (Delhi, forthcoming).
25. Athar Ali, 'Passing', p. 395.
26. Peter J. Marshall, 'Reappraisal: The Rise of British Power in Eighteenth-Century India', *South Asia*, XIX: 1 (June 1996): 71-6. See also David A. Washbrook, 'Progress and Problems: South Asian Economic and Social History c. 1720-1860', *Modern Asian Studies*, 22: 1 (1988): 57-96.

PART I
Statecraft

Lineage, State, and Symbolism of Rule in Late-Eighteenth-Century Eastern Rajputana

EDWARD S. HAYNES

The Devas (Gods) said, it is on account of our having no king,
that the Asuras (Demons) defeat us. Let us elect a king.
All consented. They elected Soma their king.
Headed by the king Soma, they were victorious in all directions.

Aitareya Brahmana 14[1]

The real power, the power we have to fight for night
and day, is not power over things, but over men.

O'Brien, in *1984* (George Orwell)

HISTORY APPEARS to thrive on a diet of firm and comfortable presupposition. Our analysis of any event or moment is all too often structured and packaged within carefully delimited expectations over *what must have happened*, and alternative scenarios are only occasionally admitted into the analysis. For South Asian history, a moment especially rich in such a process of easy assumption has been the late eighteenth century. Our analyses have been structured by easy stereotypes about the fall of one imperial system and the rise of another, and our focus on the teleological process has allowed us, all too easily perhaps, to overlook the real historical processes underway. This is in part a product of our sources and in part a process of our focus on centralized imperial processes and a general avoidance—if not outright ignorance—of local realities and dynamics.

To counter this tendency, this paper will present an examination of conflicting trends of lineage, state, and symbolism of both as they developed in north-eastern Rajputana (Rajasthan) in the later eighteenth century. In so far as documentation allows, I will examine the events of the period and the challenges that impacted those striving for survival and prosperity in the region. External powers were, often, just that: distant, alien, troubling influences to be avoided, manipulated, manoeuvred among as regional powers attempted not so much to assert new constellations of power, but to continue the balancing process which had characterized their political and economic systems for centuries.

Specifically, this paper will focus on lineage-state dynamics of the Naruka Kachhawaha Rajputs of north-eastern Rajputana, in what was becoming the Macheri/Alwar State, at the end of the eighteenth century.

The Kachhawahas and their Transition to Dhundhar, Amber, and thence Jaipur

Kachhawaha Rajput power was established through the mythic migration of the Kachhawaha lineage-head (raja), popularly known as Dulha Rai (or Dhol Rai—his personal name seems to have been Tej Karen), into eastern Rajasthan, in pursuit of this fabled love of Maroni (also known as Kumkum), the daughter of Ralhansi (also known as Ralan Singh or Salar Singh), a Chauhan Rajput chief of Lalsot, a holding of the region 75 km south-east of Jaipur. The story of Dulha Rai's love affair with Maroni has found literary form in the famous ballad of *Dhola-Maru ra Duha* of the fifteenth century. About 1071 CE (1128 VS), Dulha Rai and his father, Sodh Dev, migrated from the east and began the process of establishing their lineage presence in the new region. At this time, eastern Rajasthan seems to have been dominated politically by Bargujar Rajput clans, with most of the land in the hands of Mina cultivators. To call the Minas 'cultivators' may perhaps be a mis-statement customized to a Rajput perspective, as many local forts and other places of political power were in Mina hands, and the Mina 'tribes' in fact held significant political and economic power. The less important Chauhans in Lalsot comprised a major secondary lineage and this seems to have been important in the 'invitation' to the alien bridegroom, Dulha Rai, where the Bargujar-Chauhan tension seems to have been the determining factor. Minas, Chauhans, and Bargujars of the region all seem to have been in a position of vague subordination to the Chauhan rulers of Delhi (Dhillika). Later with the decline of the influence of the Delhi rulers, there may have been a regional drift toward independence and independent solutions to local political tensions and rivalries among the rajas of eastern Rajasthan. Before the eleventh and twelfth centuries, the major focus of political power lay with the Bargujar raja of Deoti, and it was perhaps as a counterbalance to his authority that the Kachhawaha 'foreigner' entered the political ecology of the region known as Dhundhar. To broaden the marital alliance, the raja of Lalsot granted half of the town of Dausa (about 50 km east of Jaipur and 38 km north of Lalsot), to Dulha Rai as his first territorial base in Dhundhar. He would, however, shift his capital to Khoh, 50 km west of Dausa and 14 km south of Amber.[2]

The shift in the focus of power led inevitably to a severance of the immediate influence of the Kachhawahas over Gwalior, which fort and city is said to have been left in the custodial hands of a related Parihar Rajput chieftain, the son of Dulha Rai's sister, who soon laid a claim to Gwalior that would persist for centuries.[3] The focus of Dulha Rai's activities and those of the Kachhawaha *kul* shifted to eastern Rajasthan and to the establishment of their power in that region. Under the leadership of Dulha Rai and his son Kakil Dev, a series of conquests led to the establishment of the independent state of Dhundhar by the beginning of the thirteenth century, and culminated in Kakil Dev's capture of the major fort of Amber from the Minas around 1036. However, the urban focus of Kachhawaha power would remain for some time at Khoh.[4]

This consolidation of Kachhawaha power occurred at the same time that new Muslim rulers were establishing their power in Delhi. It can perhaps be assumed that with the overthrow of the Chauhan rulers in Delhi by the new Ghurid rulers, many of the external constraints on the political ecology of eastern Rajputana were removed and new opportunities for lineage establishment appeared. In these turbulent years, ambitious newcomers such as Dulha Rai, Kakil Dev and their descendants could begin to establish a new Dhundhar Raj in the area. Across Rajasthan, Kathiawar, central India, and the central Gangetic plain, local rulers emerged—often from comparative obscurity—and claimed status as rajas and, indeed, seem even to have refined their sense of 'Rajput identity' during this period. For local Chauhan, Gehelot, Bhati, Paramar, and Kachhawaha chieftains and their lineages, the final decades of the twelfth century were a time to form, focus, and maintain new constellations of power.[5]

The opportunity to use a time of absent centralizing rule to establish a new domain continued during the reigns of seven rulers of Dhundhar after Dulha Rai. However, the eighth ruler had to face a different set of challenges. Raja Dev (r. *c.* 1290-1310) had to contend with the expanding presence of a now stable and self-confident central authority that wished to extend its rule beyond Delhi and control the chieftains of eastern Rajasthan. In 1301, the long efforts of Sultan Ala ud-Din Khalji (r. 1296-1316) and his predecessors to control the major Chauhan fort at Ranthambhor (in Sawai Madhopur district) succeeded when the fort fell into Khalji hands despite the *jauhar* of the defenders.[6] The involvement of the Kachhawahas of Dhundhar in the defence of Ranthambhor is frequently asserted and assumed, but generally unproved. What did change, however, was the formal urban expression of the state, when about 1310 Raja Dev shifted the capital city of his state from the less-defensible Khoh to the older mountainous Amber fort.[7] Not only did the fall of Ranthambhor establish Khalji power in eastern Rajasthan, but it spelled the end of the Ranthambhor Chauhan power and, perhaps, opened a political niche into which the Amber Kachhawahas could move. In addition, the frontier for expansion and conquest was closing and it would perhaps not be unlikely to find this increasingly limited political ecology reflected in internal tensions within the Kachhawaha ruling lineage as the opportunities for less divisive resolution of internal tensions became more restricted.[8]

In 1388, Maharaja Udaikarn of Amber (the fourth ruler after Raja Dev, he ruled 1366-88) died and was succeeded by his son Nar Singh Udarn. The succession was confused—legends say—by a father-son rivalry over rights to particular dancing girl (*khandi*). The story, as recounted in later Alwar chronicles, was that Bar Singh, Udaikarn's eldest son, was enamoured of the woman but his father—presumably in jest—expressed his own interest in her. With characteristic Rajput pride Bar Singh surrendered his right as bridegroom to his father, insisting that any son from that union would become the ruler of Amber rather than a more normal succession to the eldest son; thus the succession fell instead on Udaikarn's third son, Nar Singh, his only son by the disputed *khandi.* Setting aside abstract concerns with historical 'facts', the important genealogical sense of a 'right' to the Amber *gaddi* would become an important part of the understood history of Bar Singh's descendants. Indeed, the precise relation of Bar Singh and Nar Singh to their father has been much debated between historians and genealogists; different genealogical tables show different birth orders and circumstances of birth.[9]

This succession proved a major moment of lineage fission within the Amber Kachhawaha *kul.* Udaikarn's eight sons each gave origin to one of the major *sakham* of the Kachhawaha *kul* of Rajputs. Nar Singh succeeded his father on the *gaddi* (r. 1388-1428), while Bar Singh's descendants become the Naruka *sakha,* Balo's descendants became the Sheikawat *sakha,* Sheobhrama's descendants became the Sheobrahmpotas, Patal's the Patalpota, and Pitho's the Pithapota, while Pipo and Napo died without issue.[10] It is on the shifting political expressions and alliances of the Naruka *sakha* that the remainder of this study will focus.

The Naruka Emergence

Since Udaikarn's eldest son, Bar Singh, presented a potential threat within the Amber court and retained some residual claim to his parental lands, he was awarded a placating estate of eighty-four villages, known as Jhak and Mozabad (or Maujabad), an area ranging from 30 to 40 km south-west of Amber. The area seems to have been (or become) comparatively rich, as Mozabad was a major centre for indigo production.[11] Moreover, as Nar Singh was a child when he came to the *gaddi* in 1388, Bar Singh acted as regent for his young half-brother, maintaining thereby his participation in the administration. Over time, Bar Singh's family continued to play an important role in Amber politics and at times even had administrative power over the Amber region itself. By the late fifteenth century the family had established a separate power base and Bar Singh's grandson Naru gave his name to a newly established lineage (*sakha*) of Kachhawaha Rajputs, the Narukas.[12] Naru's five sons in turn gave their names to the major *khampam* of the Narukas: the Lalawat (from Lala, the eldest son, which family would become dominant in Macheri and Alwar), Dasawat (from Dasa, the thikanas of Uniara, Lawa, Garhi, and others), Tejawat (from Tej Singh, with possessions in Jaipur and Haiderhera jagir in Alwar), Jetawat (from Jet Singh, minor landholders in Jaipur and Alwar), and Chitarwat (from Chitar, unimportant in Jaipur but with minor jagirdars in Alwar).[13] Although Lala was Naru's eldest son, the descendants of Dasa became more active in continuing the familial claims on the *gaddi* and received most of Naru's lands.[15] The Dasawat Narukas and Sheikawatis were often linked in folk songs as the most contentious and troublesome groups and the metaphors were often those of hockey (*hogri*), a popular sport in the region:

Rajo Shekho, raj su, parpe nahin ariyan;
Satu seri mokali, Dasa khel dhariyan.

O Raja Shekha, with you none successfully contend;
The seven ways open (uncontested), Dasa strikes
the hockey ball.[15]

While troublesome relations such as Shekhaji and Dasa contended with the ruling lineage, Lala tacitly surrendered his ancestral claim and most of his family lands to his younger brother and contented himself with service to the established Amber chief, retaining possession of only Jhak and twelve other villages. Dasa's presumptions against Amber became increasingly militant, climaxing in his poisoning, followed by the execution of his son (Sangaji), by Maharaja Prithvi Raj of Amber (r. 1503-27). This double blow crushed the pretensions to power of the Dasawat Narukas, though they still held large and powerful estates under nominal subordination to the Jaipur rulers at Lawa, Uniara, Ladana, and in the north-eastern parts of the Jaipur territory at Garhi and Jaoli.[16]

With this apparent validation of their policy, Lala and his descendants continued their tradition of service to the Amber State and were frequently rewarded with titles, emblems of royalty, and grants of land. From the Amber perspective, the very ability to placate regionally based kinsmen with grants of land came about in large part from the growing closeness between the Amber rulers and the new dominant power—the Mughal.[17] In 1671, Rao Kalyan Singh, great-great-grandson of Lala and head of the Lalawat Naruka *khamp*, was granted lands on the north-eastern forested frontier of the Amber heartland, centring on the village of Macheri, in the region known as Narukhand, where there were already considerable Dasawat Naruka settlements. The grant seems to have come in substitution for the loss of Jhak to a rival against Mirza Raja Jai Singh (r. 1628-67); Kalyan Singh had supported the ruler in this rebellion. This initial award of land by Jai Singh's successor, Ram Singh (r. 1667-89), was expanded by grants to Kalyan Singh and his five sons so that by the beginning of the eighteenth century the lineage held some 27,000 bighas.[18] Kalyan Singh's five sons each became the progenitor of the vitally important *panch thikanas* (five residences) of Naruka power in the region. Ugar Singh founded the Macheri thikana (or *nak* in the larger scheme of Rajput lineage architecture) which was the eldest and most dominant thikana of Lalawat Narukas, Shyam Singh the Para thikana, Jodh Singh the Pai (or Nizamnagar) thikana, Amar Singh the Khora thikana, and Ishri Singh the Palwa thikana.[19]

Eventually, Kalyan Singh's descendants built a power base in the eastern part of Narukhand where a number of Dasawat Narukas were also settled. Many of these Dasawats had come into the area after the execution of Dasa by the Amber raja, and had obtained land from local cultivators in return for protection against raids from the neighbouring region of Mewat. Narukhand encompassed some 1,156.3 sq km, or about a quarter of the total area of what would become the Alwar State.[20]

Mewat had been mentioned by the contemporary chroniclers of Sultan Ghiyas-ud-din Balban's reign (r. 1265-86) and by those of the later rulers of Delhi; the connotation was chiefly the threat posted to 'settled' areas by the troublesome Mewati raiders and brigands. Mewat took its name from its inhabitants, the Meo, a Hindu (Rajput and Jat) agricultural group who had converted to Islam during the fourteenth century, especially in the reign of Sultan Firoz Shah Tughluq (1351-88).[21] More so than most of the surrounding area, Mewat was inaccessible, hilly, and heavily forested, and seems to have remained outside the effective and long-term control of any central government until well into the nineteenth century. Moreover, Mewat comprised an area of active armed opposition to central control into the twentieth century. Mewat comprised about 37 per cent of the total area of Alwar State. The entire area between Jaipur city and Delhi was alternately claimed by the two power foci, but the actual control lay with the local landlords or, move accurately, with the regional dominant cultivating classes.[22] This clearly had remained the case until Mewat and the other regions in the area were brought under central authority under the Mughal Emperors Zahir-ud-din Babur (r. 1526-30) and Nasir-ud-din Humayun (r. 1530-9 and 1555-6).[23]

To the west of Mewat lay the region known as the Raht, about 18 per cent of the total area of Alwar State,[24] settled in the tenth century by Chauhan Rajputs who had been driven out of the Delhi area by Muslim conquests and who claimed descent from Prithviraj, the last Rajput ruler of Delhi. The most important Chauhan holding in the Raht was centred on the town of Nimrana, but other smaller rajas (at Mandawar and elsewhere) retained a sizable sense of their own power and historical validity.

North of Mewat was Ahirwal, a small Ahir-dominated principality which had developed in the period of Mughal 'decline' centred on the important town of Rewari. The rajas of Ahirwal had obtained sanads granting them land and authority from Delhi, and had retained friendly relations with the Jat rulers of Bharatpur to the south-east of Narukhand.[25]

To the south of the Raht was the Wal which bordered Jaipur territory on the west and Mewat and Narukhand on the east; this hilly plateau area was controlled mainly by Sheikawati Kachhawaha Rajputs whose kinship and power alliances were with the Sheikawati of Jaipur State which enjoyed nominal—and occasionally violently defended—autonomy from Jaipur. The Wal, nevertheless, seems to have been seen as a separate region from the well-established Sheikawati area, or at the very least as an independent subregion. The Sheikawatis, as discussed earlier, also traced their descent from Maharaja Udaikarn of Amber and had historically proved almost as troublesome as their Naruka brethren. The Wal area comprised about 7 per cent of the total area of Alwar State.[26]

To the west of Narukhand was the Rajawat area, 12 per cent of the total area of Alwar State,[27] inhabited—as the name implied—by Rajawat Rajputs, who maintained close ties with their ruling kinsmen in Jaipur. These Kachhawahas traced their descent from Raja Bhagwant Das of Amber (r. 1574-89) and in many ways retained a political loyalty that reflected this genealogical link.

To the south of Narukhand was the territory of the Jats of Bharatpur, from whom much of the land in Narukhand had originally been taken. Additionally, there were two smaller recognized vernacular regions, Kather and Nahara, together encompassing some 228 sq km, or about 2 per cent to the total area of Alwar State.[28]

Although the entire area—but especially Mewat—had been alternately claimed by Jaipur and Delhi, it had only been brought under effective central political control after its conquest by Babur and Humayun. Under Akbar, the area was organized into two sarkars—Alwar, southern Mewat, and Tijara, north-central Mewat—under the subah of Agra. Faujdars for Mewat, however, continued to be connected with Delhi subah, indicating the concern for the maintenance of peace in a potentially turbulent area so near Agra and Delhi. During the reign of Aurangzeb (r. 1658-1707), the Jaipur durbar seems to have established its strong control in the southern and western areas, as grants of land were made to state servants such as Kalyan Singh Naruka. In this same period, the Alwar sarkar was formally assigned to

Maharaja Sawai Jai Singh of Jaipur as a jagir but after as few years the grant was cancelled, apparently from a fear of allowing the important fort at Alwar to remain in increasingly untrustworthy Rajput hands. From about 1720, the stabilizing force of Mughal organization in the area had declined, and considerable shifting of lands and power was under way, allowing new forces such as the Jats, and later the Marathas and British, to claim new lands and authority.[29]

The Breakaway of Macheri Raj

The senior Rajputs of Narukhand were concentrated on their estates, and the most prominent families were closely bound by a kinship and inheritance system which assured their continued supremacy; but their influence was limited to the eastern mountainous areas of Jaipur. Involvement in the politics of Jaipur, Delhi, or the surrounding areas was restricted to the provision of military service to Jaipur. The unsettled conditions of the mid-eighteenth century had begun to make this sort of service all the more important and for Jaipur—as for other states—the local landholders on the frontier areas had become both more important to stability and more dangerous to that same stability.

Following the tradition of the Lalalwat Narukas of Macheri, Pratap Singh Naruka, the son of Mohabbat Singh, entered the service of Maharaja Madho Singh of Jaipur (r. 1751-67) in 1751. Pratap Singh was born in 1740 and succeeded his father as thikanadar at the young age of sixteen. While his meagre personal holding of two-and-one-half villages in central Narukhand scarcely gave Pratap Singh a powerful economic or territorial base, his kinship ties and military service to Jaipur soon made him powerful within the court. Within a few years he had made his reputation by subduing his turbulent Dasawat kinsmen at Uniara in southern Jaipur and by breaking the Maratha siege at Ranthambhor, and was rewarded with the increase of his estate in Narukhand to four villages and with an elevation to a place of ceremonial prominence in durbar.[30]

The sudden rise of the young Naruka to such potential power irritated the other Jaipur jagirdars, and plotting began against him. When this jealousy took the form of assassination attempts, apparently carried out with the approval of the maharaja (it appears that he had been reminded of the distant claim of the Narukas on the Jaipur *gaddi*), Pratap Singh left Jaipur in 1765 and took sanctuary in Bharatpur, but not before cautioning his kinsmen in Narukhand to remain loyal to the Jaipur *gaddi.* It is difficult to sense clearly Pratap Singh's motivation, but traditional histories convey a sense of an unfairly attacked loyal servant suffering under the jealousies of his master's non-Rajput bureaucrats.[31] Pratap Singh's jagir in Narukhand was sequestered by Jaipur, but he received lands from the young Bharatpur ruler, Jawahar Singh (r. 1763–?), for his maintenance and in return for military services. After only two years of exile, Pratap Singh returned to Jaipur a few weeks before a Bharatpur invasion of Jaipur. As he had filled a high-level military position in Bharatpur, it seems likely that this homecoming to Jaipur was sweetened by a familiarity with Bharatpur battle plans. The invasion was repelled, and this timely defection, combined with his command of the Jaipur troops, restored Pratap Singh to his position in the court, and his jagir in Narukhand was immediately restored to him.[32]

Shortly after the victory, Maharaja Madho Singh of Jaipur died and was succeed by Prithvi Singh, a minor. As was the usual Rajput custom, a council was formed to administer the state during this minority. Khushaliram Bhora, a minister in the Jaipur government, become a prominent and active member of this regency which apparently served to increase the influence of his patron, Pratap Singh Naruka, with whom he had shared exile in Bharatpur.[33] Generally Pratap Singh's power in Jaipur expanded until his faction was able to gain supremacy over the other that had emerged in the state during the minority.

> Using Bhora's party as his tool, he controlled the administration and gained everything that he desired without bearing the responsibility of any office in the state . . . he was in the end left in supreme control, as the helpless people realized that he alone could save the royal house from Mughal greed and baronial anarchy alike.[34]

The characteristic prose of Jadunath Sarkar, cited above, needs careful examination. Certainly, Pratap Singh was able to control the state during the period of conciliar rule, but this was not an uncommon occurrence and was more akin to 'baronial anarchy' than a factor preventing it. In any state, factional bonds of kinship and region constantly worked against any central regime, but the raja was generally able to keep these interests under control. However, during a minority, by virtue of their council membership, the jagirdars were presented with an opportunity to resurrect their other loyalties and factional alignments and vie openly for influence. This was a common pattern in the Rajput states but was especially acute in Jaipur, where the clan structure of the Kachhawaha Rajputs, and the common practice of partitioning inherited lands, were predisposing factors toward such lineage alignments. As Sir Alfred C. Lyall later would observe:

> They have never formed a state under one tribal leader and they still continue in the molecular condition of an uncertain federation of family groups of different magnitudes, usually dividing and subdividing the land down to the point consistent with some kind of cohesion for self-protection and recognition of a head to each family.[35]

Thus, Pratap Singh Naruka had been able to gain control over the Jaipur government through his status as head of a powerful lineage with an economic base, a long-standing claim to power, personal achievements, and the coincidence of minority. Not surprisingly, his increased power again engendered rivalry among the other jagirdars until, in late 1777, there was another assassination attempt, and Pratap Singh Naruka was forced to leave Jaipur and return to his lands in Narukhand. His indirect control over Jaipur affairs, however, was maintained for some time.[36]

While Pratap Singh continued to profess loyalty to Jaipur during the minority of Prithvi Singh, he had also been expanding his territorial holding in the eastern parts of the state and since 1768 he had been capturing and constructing forts throughout Narukhand, the Wal, and the Rajawat country, as well as seizing territory from Bharatpur. By 1775, he had begun to impinge on Mewat, which was still viewed by Delhi as its territory. In November of that year, Pratap Singh Naruka captured the powerful fort at Alwar and redefined his power within Narukhand

and, in essence, established the State of Macheri as independent from Jaipur.[37]

The basis of the political and economic system among the Rajputs of Macheri, later known as the Alwar State, was the jagir system, landholdings which were fairly small in comparison with earlier periods and other areas of the Indian subcontinent, averaging 1,000 bighas of cultivable land each, with the largest holdings around 13,000 bighas. In Rajput terms, a jagir was an assignment of land, with or without condition of military service, granted in recognition of meritorious service to the state. Generally, these awards of land were given to kinsmen of the head of the ruling lineage. Most jagirdars had the responsibility of providing soldiers to the state and a total of 876 horsemen, the major military force of the state, were furnished in this manner. Almost without exception, the jagirs were inheritable but could be transferred or resumed by the raja, although this was rarely done, and over time the jagirs came to be regarded as personal property of the allottees. The latter ranged in social status from large landlords to small cultivators, enjoying the status of jagirdar and thakur (landholder) mainly because of kinship with the ruling family.[38]

Given his control over the Jaipur minority, there was no immediate questioning of Pratap Singh's territorial expansions, but a serious challenge came from his own kinsmen in the southern part of Macheri. The greatest problem was with the powerful Dasawat Narukas in Narukhand who held control of the important forts at Ramgarh and Lachmangarh, and opposed Pratap Singh's claims to superiority. As the opponents to Pratap Singh capitulated or were executed, their holdings together with the newly conquered lands near Alwar city were redistributed to the Naruka families who had supported Pratap Singh in his conquest. In addition, a large number of non-Naruka Rajput landholders, often at the level of zamindar or village headman, lost their lands; in such instances, which often involved Chauhans, the holdings were redistributed to other classes, often non-Rajput to secure their loyalty to the new regime. All together, around 40,000 bighas were assigned by Pratap Singh to his followers as jagir holdings.

Seven Naruka jagirs in Narukhand, mostly non-*barah kotri*, survived the reorganization and conquest of Pratap Singh. Excluding the *khalsa* holdings of Pratap Singh, which weredirectly under central control, only three *barah kotri* jagirdars (Bijwar, Garhi, and Khora) continued to hold land under their original sanads from Jaipur. Most of these pre-Pratap Singh grants were in the areas of eastern Narukhand where the new raja had first built his power base, and, on the average, were around 5,000 bighas, of which nearly 4,000 were cultivable. It seems to have been fairly good land, with a total value of 44,000 *tan*, nearly Rs. 17,000.[39] A total of 102 horses were represented by these seven jagirdars.

To build his own following and to secure the loyalty of his kinsmen, Pratap Singh awarded nine jagirs, a total of twenty-four villages. These jagirs were smaller than the earlier estates, but had a larger percentage of cultivable land and a much larger *tan*.[40] In all, these new grants provided an additional 98 horses for Pratap Singh's increasingly necessary army. In general, the jagirs were awarded from newly-conquered land in the Alwar and Rajgarh areas to *barah kotri* families who had not previously held land in Narukhand.[41]

Thus, drawing from kinsmen who had not previously held significant land, despite their military and political importance, Pratap Singh Naruka was able to create a new landed class to supports his rule. Those jagirdars who predated his seizure of power were forced to acknowledge his supremacy, either on the voluntary basis of kinship affinities or under threat of military strength, or to forfeit their lands to the new jagirdars who had aided Pratap Singh in his conquests. In this process, he brought about a significant shift in the political status among the Rajputs of Narukhand. Previously, most of the land had been held by the Dasawat Narukas, as the original Lalawat territorial base had been farther to the west. Thus for the Dasawat Narukas, as well as for the non-Naruka Rajputs (Chauhans, Rajawats, or Sheikawatis, for example), the conquest of Pratap Singh must have seemed the actions of a comparative newcomer, as an attempt to generate a powerful landholding class to provide a political base and ideological legitimacy for his rule, to protect it from internal and external challenges, and to produce a base for possible further territorial expansion. Pratap Singh's redistribution of lands in Narukhand and surrounding areas had also conversely acted to introduce a new element of instability to his power, while seeking to sustain it. By dispersing military and economic power among a number of subordinate kinsmen, the tendency toward local independence was encouraged, and at the very least, the authority of the lineage head remained vague, as the limits of his power depended on the raja's ability to control his kinsmen.

Counterpoised to these newcomers were the indigenous landholders of the area which Pratap Singh had conquered. The pre-existing jagirdars who held their lands under the authority of Jaipur State had to be appeased or conquered. Pratap Singh experienced special difficulty with the Chauhan and Dasawat Naruka Rajput landholders of the area, many of whom lost their estates, which were then redistributed by Pratap Singh in jagir to his kinsmen and supporters. Opposition was also encountered from the non-Rajput cultivators of the land that Pratap Singh claimed [mostly Meo, Ahir, Mine, Gujar, Jat and Khanzada (Muslim) Rajput], some of whom continued to oppose any centralized control of their villages until well into the twentieth century.

In addition there was also a small non-Rajput bureaucracy which served Pratap Singh at the time of the foundation of the state of Alwar. These early state servants were mostly, like Pratap Singh and his newly created jagirdari aristocracy, refugees from Jaipur service, and provided useful ties outside the state (to Jaipur and Delhi, for example). These ties and machinations in fact comprised much of Pratap Singh's foreign policy and provided the means for him to protect his territories from outside danger. Since these non-Rajput administrators had no clearly defined place within the lineage relations or landholding system of the Alwar Rajputs, they owed little loyalty to the ruling lineage as such when their personal or fictional goals could be better served by independent action; but, as the Rao Raja was their sole patron within the state, their personal loyalty to him was linked to their continuance in office.[42] All parties in Alwar—Rajput and non-

Rajput alike—attempted to utilize both internal and external linkages and pressures to obtain their own continuance in service and power, and appear to have cooperated with Pratap Singh only insofar as his goals coincided with their own or—in the wider Rajput case—with the best interests of their lineage as a corporate group.

The striking of coins, the *sikka,* was one powerful way for a ruler—especially during the turbulent eighteenth century—to proclaim his independence, to make tangible his breakaway from a nominal superior, and establish a sort of political legitimacy.[43] Pratap Singh Naruka chose the minting of rupees as one of his first acts in his gradual shift toward independence from Jaipur. Perhaps as early as 1761, even before he had constructed the fort at Rajgarh or otherwise broken with Jaipur, Pratap Singh issued a rupee in the name of Emperor Shah Alam II (Ali Gauhar), Jalal-ud-din (r. 1759-1806) from his mint in that city. This coin, a fairly typical late Mughal piece, had on the obverse *Sikka mubarak badshah ghazi shah Alam* (auspicious coin of the victorious Emperor Shah Alam) and on the reverse *zarab rajgarh sanah julus maimanat manus* (struck at Rajgarh in the second year of his fortunate reign).[44] While the legend claims the coin was struck in the second year of Shah Alam's rule, it is quite possible that this coin was 'back-dated' to give even greater chronological depth to Pratap Singh's claim to independence and the *sikka.*[45] Alwar had been used as a mint much earlier in Indian numismatic history, and had seen silver *tankahs* coined there in the name of Balban in AH 664 [AD 1265-6, in what seems to have been a conscious attempt to establish legitimacy by expanding widely the minting of coins in his name into the districts (*khitta*) around Delhi]; the mint at Alwar also had a copper coinage under Sher Shah Sur and Islam Shah Sur, about 1543-8.[46] Pratap Singh Naruka of Alwar struck both silver rupee and copper *paise* (or, locally, 'Rao Sahi Tanka') coins in the name of Shah Alam.[47]

Even before Pratap Singh's open break with Jaipur, the aspiring raja attempted to express a degree of independence when he built onto his ancestral holdings at the village of Macheri to lay out plans for the expanded city of Rajgarh in 1765. He saw this new city as a mark of this independence and ordered the construction of a new fort and street system which, drawing on the example of Jaipur for politicized public architecture and urban planning, also incorporated elements from Mughal architecture. In 1770 Pratap Singh Naruka constructed his new and impressive fort at Rajgarh (at the core of the geographical region of Naruka power in Alwar). Even after his seizure of the city of Alwar in 1775 and the gradual transfer of the seat of administration to this older Pathan city (some 20 km to the north), his base of ceremonial power remained in Rajgarh.[48]

In the Rajgarh fort, frescoes were added in the Shish Mahal which functioned as the ceremonial centre (serving as a hall of public audience, as we can reconstruct its eighteenth-century structure and function today). This was perhaps the most publicly accessible area within the fort (most were not), and thus, appears to have been designed to impress kinsmen potential rivals, as well as the 'public' at large. While there is some evidence that the extant frescoes were completed (or refurbished) during the reign of Pratap Singh's successor, Bakhtawar Singh, it is apparent that such an artistic venture served political as well as aesthetic purposes.[49] The Shish Mahal frescoes today are faded and damaged by vandalism and the climate, but they are clear enough to be identified as to subject and intent.[50]

In October 1866 when the French traveller Louis Rousselet passed through Rajgarh, the buildings may have had tattered draperies but the Shish Mahal paintings were still very bright:

> The principal hall is inlaid with pieces of glass of different colour, amongst which are placed beautiful golden arabesques; and the panels are ornamented with curious frescoes representing the principal Raos of Matcher [Macheri] and are mythological and other scenes. These frescoes are executed with great delicacy, and most of them contain thousands of figures. There is a verandah in front of this hall, supported by fine marble pillars, the dome of which, worked in stucco, is made to resemble a golden curtain embroidered with flowers and animals. On the right-hand side of the verandah hangs a superb picture, representing the descent of King Pertab Singh [*sic*] into the Elysian fields where Krishna reigns; on the other side there is a fresco of the same dimensions, representing the enthronement of Pertab Singh, presided over by Krishna.[51]

While Rousselet's metaphors are (at best) mixed this identification of Krishna is somewhat suspect, and his 'Elysian fields' defy location in the surviving frescoes, the political statement of the paintings is clear: the rebel chieftain of Macheri has been transformed into the raja of Alwar under divine sponsorship. Indeed, it cannot be coincidental that this message is delivered in the entryway, one of the most publicly viewed areas of the Shish Mahal. Whether portrayed in armed procession—mounted on an elephant with his troops and retainers clustered on the ground about him—or in formal durbar with courtiers and dancers, Pratap Singh Naruka was shown with all the characteristics of a ruler, and any who doubted his status had only to look around the Rajgarh Shish Mahal. It was, in fact, to the courtyard in front of the Rajgarh Shish Mahal that Pratap Singh brought his most potent rivals for conferences and, frequently, for subsequent execution.[52]

Although the most important regional town, Alwar, had been captured by Pratap Singh in November 1775, the focus of state administration was not shifted to it until late in his reign (Pratap Singh's *chhatri,* or cenotaph, is near the Alwar fort, not at Rajgarh). The Alwar fort, some 300 m above the town of Alwar, was substantially refurbished and extensively repaired and internal construction was added by Pratap Singh's successor, Bakhtawar Singh.[53]

The Assertion of Alwar

In 1778, Maharaja Prithvi Singh of Jaipur died and was succeeded by Sawai Pratap Singh, also a minor.[54] It was customary for all subordinate landholders to attend the ceremony installing the new ruler on the Jaipur *gaddi* in order to demonstrate their support for the new reign, but one jagirdar of note, Partap Singh Naruka, was absent from this event. As the ruler was a minor, the earlier minority council was continued with Pratap Singh's agent, Khushaliram Bhora, holding increased powers as first minister.[55] Pratap Singh Naruka was able to maintain his independence of Jaipur through his continuing influence in the administration to the state. He also established good relations with Bharatpur by aiding that ruler in regaining parts of his land that had been taken by the Marathas.[56]

Pratap Singh, was able to establish and maintain the state of Alwar only by a careful balancing of opposing external and internal power alliances. To the south-west of his kingdom lay Jaipur, temporarily weakened by the minority of its maharaja and ruled by a regency council, and to the north-east lay Delhi, the seat of atrophied Mughal authority. Much of Pratap Singh's success in this period of 'anarchy and chaos' can be explained by the absence of a strong imperial power that could maintain order and restrain such adventurers in their breakaway efforts.

When Pratap Singh asserted his autonomy from Jaipur in 1778, his political base in Alwar was laid on the uncertain allegiance of Rajpur families bound to him either as their lineage head or as their affinal patron. Many of these families, like Pratap Singh himself, were exiles from Jaipur and therefore relied on the Naruka leader for the continuance and success of their lineages. These Rajput families (mostly his closest kinsmen of the Lalawat Naruka *khamp*) numbered fewer than fifteen, but constituted the core of the corporate armed might by which Pratap Singh obtained and held power in his fledgling state.[57]

Perhaps one result of Pratap Singh's increasingly independent course was the drawing of Delhi's wavering gaze even more closely to Macheri affairs. There had been little initial concern in Delhi over the Naruka Rajput's seizure of those areas in Mewat that were held directly by the emperor as *khalsa* lands. In 1778 a campaign was launched against Macheri under Mirza Najaf Khan, the *mir bakhshi*, or paymaster general. Raja Pratap Singh was besieged at Lachmangarh and nearly captured. In an attempt to obtain relief, both Macheri and Jaipur sent envoys to Najaf Khan's rivals in Delhi to negotiate a separate peace. As any damage to Najaf Khan's position served his rivals' goals, a *proforma* repudiation of the campaign into Rajputana was issued in the name of the Emperor, Jalal-ud-din Shah Alam II 'Ali Gauhar'. In earlier days of significant Mughal power, Pratap Singh's territorial claims so close to Delhi would have been quickly and decisively countered and the authority of Jaipur restored. The repudiation of the campaign against Pratap Singh, while it failed in deposing the *mir bakhshi* from power, certainly lightened the military pressure on Macheri, which was ordered to pay an immediate tribute of Rs. 3 lakh to Delhi, plus an additional Rs. 3 million over the next three years.[58]

Even this, while certainly better than total defeat, was more than the new raja of Macheri could bear, since he had no funds. On the urging of Khushaliram Bhora, the Jaipur court advanced the initial payment to Pratap Singh Naruka. The aim of this has been said to be 'to keep away the *mir bakhshi* and also to oblige Pratap Singh who was a constant menace to the Jaipur State'.[59] But there may indeed have been more to this generosity than Bhora's desire to aid his former compatriot, and Jaipur court politics probably played an important role. When almost immediate repayment of the loan was demanded, Pratap Singh refused, seemingly encouraged by his prime minister, Khushaliram Haldia, and ex-official of the Jaipur court. Bhora thereupon called for debt-collecting assistance from Delhi and an army was sent out under Zain-ul-Abidin Khan (Najaf Khan's great nephew).[60]

Again Pratap Singh Naruka's State—and probably his life—was saved by the politics of the Mughal court. Still perturbed at the effect this campaign could have on Najaf Khan's career, the *mir bakhshi's* rivals began to question why he had sent no tribute or revenue to Delhi, and urged the emperor to launch an expedition into Rajputana to investigate the situation and possibly to relieve Najaf Khan of his command. This threat gave the *mir bakhshi* sufficient cause to conclude a speedy peace with Pratap Singh and to hasten back to accompany the imperial camp on its tour. The tribute from Macheri was presented in person to Shah Alam, in return for which Pratap Singh Naruka was granted a sanad to hold Macheri directly as a jagir from Delhi with the confirmed title of Rao Raja.[61] Shah Alam's expedition to the west was finally defeated and retreated to Delhi in some disarray, and Mirza Najaf Khan was recalled to Delhi to take charge of defence matters. Pratap Singh soon secured the patronage of his agent in Rajputana and used him to further Macheri's interests in Delhi.[62]

Meanwhile, Rao Raja Pratap Singh Naruka was attempting to maintain his waning influence in Jaipur, since it seemed that any period of stability might result in an attempted reannexation of Macheri, regarded by Jaipur as a wayward kinsman. Pratap Singh was able to retain his agents in Jaipur in the administration and encouraged the harassment of Jaipur by the Mughal military forces, giving Alwar an added dimension of defence security.[63]

In 1786, a new force entered the political scene in eastern Rajputana, Mahadji Sindia. A Maratha and prime representative of the Maratha rise in western India, Sindia had been invested with the title *vakil-i-mutlak* (or 'regent of the empire') by Shah Alam in 1785. Sindia invaded Jaipur in 1786, and it seems that Pratap Singh played a large role in encouraging this enterprise, since he was one of the three administrators appointed to oversee the collection of Rs. 6 million tribute from Jaipur and the reassignment of some jagirs.[64]

By the last to the eighteenth century, yet another external influence had entered the already complicated situation in Rajputana: the East India Company. Maharaja Sawai Pratap Singh of Jaipur had unsuccessfully attempted to hire a British brigade to use against the Marathas.[65] Pratap Singh Naruka seems to have realized that a new factor had entered the political equation for as early as 1790 he had approached the Company, attempting to establish friendly relations.[66] It is easier to understand Jaipur's willingness to approach the British; the Marathas used foreign troops, and it would only be reasonable for Sawai Pratap Singh to seek similar assistance. But for Alwar, such an explanation is insufficient; Pratap Singh and Mahadji Sindia were at least nominal allies, and it can be argued that the Alwar ruler was seeking another source of support for his kin-based state system.

On 26 September 1791, Rao Raja Pratap Singh Naruka of Macheri died; before his death he had adopted a successor, Bakhtawar Singh, from the Thana family of the Para thikana. This family was not a *thikana* head but a junior branch. Such a selection served to broaden the base of support for the Alwar ruling house by appealing to the lesser jagirdars; also, had a successor been selected from the leading *panch thikana* families of Bijwar, Khora, Para, Palwa, or Pai, severe rivalry would have been unavoidable and would almost inevitably have threatened the uncertain basis of internal legitimacy which had supported the state. Yet the Thana family had sufficient antiquity (the jagir had been granted by Jaipur in 1727) to be acceptable to most of the established jagirdars. The challenge for Bakhtawar Singh, of course, was to gain the acquiescence for this rule—if not the outright support—not only from the major Alwar jagirdars, but also from the potentially hostile surrounding powers.

Before the late eighteenth century, it would probably have been impossible for a leader such as Pratap Singh Naruka to establish his independence from his parent state. Normally, subordinate lineages within a state such as Jaipur would be kept under control by constraints operating outside the Rajput state structure. In earlier stages of the evolution of a state, soon after the settlement, the chief and his kinsmen would start

> upon an interminable career of feuds and forays, striving externally to enlarge their borders at the cost of their neighbors. When the land grew to strait for the support of the chief's family, of the sept, that is, when there were not vacant allotments, a landless son of the chief would assemble a band and set forth to make room for himself elsewhere. If he was lucky, he found his room; if not, the family was rid of his company; in either event he never came back.[67]

When the frontier disappeared, it became more difficult for cadet lines to make an independent place for themselves. But there was more to the process than the simple unavailability of land. Jaipur city is located only 240 km from Delhi. As long as the overshadowing Mughal power persisted the political system in eastern Rajputana lost its flexibility so that the status quo was maintained and even fairly inaccessible areas such as Mewat were temporarily stabilized. Such a system also tended to be self-perpetuating, for as this pressure grew, 'the office and personage of the lineage raja and the basis of the power and wealth of the lineage elite become established'.[68] Thus, the restrictions on an ambitious cadet line and on its leader were increased, and the lineage would either merge and accept its subordination or usurp the power and position of the lineage elite in its time of weakness. By acquiring a revenue base independent of that of the ruling house, the cadet lineage could greatly heighten its chances of a separate existence. In other periods and in areas directly under central British control, this fiscal independence was generally achieved by a separate revenue settlement with the central government.[69] For Pratap Singh, however, his economic base was achieved through kin-concentration in a remote area not under the secure control of any central power. Perhaps the major factor in Pratap Singh's ability to sever ties with Jaipur and to create an independent state was the comparative lack of any external force, whose influence would have stabilized the political ecology of the area and whose military force would have restored the status quo before the cadet raja could generate an economic and military base by establishing his own kinsmen on the land and joining their interests to the continuation of the newly created state. Certainly, there was no stabilizing force in eastern Rajputana in the 1770s, for the Mughal power in Delhi was too weak to respond immediately. In addition, any possible interference by Jaipur in the seizure of a part of its territory by a cadet line was unlikely, because of the continuing minority largely controlled by Pratap Singh Naruka. Under a strong Mughal power, possibilities for the expansion of territory and authority by a powerful cadet lineage had been removed, and this external pressure, together with the internal tensions produced by the increasingly political entrenchment of the Jaipur ruling elite, had closed off competition among the junior lineages. In such a time of dual weakness, it was possible for a lineage head such as Pratap Singh to utilize internal rivalries and diffusion of power to create a new state in eastern Rajputana. But having thus established himself, the vital task remaining for Pratap Singh Naruka was to maintain his authority while extending his holding; in short, to seek internal and external legitimacy for the new Alwar State.

The Structure of Rajput Power in Alwar

The kinship nobility in the Alwar State held its claim to power by virtue of its genealogical ties to the ruling lineage and its economic base in the various tenurial systems in the state. The granting and regulation of landholding within this ruling elite enabled the Alwar raja to manipulate both internal and external relationships and to maintain a class which owed its status to him and would, therefore, serve as a legitimizing force for his regime.

It is important to note that, despite larger issues of power, politics, and—perhaps—religion, the balance of population strength did not lie with those who would dominate the history of the region. Perhaps this is not surpassing, but it needs to be remembered to understand the wider political ecology of the region. In the 1891 census—perhaps the only reliable count of what the British came to call 'caste'—the largest single caste in Alwar State (over 12 per cent of total population) was the Meo, the nominally Muslim dominant cultivating class of Mewat.[70] The only other castes representing at least one-tenth of Alwar's total were the Chars (about 11 per cent) and Brahmans (10 per cent).[71] Other 'significant castes'—here defined as over 20,000 individuals out of a total recorded population of 7,67,786—were the Ahirs (8 per cent), Minas (6 per cent), Gujars (6 per cent), Baniyas (5 per cent), Jats (4 per cent), Rajputs (4 per cent), and Malis (3 per cent).

The Rajput population—insignificant in absolute number but all-important in political impact—was comparatively small, only 27,552 individuals, some 3.9 per cent of the total. Of these the largest single Rajput *kul* was—perhaps not so surprisingly—the Kachhawaha, with some 10,500 individuals, 1.4 per cent of Alwar's total population, and 34.8 per cent of the Rajput population of the state. The only other significant Rajput populations were the Chauhan Rajputs (9,200) and Muslim Rajputs (4,600).[72]

Of the politically dominant Kachhawahas, the 1891 census shows the ruling Narukas as the single largest *sakh* (42.7 per cent of the Kachhawaha, 14.8 per cent of the Rajput, but only 0.6 per cent of the total population).[73] The only other significant Naruka group was the Sheikawat *sakh*; all other Kachhawaha *sakham* were below 5 per cent of the Rajput population.

In what may seem a somewhat strange—and politically significant—distribution (especially for those specialists in other areas of Rajwara and Rajasthan), Bhats and Charans, the traditional genealogist castes, were almost entirely absent in Alwar in 1891. Bhats comprised only 560 individuals. Charans were even fewer: 401 individuals recorded.

One of the important methods by which states such as Alwar had been able to establish and sustain their internal structure was through the dynamic structuring and restructuring of a changing set of modes of interaction which replicated and strengthened the older norms of the state and the face of statecraft as the rulers wished it to be presented. As the nature of the Rajput State and of interrelationships within the corporate kinship elite that comprised the relevant polity changed, so were the patterns of ceremonial interaction manipulated and altered. Not only was it necessary for the relations among the ruling (predominantly Rajput) elite to be structured by and subsumed within these increasingly ritualized patterns, but it was also required that extra-lineage interests (whether those of the Brahmans, Baniyas, or British) be likewise incorporated into the overarching state through careful structuring of patterns and symbols of the state in all its forms.[74]

The characteristic institution of political, military, and economic institution of state and lineage power was the jagir. By the eighteenth century, the term already had a long history in South Asia. Unlike the earlier Afghan and Mughal jagir, the jagir of eastern Rajputana was a hereditary land grant, free of any substantial tribute or revenue requirement, and effectively transferable or resumable by the raja only at his own risk.[75] By the end of the nineteenth century, there were 129 jagirs in Alwar; almost all were held by Rajputs and were clustered in the southern part of the state, in Narukhand, the traditional heartland of Rajput power in Alwar. These estates comprised 14 per cent of the total area of the state, but included some of the best agricultural land and most valuable natural resources. The *khalsa*, or directly administered revenue-producing area of the state was 77 per cent of the total area; this land, mostly held by Meos and Ahirs, was under the nominal control of the raja and provided the bulk of the state's revenue.

The basic function of the jagirdari system in Alwar was the furnishing to the state of a military force specified in the original document which bestowed the land. Theoretically, the jagirdars were responsible for providing 876 horses, riders, and the maintenance for both; but in reality, only 572 horsemen had this service enforced. Most were required to perform actual military service in alternate six-month periods, but some were excused even this duty. Of these, 82 horsemen (*khasa, ambari,* and *naraka nishan*) were retained for the personal use of the jagirdars who were responsible for them, but these troops were liable for regular (but not very regular) inspection by state officials who would ascertain their readiness to serve them when required. The service of the remaining 304 horsemen was not rigorously enforced. Some were not liable for state inspection but were maintained in the villages and could be called into state service in times of special emergency (the 57 *sharista nahin sadawan*). For a number of jagirdari tracts, the yield of the land had declined since the original grant and therefore the thakur could not provide the specified force (*kamin singha*); a total of 151 jagirdari horsemen had thus been relieved of the responsibility of either service or maintenance by the thakurs. The remaining category of non-furnished horse were those whose service had been excused because of some special service given to the state by the jagirdar (the *mafi* horse).[76]

In return for their grants, the Alwar jagirdars (nearly half of whom were Naruka Kachhawaha Rajputs) provided the raja with a nominal force of almost 1,000 horsemen. During the eighteenth and early nineteenth century, it was primarily this armed force that allowed Pratap Singh and his successors to obtain and maintain his *gaddi* against challenges from Jaipur, Delhi, and the Marathas. By the mid-nineteenth century, however, the Alwar jagir horse became both unnecessary and ineffective; whenever the promised horsemen actually arrived, they were considered an open joke by all who viewed them. While the Rajput jagirdari system is often taken—on this narrow military condition—to resemble European feudalism, the value of the jagir system went far deeper. It was felt that only with the support of the jagirdars had the Macheri estate gained political security, and therefore, the senior jagirdars had a rightful claim to power within the state. The only standing troops under the direct command of the raja were the ruler's personal bodyguard (mostly younger non-inheriting sons of senior jagirdars and the small state artillery (mostly non-Rajput, and by the 1850s predominantly Muslim). Even this bodyguard was open to jagirdari influence, as membership in it was regarded as the hereditary right of younger sons of jagirdars and other significant, but non-jagirdari, Rajput families. Thus, while the ruling lineage had a large economic base (most of the cultivated area in Alwar was held directly by the durbar as *khalsa* land), the raja only had an insignificant military force independent of the jagirdars. As long as the Thakurs continued to support the raja, the reliability of the army was assured, and, therefore, there was no reason to form a standing army within the state. Indeed, with the small Rajput population focused in political and military terms on the ideal of jagirdari military service, there was little ideologically satisfying population to draw upon to form a new standing army. This would become necessary only if it was desired to displace the jagirdars from their positions of political importance within the state.

Since the Rajput kinsmen of the raja, the head of the ruling lineage, held to the historical tradition of their participation in the foundation of the state and, thereby, held onto a claim to involvement in the welfare of their state, the jagir system acted to bind them to the ruler, to give them a role as subordinate rulers of a portion of the lineage territories, to link them to the symbolism and *dharmic* nature of the raja, and to reconfirm their genealogical status through the conferral of delimited military, economic and ritual power. It is important to recall that, even in the European case, one of the marks of a feudal system was a resort to the bonds of at least surrogate kinship.

Similar questions of power relationship existed between Alwar jagirdars and the raja, who was seen by his kinsmen as lineage head, not as sovereign ruler. This claim was strengthened by the fact that the jagirdars were collectively responsible for the only significant military forces in Alwar. Despite their sizable share in the foundation and administration of the Alwar State and their responsibility for its military forces, the jagirdars had a small economic base. Nevertheless, there is some evidence that the jagir villages had a disproportionate share of the rich non-agricultural natural resources of the state, and that there were effective (if more repressive?) conservation measures in place.[77]

The Alwar jagir holdings were concentrated in the southern tahsils of the state, with the three southern tahsils of Ramgarh, Alwar, and Lachmangarh containing almost two-thirds of the

Alwar jagirs. Likewise, individual lineages tended to be concentrated in the same area, increasing the stability and cohesion of these kinship landholding structures. The holdings ranged from one to ten villages, average holdings being one to two villages of about 1,000 bighas cultivated area. There were a few very large jagirs, but only ten thakurs held more than three villages; the most valuable jagir in state was the *barah kotri* family of Para, representing an annual income of about Rs. 13,000 at the time of its award by Jaipur in 1774.

Little evidence is available on the subtenurial system within the jagirdari estates. The arrangement a jagirdar might make with his tenants was outside the authority of the central government, for despite the nominal control of the raja over all land in the state, the jagirdars were given independent proprietary right in their estates. The jagirdar's share was taken from the cultivator according to the complicated set of cesses and rights. In the 1870s, the thakur's fair share comprised: one-third of the gross produce of the land, one additional *seer* (0.9 kg) for every maund (37.1 kg) of production, one day's work from every plough to cultivate the jagirdar's private lands, a load of green corn from the irrigated lands around every well, Rs. 2 for every marriage in jagir, the grass corn and wild produce of the uncultivated land, and approximately Re. 1 for each bigha of fallow land. Of course this complicated share dependend on the ability of the jagirdar to take it. By the 1870s an alternative arose, in which the jagirdar simply set a fixed rent, either in cash or in kind, on the land of his holdings. The thakur would decide at each harvest how that particular installment of the rent would be taken, and thereby attempt to maximize his share. This uncertain revenue responsibility was opposed by the cultivators, and in order to keep them on the land, a choice between payment in cash or kind was usually offered.[78] The amount taken by the jagirdar was not in proportion to his responsibility to the state, to the prevailing cost of grain, or to the general prosperity of the area. This system was more oppressive to the cultivators than the conditions in *khalsa* territory directly under the raja or those areas under the direct revenue administration of the British, where the demand was fixed and invariably taken in cash. The tenurial system in jagir estates in Rajputana has been described:

> The majority of the tenants in the jagir areas did not know what security of tenure, fixity of rent and fairness of rental meant. The majority of them were 'tenants-at-will' and lands were let out to the highest bidder, resulting in unhealthy competition and rack-renting and deterioration of land.[79]

While the particulars of this generalization still require careful examination, it is clear that the Alwar central administration saw the nature of tenure under its jagirdars as none of its legitimate concern, and these kinsmen-landowners generally were left unregulated on their own lands.

Lineage and the Power of the Thikana and the Jagir

Among the Alwar jagirdars, those of highest status were the families most closely related to Pratap Singh. Over time, these families had become the *panch thikanas*, or 'five residences' and their descendants formed the core of Lalawat Naruka power in Alwar. Borrowing a term from the Jaipur durbar, the twenty-five families (*nakas)* of the *panch thikanas* called themselves the *barah kotri*, or 'twelve chambers'. Among the families of the Naruka *barah kotri*, succession to the jagir estate was generally by primogeniture, whereas other jagirs (especially non-Lalwat-Naruka jagirs) were usually dividend among the sons on the jagirdar's death. The latter produced a complex arrangement of shares and share-holders under the nominal control of the eldest (or most powerful or competent) son and his descendants, who maintained the ceremonial rank and status of jagirdar, the other sons being simply shareholders in the divided estate. Thus, the power of the *barah kotri* remained concentrated and their genealogical and ceremonial status was reconfirmed by there undivided estates, while the economic and the political base of the other Rajput jagirdars was diluted by numerous divisions and subdivisions of the land and of the power derived from it.[80]

Higher in status than the non-*barah kotri* Narukas were those jagirdars who held the honour of *tazim*, that is, of being received by the raja in durbar, or formal court, while he was standing. These ceremonials of the durbar served in large measures as a reconfirmation of status achieved in economic or military terms, and were important visible evidence of these factors. The greatest political power in the state lay with the *barah kotri* Naruka jagirdars—borrowing a term ('twelve chambers'), if not a number, from Jaipur usage—and with those non-Naruka jagirdars who held the honour of *tazim*, that is of being received in durbar by the raja while he was standing. The honour was symbolized by the jagirdar's right to wear a gold bracelet on his right ankle. However insignificant such a thing may appear today, this not-so-simple honour proved a major point of contention and constituted a significant mark of honour. On the one hand, while these jagirdars were the most important supporters of the raj, but at the same time they were the ruler's most potent rivals. In the formal court ceremonials, the precise relationship of the elite representatives of the major lineages of the state to the raja was clearly drawn. Indeed, any betterment in status through increased landholding or the confidence of the raja would be mirrored in the award of *tazim* or other honour in the durbar. The durbar ceremonials also served as a visible reminder of the cooperative and mutually supportive nature of the state, in which the raja was expected to consult with his kinsmen and other state elites. While the ceremonials were the visible indicator of this status, they were often a revalidation of power and authority based in kinship ties, valuable landholdings, the number of horsemen provided to the state, or the antiquity (and, presumably, inviolability) of the jagir. In Alwar there were seventeen *tazimi* jagirdars, eight of whom were *barah kotri*: Bijwar, Palwa, Para, Pai, Khora, Thara, Khera, and Srichandpura. These may be considered the most powerful *barah kotri*, representing the *panch thikana* families and their major branches. Garhi, which provided 20 horses to the state, was the only *tazimi* Dasawat Naruka jagirdar. The non-Naruka *tazimi* jagirs were: Salpur (Rathore, 28 horses), Sukhmeri (Rathore, 11 horses), Rasulpur (Rathore, 5 horses), Tsing (Badgujar, 4 horses), Chimraoli (Gaur, 24 horses), Kankwari (Jadon, 9 horses), and Mokanpur (Jadon, 3 horses). Also, nine smaller thakurs of sub-jagirdari status held *tazim*, chief among whom was the Dasawat Naruka family of Jaoli.[81]

Jaoli's status, however, was extraordinarily uncertain and

constantly debated. It seems that the family first received grants of land about 1720, but may have existed only as a large cultivator, although its villages were held on formal lease from Jaipur. At the time of Pratap Singh Naruka's rise to power, the Jaoli holdings were first seized and then restored in return for the annual payment of a communication fee, but without any obligation to supply horses to the state.[82] Jaoli was a fairly large grant concentrated in Lachmangarh tahsil and holding, by the late nineteenth century, around 13,000 bighas. Officially, the estate was classed not as a jagir but as an istramdar holding, a terminal arrangement where the land was held without military obligation and was assessed for the payment of land revenue at concessional rates. Jaoli's actual status seems to have been much close to a *jaidad* jagir, as the fee paid to the durbar was more of a payment in lieu of military requirement then a revenue settlement; it is certain that the assessments of the value of the estate were not decided through normal revenue processes. Similar confusion over conflicting claims to status existed among other Alwar jagirdars, especially Dasawat Naruka families and non-Naruka had been displace during Pratap Singh's realignment of the area's revenue, military, and political structures.[83] Such conflicts underlined the uncertain status and power distributions below the level of *barah kotri* jagirdars in Alwar.

The Gaddi and the Durbar as Manifestations of the State

In Alwar, the *gaddi* and durbar saw the acting-out of changing political relationship and rivalries within the state and served as a mirror of power relationships. The involved ceremonials of the state served in large measure as a reconfirmation of genealogical, military, or economic status among the elite. In the rituals of the durbar, the precise relationships among the lineage head of the ruling lineage, his relatives, and the other elite groups of the state were given visible form and substance. Any increase in status through marriage, augmented landholding, or the renewed confidence of the ruler would be mirrored in the award of *tazim*, titles, or other honours by the durbar. These ceremonials served as a visible reminder of the corporate nature of the Rajput State, in which the raja was expected to consult with his kinsmen, the other Rajput landholders, and the most prominent representatives of the non-Rajput elite (including state servants, prominent commercial families, and non-Hindu religious leadership) to obtain a consensus on what constituted the welfare of the state, the lineage territories which had been conquered with the aid of senior jagirdars. These were the most powerful families in the state, in many ways of equal power and importance to the raja, who might be—at best—the first among equals, at least in the estimation of the *tazimi barah kotri* jagirdars. In Alwar, there was only one *tazimi* non-*barah kotri* Naruka jagirdar, while seven non-Naruka jagirdars held this honour (descendants of non-Narukas who had supported Pratap Singh). Other prominent Rajput landholders of sub-jagirdari status could be awarded this honour, and in the 1880s nine such thakurs had; this award usually led them to claim jagirdari status based on family tradition or occasionally fraudulent documentation.[84] While the honour of *tazim* could be awarded to non-Rajputs, it was extremely rare in Alwar usage until the 1870s, usually being reserved for the Brahman *rajpurohit* ('royal chaplain', very loosely translated, who was often a non-resident of the state) and, quite rarely, for senior non-Rajput civil servants. In one case, the honour was awarded to a prominent Muslim sword-maker and damascer. This granting of *tazimi* status to non-jagirdars was frequently opposed by the senior families who seem to have viewed such actions as an infringement on their traditional relationship of the raja.

In Alwar, there were thus seventeen *tazimi thikanas*, eight of which were among the *barah kotri*, viz., Bijwar, Palwa, Para, Pai, Khora, Thara, Khera, and Srichandpura thikanas. These were most powerful families in the state, in many ways of equal power and importance to the raja, who might be—at best—the first among equals, at least in the estimation of the *tazimi barah kotri* jagirdar.[85]

The central institution of ceremonial interaction was the durbar or formal court or levee. Derived from mixed Persian and Sanskrit (a more dubious derivation, but often claimed in the Rajput states as a possible mode of cultural and ideological validation), a standard dictionary runs: 'A house dwelling; court, area; hall of audience, court; holding of a court, levee; royal audience; the executive government of native state.'[86] This definition aptly summarizes the breadth of state symbol and power that the durbar represented, combining the place for the ceremonial drama of the principality, the acts and formal relations of that ceremonial, and the ruler who was, if not the focus, the chief actor in that ceremonial.[87]

While the formal court ceremonial of the durbar was a vital statement of the public ordering and relationship of power within the state, the changes in large political reality were also mirrored in other public and semi-public ceremonials (Diwali, Dussehra, and other festivals, 'royal' patronage for the public arts such as wall-painting or music/dance performance), in the delimited princely prerogative to coinage or to the award of titles or decorations to state subjects, or even in the spatial location for structured ceremonial interaction, in the architectural tansition from hill-top fort to garden place. Changes in all these modes of public interaction, of a public emblemization of the existence of power relationships were reflections of the health and strength of the underlying political institutions. As the nature of institution changed, these ceremonials were modified and as the imperial presence of the British extended onto the princely states from the early nineteenth century, representations at all levels were changed to reflect new constellations of power.

An important public means of expressing power relations within the state and for refocusing these relations on the ruler was the public ceremonial of durbar and, in addition, of festival observances in which the ruler took an important role as head of his people. The narrowly ceremonial private observances of the formal levee were less useful than the festival or other observance in obtaining public notice and support, but from the point of view of the raja, the relevant 'public' whose loyalty had to be regulated and ordered was his kinsmen, the nobles and 'aristocrats' of the state. To subordinate their power and reinforce an appearance of authority even as the raja strove to diminish their rights, the formal rankings and ceremonials of the durbar became an important area of elite political interaction. In other cultures and historical moments, similar roles for state ceremonial have been observed; John Wolf has noted in the France of Louis XIV:

> All of the bowing and scraping, the pretensions to grandeur, could not conceal the fact that Louis had separated real power from social prestige. . . . [The nobles] were offered social prestige, ceremonial importance, grandeur—if they would act out rules that would supply the mystique for the king's exercise of power.[88]

Similarly, the disputes over ranking, seating precedence, even of simple access to durbar provided a means for mobility and for challenging the rights (and power) of rival families within each Rajput State as much as they did in Europe.

While there was a heritage of durbar that linked each state to the Mughal court, it is misleading to see the Mughal rituals as providing the direct model for Rajput activity. In ceremonies, as in most areas, the Rajput States joined their own traditions to only some of the Mughal paramount power. While details of pre-'Muslim' Rajput practices are unclear, it does seem that even under the Pratihara rules of the eighth century, there were established standards of ceremonial interaction, with institutions of both public and private court ceremonials (the *mahasthana* and the *abhyantatasthana*).[89] By at least the early eighteenth century, this earlier repertoire of ceremonial had been augmented by Mughal practices, and later one finds British additions.[90]

For the states themselves, the earliest and most powerful symbol and unifying representation of the state and its unity was the formal durbar court ceremonial, in which the ruler, his senior kinsmen, the most important non-kindred subordinate landholders, representatives of the commercial and religious community, and even the resident British official were assembled in a spatial arrangement that symbolized their power relationships to the state. The details of seating arrangements, who would be received in durbar in what fashion, and details of ritual rights and duties were all carefully outlined and delimited and, if challenged, could become a focus for debate and rivalry within the state. Access to the ruler came at the durbar and, in some states, actual state business was conducted there until it was relocated to the growing semi-bureaucratic forms of a Westernized 'rational' administration.

The willingness of the ruler's kinsmen to summit to this durbar ceremonial, to literally take their traditional places of subordination in the state, was a major factor underlying the very form and function of the state. Even on an imperial level, the tenets of British policy held that in India, as

> In Europe, in the case of ceremonies in which ambassadors or other high officials or commanders take part, it is understood that if the salutes and other honours and the relative rank of the representatives of the different nations cannot be adjusted by pre-arrangement, the dissenting party will withdraw from the ceremony. But this form of protest is not open to rulers of native states. To attend a ceremonial assemblage at the behest of a superior is an acknowledgement of allegiance; to be willfully absent without excuse is a mark of disrespect amounting to contumacy. . . . As the right of protest which equal powers possess is disallowed, it is all the more incumbent on those who advise on the conduct of our Oriental ceremonies to be careful to give every chief his due.[91]

Likewise, to refuse to appear for a ruler's durbar, or—perhaps worse—to behave improperly was a sign of contumacy and disobedience, virtually tantamount to a rebellious declaration of independence.

Sub-Jagirdari Landholding and Authority

The other important category of revenue-free lands in Alwar were the *mafi* grants—villages or isolated plots of land granted to individuals or institutions to provide maintenance for the awarded. There were around one hundred full-village *mafi* grants concentrated in Rajgarh and Alwar tahsils. Grants smaller than full villages, generally of isolated plots of land, comprised a total of around 80,000 bighas, mostly in Alwar, Rajgarh, and Lachmangarh tahsils. Many of these *mafi* grants were awarded to Brahmans or temples in the form of religious charity, and a number of these estates were comparable to the average jagir holding of around 1,000 bighas. Charitable *mafi* grants were often termed 'copper-plate grants', since many of the grants were of such antiquity that the original *sanads* of award were said to have been engraved on copper plates (although forgery seems to have been fairly common here). Other *mafidari* awards were to various administrative classes in the state, including *qanungos* (record-keepers) and *chaukidars* (village watchmen), and served as salary for these important village servants. Some *mafi* estates were granted to Rajputs for their personal maintenance in recognition of past or present services to the state. Frequently these awards, *kabila kharch mafis*, were not clearly distinguished from jagir holdings, although they were much smaller than the most prestigious jagirdari grants. Also, *mafi* grants involved the payment of an annual fee to the government to replace a part of the revenue lost by the award, but it seems that many Rajput *mafidars* (for example the Narukas of Madhogarh) were able to sustain a claim to jagirdari status by economic strength and political influence within the state.

The remainder of the state was *khalsa*, that is, land liable to direct revenue assessment by the durbar. The lightest demand was on the *istramdar* tenure, which was usually enjoyed by larger Rajput landlords whose holdings predated the introduction of Lalawat Naruka authority into the area. These lands were assessed, but concessional terms were extended to the privileged *istramdars*. The most common tenurial system in the state was *pattidari*, in which the shares in the land were determined by custom, and an individual's share of labour and produce was specified. Among the cultivating classes in the north-eastern tahsils, especially the Meos, Jats, and Ahirs, the *bhayacharya* system was common, and the land was held jointly by lineage, caste, or other group of identification, without any reference to shares. Only about one-tenth of the *khalsa* area was held by landlords or zamindars, and in most cases was jointly held by a number of zamindars rather than by a single landlord, as was the practice in other parts of north India.

There is little evidence of political participation among these non-jagirdari classes, although powerful regionally concentrated groups such as the Meos were always considered in any programme which involved the revenue system. The Meos were the single largest cultivating class in Alwar, and altogether they held major proprietary rights in one-third of the *khalsa* villages of the state. Their homeland, the area of Mewat, had only recently and marginally been brought under authority, and their potential political mobilization, either to rebellion or recalcitrance in revenue payment, was an unknown factor in the political and economic system of Alwar.[92]

The jagirdars were neither the largest nor the richest land-holding class in Alwar, for other cultivating classes (Meos or Ahirs, for example) held more land, but they did have a significant claim to participation in the polity and the administration of the state. The most important group of jagirdars were the *barah kotri* Narukas, who together with their own kinsmen possessed a lineage tradition of participation in the foundation of the Alwar State. By virtue of their relation to the ruling Macheri lineage, they viewed the raja as first among equals, as responsible to them in their role of ideological supporters of the state as they were to him as the head of their lineage. The non-Naruka jagirdars were not directly tied to the raja by consanguinity, but many were bound to him through the clan exogamy practiced by the Rajputs. Many of these other jagirdars also owed their status to the Naruka lineage elite, as their estates had been received as reward for their services to Pratap Singh and his successors. There were many non-Naruka Rajputs who had been displaced from property and power at the time of the state's foundation and consolidation; resenting the Naruka hegemony in the area, they looked for some way to restore their influence in local and perhaps state affairs.

Power, Land, and Lineage: Contradictions within the State

The only power the Alwar jagirdars enjoyed other than their traditional supportive role in the state lay in their provision of the bulk of the army. There was no standing army in Alwar, and therefore no significant military force which was responsible directly to the raja without reference to his kinsmen. Therefore, despite their small territorial and economic base, the Alwar thakurs had the powerful traditional lever of kinship and military necessity through which they could influence and participate in the politics of their state.

Their participation was not usually institutionalized in bureaucratic appointments, but was a potential influence in a system of consultation and contact with Alwar ruler, viewed as first among equals by even the non-Naruka thakurs. This traditional pattern of diffused power produced an unstable political structure at the upper levels, and the successors of Pratap Singh had sought sources of external legitimacy and internal political strength to confirm their hold over the state and to protect against external threats. The Alwar rajas sought to consolidate political power and reduce the influence of these traditional internal co-sharers, and therefore external administr-ators were introduced into the state, together with new institu-tions and administrative techniques. This served to remove the jagirdars and even the traditional state servants from power and replace them with a new bureaucratic class not responsive to traditional political sensitivities, but responsible only to the raja's consolidating sovereign authority.

The Unravelling of the System

British links with the eastern Rajputana States such as Alwar had been opened out of military necessity. Much of the growing British presence in and attention to the region was the result of campaigns against the Marathas, as the problems of north Indian hegemony were advancing toward resolution. The special enemy in the Alwar region was Mahadji Sindia. On 1 November 1803, Lord Gerald Lake defeated Sindia's troops near the south-western Alwar village of Laswari; in this victory, he enjoyed the military assistance of a small contingent of Alwar troops. Two weeks after the victory, on 14 November, Lake concluded a treaty between the East India Company and Alwar. Rao Raja Bakhtawar Singh agreed to cooperate with the Company if it or its allies were at-tacked and, in return, the Company agreed to manage Alwar's external relations, but not to interfere in foreign affairs. The boundary between these two activities was left delightfully vague.[93] Perhaps the most important aspect of this treaty came in a *sanad* which followed within a few weeks of the signing: as a pecuniary reward for his support of the British, the Alwar ruler was awarded more territory: the areas of Rath (north-west of Alwar city with many Chauhan Rajput landholders), Haryana, and parts of Mewat. Soon after the initial transfer, Haryana was exchanged for more territory in turbulent Mewat, including the area of Tijara and territories west of Rajgarh.[94]

By 1805, however, the British were seriously reconsidering the wisdom of their wartime treaty with Alwar, as well as their similarly occasioned pact with Bharatpur. In Alwar's case, no sufficient reason could be produced to justify reneging on the treaty. In the following years, with the decline of British interest and influence in Rajputana, a political vacuum was created into which the states moved with their own diplomatic arrangements. In 1807 Alwar led an attempt to bring about an alliance among itself and Jaipur, Sindia, and Holkar, but this scheme failed.[95] With the collapse of this particularly far-fetched plan, Bakhtawar Singh tried to stir up discontent in Jaipur State by conspiring with Khushaliram Bhora and Muhammad Shah Khan to gain control of the Jaipur administration by activating Jaipur-Jodhpur rivalries. In 1811 Alwar forces were dispatched to add armed persuasion to the plotting but were quickly withdrawn under the insistence of the Government of India, who considered such activities irregular under the terms of Alwar's treaty obligations of 1803. On 16 July 1811, Charles Metcalfe, the British Resident at Delhi, took an assurance from Bakhtawar Singh that the Maharao Raja would not conclude agreements with any third party without prior permission of the Government of India.[96] This British restriction did not prevent, the next year, an Alwar attack on Jaipur that captured two forts, but the following year the Delhi resident compelled the Maharao Raja to return them.[97] Bakhtawar Singh's policies in the later years of his reign produced domestic difficulties for Alwar, he launched a series of attacks against Alwar's sizeable Muslim population, the Meo agriculturists, most of whose territory had only recently come under central control after being received by Alwar in 1805. It seems Bakhtawar Singh was attempting to collect revenue regularly, and this was opposed by the independent Meos. His reaction was consistently brutal and caused alarm among the Muslims of Delhi, who threatened an invasion of Alwar. The Mughal Emperor, Bahadur Shah, too was disturbed by the conditions in Alwar and complained to the British agent.[98]

From the point of view of British policy toward Alwar and the other Rajputana states, these years were a period of benign neglect in which older feuds, jealousies, and diplomatic arrangements were allowed to reappear and displace the British presence as a governing factor in state affairs. In the case of Alwar, the major thrust of this feuding in the guise of foreign policy was to weaken Jaipur, and search out another source of strength and external legitimacy to replace the British attention that had turned away from Rajputana. The British noticed a prince only when his policy posed a threat to them, or an embarrassment to their basic rule of maintaining the status quo, of minimizing the actual and potential conflict between the native princes who were firmly and harmlessly bound to the 'Raj' by their treaty obligations. From the point of view of internal Alwar affairs, the acquisition of the new territories in 1805 had reopened the frontier for senior branches of the family, as well as junior, on whom the pressure of the changing political ecology had begun to fall. After 1805, Bakhtawar Singh granted six new jagirs, all but one to *barah kotri* families. It was no longer necessary to purchase the support of younger families with new lands; the need now was to reassure important cadet lines of their continued power by giving them a secure base, ideally on the fringe of the political core areas of the state. It can be argued that this was also an attempt to anticipate the demands for a reaffirmation of traditional jagirdari status which began to come as the relationship between the Maharao Raja and the jagirdars altered, because of the development of the raja's and lineage elite's superordinate status within Alwar and because of the hovering presence of the imperial power to legitimize, oversee, and pacify internal as well as external affairs.

It was perhaps in an attempt to remove the routine management of the state from such dangers of disputed succession and from excessive jagirdari influence that the Alwar rulers began to place increasing trust in newly-imported non-Rajput state servants. As late as 1811, the Alwar ruler was being aided in his administration by the same families who had served Pratap Singh.[99] After Bakhtawar Singh's death and the intense stresses of a subsequent disputed succession, two competing bureaucratic factions emerged, each supporting one of the rivals for the *gaddi.* One faction, led by Nawab Ahmed Bakhsh Khan, supported Balwant Singh, Bakhtawar Singh's 'natural son' by a Muslim 'concubine'. He had come to Alwar from Ferozepore Jhirka and had the support of the small Alwar standing army and the British resident at Delhi. Banni Singh, the senior jagirdars' choice for the *gaddi* and Bakhtawar Singh's nephew from the *tazimi barah kotri* house of Thana, was supported by three prominent state servants, Dewan Ramu Khwas and his sons Mullah Khwas and Nandlal, both of whom would later succeed their father as *dewan* (first minister) under Banni Singh.[100]

Like his predecessor on the Alwar *gaddi,* Bakhtawar Singh had no heir. He had approached the Government of India on several occasions for permission to nominate his illegitimate son Balwant Singh, his successor. Such approval did not come, as the Government considered such a decision beyond the limits of its reasonable concern. Additionally, the matter was complicated by the fact that Balwant Singh was born of one of Bakhtawar Singh's Muslim concubines, a situation of which the thakurs, the lineage elite, disapproved. In 1815 Bakhtawar Singh died, and this problem, still unresolved, flared into an open succession dispute, a crisis which would reverberate through Alwar's politics until at least 1857.

By the early years of the nineteenth century, the Alwar Naruka jagirdars enjoyed a relationship with their lineage head similar to that which Pratap Singh Naruka had shattered when he broke away from Jaipur to found his own kingdom. While the later imposition of British paramountcy would act to destroy the fluid frontier into which troublesome cadet lineages might have been dispersed before the late eighteenth century, this new presence seems mainly to have acted to increase internal tensions and rivalries within the state. All senior Alwar jagirdars were a potential challenge to the raja. They shared both understood history and 'blood'; their relation to the state and to the ruling lineage gave them the duty to participate in the governance of the state and, perhaps, the accompanying 'right to rule'. One British official would later observe that

When a Rajput chief has managed to cut away all round himself the power and independence of his kinsmen, the state topples over at the first vigorous push like any other ephemeral Asiatic Principality. It is sound political as well mechanical truth that you can have no real support without resistance, or the capacity to resist.[101]

Even if the state avoided this predicted collapse, the underlying ideology of the Rajput raj would be placed in the gravest of dangers.

This ideology was, of course, a comparatively recent creation. It did not, as some would assert, extend back to the hoary days of the *Mahabharata.* Neither was it a creation of British—or even Mughal—paramountcy. The nature, structure, and symbolism of the state was a creation of contending Rajput lineages from their great time of opportunity that the late eighteenth century represented. It is in this way, perhaps, that we can best understand the end of the eighteenth century: as a time of opportunity which would soon be extinguished by a centrally imposed inertia which seemed to the central power to be no more than rightful 'stability'.

NOTES

* The research presented in this paper has been supported by grants from the American Institute of Indian Studies, the National Endowment of the Humanities, and the Winthrop University Research Council.

1. *Aitareya Brahmana*, tr. Martin Haug as *The Aitareya Brahmana of the Rigveda*, extra vol. 4 in *Sacred Books of the Hindus*, series ed. B.D. Basu (Allahabad, 1922), p. 23.
2. Sharma, *History of Jaipur*, pp. 18-22; Bharghava, *Rise of the Kachhawas in Dhundhar*, pp. 5-6; Sarkar, *History of Jaipur*, pp. 11-12, 21-3, and 28 (nn 2 and 3); Shymaldas, *Virvinod*, 2: 1238-9; Gehelot, *Rajputane ka Itihas*, 3: 59-60; Tikkiwal, *Jaipur and the Later Mughals*, pp. 1-2; Tod, *Annals and Antiquities of Rajasthan*, 3: 1329-32; India (Republic), Rajasthan, *Rajasthan District Gazetteers*, vol. 26, *Jaipur*, comp. Savitri Gupta (Jaipur, 1987), pp. 25-6, 899-901, and 912-13; and Sham Singh Ratnawat, *Kachhawan ri vanshavli: A Genealogical [sic] Account of the Kachhawa Nobility* (Jaipur, 1981), pp. 1-4. An otherwise valuable work, but one which unfortunately does not contribute much to the present discussion, is Dinesh Chandra Shukla's *Early History of Rajasthan* (Delhi, 1978). A recurring pattern in the historical understanding of this period and this process is one of the outsider 'invited in' as a mediator or pacifying conqueror among an

otherwise unorganized or turbulent socio-political scene. To restore peace in the midst of turbulence was part of the 'job description' of the raja. There is inevitably confusion and contradiction in this realm of bardic history. For example, the Dulha Rai accounts are replicated in as many as three separate eras. In some accounts, he is even described as fleeing in romantic disguise to Dhundhar as 'the last survivor of the siege of Narwar'; see Markhand Nandshankar Mehta and Manu Nandshankar Mehta, comps, *The Hind Rajasthan or the Annals of the Native States of India*, 3 vols. (Bhandara, 1896; rpt. Delhi, 1985), 1: 191-3. Here, I have tried to disentangle the story—as it came to be understood—merely as a background and as an established and understood pattern of migratory state conquest and formation. Despite Sarkar's impassioned defence of the literal truth of traditional histories (*History of Jaipur*, pp. 27-8, it is more important to try to discern the impact of these tales than to defend slavishly the absolute accuracy of any account, be in 'traditional' or 'contemporary'.

3. Sharma, *History of Jaipur*, pp. 21-3; and Tikkiwal, *Jaipur and the Late Mughals*, p. 1.
4. Ratnawat, *Kachhawan ri Vanshavali*, pp. viii, 5-6, and 114-20; Sharma, *History of Jaipur*, pp. 22-7; Bharghava, *Rise of the Kachhawas in Dhundhar*, p. 6; and Sarkar, *History of Jaipur*, pp. 23-4. State nomenclature is a problem. The oldest name, Dhundhar, is a traditional regional reference and might best reflect the customary view of the state. Later names, however, were based on the idea of the centrality of the capital city in the functioning of the sate and the older Dhundhar Sate changed into Amber State (with the shift of administration to Amber in the fourteenth century) and, finally, to Jaipur State (with the foundation of the new city in 1727). Similar problems of urban name exist with Mewar and Marwar States, which have become more commonly known after the names of their capital cities, Udaipur and Jodhpur, respectively.
5. Ahluwalia, *Muslim Expansion in Rajasthan*, pp. 15-39.
6. India (Republic), Rajasthan, *Rajasthan District Gazetteers*, vol. 23, *Sawai Madhopur*, comp. Savitri Gupta (Jaipur, 1981), pp. 30-2 and 540-3.
7. Sharma, *History of Jaipur*, pp. 29-30; and Ahluwalia, *Muslim Expansion in Rajasthan*, pp. 83-9.
8. S.L. Nagori, *Alwar Rajya ka Itihas (1775-1857)* (Jaipur, 1982), pp. 9-17.
9. P.W. Powlett, *Gazetteer of Ulwar* (London, 1878), p. 13; and Nagori, *Alwar Rajya ka Itihas*, pp. 17-18.
10. Ratnawat, *Kachhawanri Vanshavali*, pp. xiv-xv, 35-6 and 134-6; and Bahadur Singh, *Kshatriya Vanshawali* (Jodhpur, 1987), pt. 2, p.14.
11. Powlett, *Gazetteer of Ulwar*, p. 13; Gehelot, *Rajputane ka Itihas* 3: 60, 252-3; Nagori, *Alwar Rajya ka Itihas*, p. 17; and Futeh Singh Chanpawat, *A Brief History of Jeypore* (Agra, 1899), pp. 18-19. By the sixteenth century,

Mozabad produced 400-500 maunds (around 17,000 kg) of indigo annually; see Irfan Habib, *Atlas of the Mughal Empire: Political and Economic Maps with Detailed Notes, Bibliography and Index* (Delhi, 1982), Plates 6A and 6B, and p. 20.

12. Nagori, *Alwar Rajya ka Itihas,* p. 18. As suggested earlier a good bit of this discussion is based in Fox's *Kin, Clan, Raja and Rule,* especially pp. 14-57. In general, when I speak of a 'family', I do not, of course, refer to single hearth-sharing unit, but rather to a larger corporate lineage structure which may include a number of functionally closely related households.
13. Powlett, *Gazetteer,* p. 13; and Nagori, *Alwar Rajya ka Itihas,* p. 19.
14. An interest recurring metaphor in Naruka—and other Rajput—genealogies is that of the rightful son being deprived of or resigning his deserved position in favour of a younger sibling.
15. Quoted in Powlett, *Gazatteer,* p. 46. The phrase 'strikes the hockey ball' can also be interpreted as 'practices dacoity' and this dual reading is particularly instructive. For background on the nature of the Sheikawati challenge, see Tod, *Annals and Antiquities of Rajasthan,* 3: 1378-427.
16. 'Ek Itihas Premi', *Poorvi Rajputana tatha Jeypur ke Deshi Naresh* (Banaras, 1942), pp. 37-8 and 117-19; Mehta and Mehta, *Hind Rajasthan,* 2: 198 and Powlett, *Gazetteer,* pp. 120-1.
17. Tikkiwal, *Jaipur and the Later Mughals,* pp. 2-11; Ratnawat, *Kachhawan ri Vanshawali,* pp. xvi, 57-9 and 153; Nagori, *Alwar Rajya ka Itihas,* pp. 19-20; and Sarker, *History of Jaipur,* pp. 31-41 and 218-20. An excellent detailed survey of the system at work is provided by Satya Prakash Gupta, *The Agrarian System of Eastern Rajasthan (c.1650-c.1750)* (Delhi, 1986).
18. Powlett, *Gazetteer,* pp 13-15 and 120-1; and Nagori, *Alwar Rajya ka Itihas,* p. 20. Another interesting 'coincidence' of Rajput genealogies in general and Naruka descent in particular is the frequency of five-son sets, especially in the seventeenth and eighteenth centuries. Kalyan Singh is said in some sources to have had six sons, but only five 'had issue'; in any event, any message of the sixth son has been excluded from most *vamshavalis.* This recapitulation of the five Pandava brothers (of the *Mahabharata*) cannot have been coincidental and likely was not ignored much later in a period where a strong mythic base to one's descent would be most comforting indeed.

    The bigha is frustrating unit of measure throughout northern India, one that can assume many divers meanings. In Alwar the most common bigha was the bigha of about 1/4 ha, or approximately 5/8 acre.
19. Powlett, *Gazetteer,* pp. 14-15; and Nagori, *Alwar Rajya ka Itihas,* pp. 20-1.
20. Powlett, *Gazetteer,* pp. 120-1; Nagori, *Alwar Rajya ka Itihas,* p. 2. While Narukhand is (strangely or significantly?) not mentioned, an especially valuable source for the 'vernacular regions' of the area is Joseph E. Schwartzberg, 'Folk Regions in Northwestern India', pp. 205-35 in *India:*

Culture, Society and Economy; Geographical Essays in Honour of Prof. Asok Mitra, eds. A.B. Mukerji and Aijazuddin Ahmed (Delhi, 1985).

21. Powlett, *Gazetteer,* pp. 124-5.
22. For more information on the Meo and on Mewar, see Abdushshakur, *Tarikh-i-Mev Chatri* (Delhi, 1975); Pratap C. Aggarwal, *Caste, Religion and Power: An Indian Case Study* (Delhi, 1971); and Hashim Amir-Ali, *The Meos of Mewat: Old Neighbors of New Delhi* (Delhi, 1970).
23. Powlett, *Gazetteer,* pp. 1-8; Nagori, *Alwar Rajya ka Itihas,* p. 2; and Schwartzberg, 'Folk Regions', pp. 212-13, 216-17, 224, and maps.
24. Powlett, *Gazetteer,* pp. 1 and 121-2; and Schwartzberg, 'Folk Regions', pp. 212-13, 217-19, 230 and maps.
25. See M.S.A. Rao, 'Rewari Kingdom and the Mughal Empire', in *Realm and Region in Traditional India,* ed. Richard G. Fox (Duke University Programme in Comparative Studies in Southern Asia, Monograph and Occasional Papers Series No. 15, n.p., 1977), pp. 79-89. The original unrevised conference version, presented to the conference on 'Realm and Region in Traditional India', Duke University, Durham, NC, 13-15 April 1973, has also been of value. See also Schwartzberg, 'Folk regions', pp. 212-13, 215-19, 225 and maps.
26. Powlett, *Gazetteer,* p. 1; Nagori, *Alwar Rajya ka Itihas,* p. 2; and Schwartzberg, 'Folk Regions', pp. 212-13, 218 and maps.
27. Powlett, *Gazetteer,* p. 1; and Nagori, *Alwar Rajya ka Itihas,* pp. 2 and 6. Like Narukhand, Rajawat was not characterized by Schwartzberg, 'Folk Regions'.
28. Nagori, *Alwar Rajya ka Itihas,* p. 2.
29. Powlett, *Gazetteer,* pp. 1-15; R.H. Jennings, *A Short Account of the Alwar State, 1899,* revd. edn. (Alwar, 1899), p. 2; Abul Fazl-i-'Allami, *'Ain-i-Akbari of Abul Fazl-i-'Allami,* vol. 2, *A Gazetteer and Administrative Manual of Akbar's Empire and Past History of India,* 2nd edn. (Calcutta, 1949), p. 202; and Irfan Habib, *An Atlas of the Mughal Empire,* Plates 6A and 6B and pp. 16-20.
30. Gehelot, *Rajputane ka Itihas* 3: 225; Nagori, *Alwar Rajya ka Itihas,* pp. 21-7; Alex S. Faulkner, *An Historical Sketch of the Naruka State of Ulwar in Rajputana* (Calcutta, 1895), p. 10; Powlett, *Gazetteer,* pp. 15 and 176.
31. Shymaldas, *Virvinod,* pp. 1377-8 quoted in Gehelot, *Rajputane ka Itihas,* 3: 255; Nagori, *Alwar Rajya ka Itihas,* pp. 26-8; Sharma, *History of Jaipur State,* p. 189; and James Tod, *Annals and Antiquities of Rajasthan or the Central and Western Rajput States of India,* ed. William Crooke, 3 vols. (London, 1920), 3: 1360.
32. Gehelot, *Rajputane ka Itihas,* 3: 255-6; Nagori, *Alwar Rajya ka Itihas,* pp. 28-47; Jadunath Sarkar, *Fall of the Mughal Empire,* 4 vols. (Calcutta, 1950), 3: 116, 232, and India (Republic), Rajasthan, *Rajasthan District Gazetteers,* vol. 6, *Alwar,* comp. Maya Ram (Jaipur, 1968), p. 61. To a considerable degree, Sarkar's *Fall of the Mughal Empire* and his *History of*

Jaipur contain duplicated information when they relate to Jaipur affairs during this period.

33. Tod, *Annals and Antiquities,* 3: 1361-2.
34. Sarkar, *Fall of the Mughal Empire,* 3: 232.
35. Alfred C. Lyall, *Asiatic Studies: Religious and Social* (London, 1884), p. 218. This chapter, 'The Rajput State of India', was originally published anonymously in *Edinburgh Review,* 144 (July 1876): 169-203.
36. Sharma, *Jaipur,* pp. 188-91; and Sarkar, *Fall of the Mughal Empire,* 3: 230-1.
37. Faulkner, *Ulwar,* pp. 16-18; Powlett, *Gazetteer,* p.16; Gehelot, *Rajputane ka Itihas,* 3: 257-8; Sharma, *Jaipur,* p. 190; and Mehta and Mehta, *Hind Rajasthan,* 1: 395-6. Hereafter, Macheri and Alwar are used as synonyms for the state established by Pratap Singh Naruka; Macheri is the earlier name. A distinction, however, should be made between the *state* and the *city* of Alwar.
38. The military force provided to the central power was expressed in terms of 'horses', but this included more than the animal and implied the rider and supplies for both.
39. *Tan* is a measure of the value of a grant at the time of the award; one *tan* equals approximately 6 anas (3/8 rupee). In the *sanads* awarding the jagirs, the value of the land at that time is expressed in terms of *tan* and represents the revenue lost to the state by the award of the jagir, which would then not pay revenue, but rather supply troops.
40. Mean area 4,431 bighas (1,108 ha); mean cultivated area 3,691 bighas (923 ha, or about 83 per cent cultivated); mean *tan* 10,887.
41. Pratap Singh granted jagirs as follows: Para, two; Khora, three; Palwa, two; non-*barach kotri,* two. Only Khora thikana had held a jagir in Narukhand before 1775. Five jagirs were near Rajgarh, three near Alwar, and one near Lachmangarh; the location of the remaining jagir is unknown.
42. Tikkiwal, *Jaipur and the Later Mughals,* pp. 144-7; Sarkar, *Fall of the Mughal Empire,* 3: 118-20; Gehelot, *Rajputane ka Itihas,* 3: 258; and Sharma, *History of the Jaipur State,* p. 194. Throughout, I have attempted to maintain the terminological and ideological exactitude of titles for rulers; in general terms (for Alwar) these are in an approximate rising scale from thakur, to *rao,* to raja, to *rao raja,* to *maharao raja,* to—finally—the more common maharaja. I have also used 'raja' as an all-purpose generic term.
43. See the very valuable John S. Deyell and R.E. Fryckenberg, 'Sovereignty and the "SIKKA" under Company Raj: Minting Prerogative and Imperial Legitimacy in India', *The Indian Economic and Social History Review,* 19 (January 1982): 1-25. Given the rather severe editing of this paper, it has also been useful to consult the earlier version, presented to the Fifth European Conference on Modern South Asian Studies, Leiden, The Netherlands, July 1976.

44. See William Wilfrid Webb, *The Currencies of the Hindu States of Rajputana* (Westminster, 1893; rpt. Varanasi, 1972), p. 111; and Colin R. Bruce II, John S. Deyell, Nicholas Rhodes, and William F. Spengler, *The Standard Guide to South Asian Coins and Paper Money since 1556 AD*, 1st edn. (Iola, 1982), p. 123 although only the issues of 1763, 1777, and 1782 are listed here.
45. Alwar had been a mint before, but Rajgarh was a mint only for Pratap Singh's emerging state.
46. H. Nelson Wright, *The Coinage and Metrology of the Sultans of Delhi* (Delhi, 1936; rpt. Delhi, 1974), pp. 59, 80, 291-2, 342 and 386-7.
47. See Webb, *Currencies of the Hindu State of Rajputana*, pp. 111-12 and 114; and Bruce et al., *Guide to South Asian Coins*, pp. 123-4.
48. Powlett, *Gazetteer*, p. 16; Jeysingh 'Neeraj', ed., *Vinay: Alwar Ank* (Alwar, 1969), p. 150; India (Republic), Rajasthan, Department of Archaeology and Museums, *As Stones Speak in Alwar* (Jodhpur, *c.* 1965), p. 12; and personal observations 1985.
49. Jeysingh 'Neeraj', 'Alwar ke bhitti-chitra', *The Researcher*, 12-13 (1972); 39-42; and 'Neeraj', *Vinay*, pp. 150-1.
50. Personal observations, 1985.
51. Louis Rousselet, *India and Its Native Princes: Travels in Central India and the Presidencies of Bombay and Bengal*, rev. and ed. by Lt. Col.{?} Buckle (London, 1876), pp. 250-1.
52. Similarly, such messages are expressed in the Jaipur Sate region of Sheikawati where, had it not been for the presence of British imperialism, similar decentralizing centrifugal forces may have prevailed, particularly in subordinate jagirs such as Sikar. See Francis Wacziargh and Aman Nath, *Rajasthan: The Painted Walls of Shekhavati* (Delhi, 1982); and Robert W. Stern, *The Cat and the Lion: Jaipur State in the British Raj* (Leiden, 1988), especially p. 265.
53. India, Rajasthan, *As Stones Speak in Alwar*, p. 5: and Powlett, *Gazetteer*, p. 156.
54. To avoid probable confusion, Pratap Singh (Macheri/Alwar) has been referred to as Pratap Singh Naruka or simply as Pratap Singh, whereas Pratab Singh (Jaipur) has been called Sawai Pratab Singh or Pratab Singh. In actuality, the Hindi names are the same (Pratap Singh), but this would be too confusing.
55. Tod, *Annals and Antiquities*, 3: 1361-2.
56. Sarkar, *Fall of the Mughal Empire*, 3: 116; and Mehta and Mehta, *Hind Rajashan*, 1: 206-7.
57. Throughout, information on Alwar's jagirdari families has been drawn from Alwar (Rajputana), *Jagir History showing Naruka Clan of his Highness' Government, Alwar* (Alwar, 1933); 'Ek Itihas Premi', *Poorvi Rajputana tatha Jeypur ke Deshi Naresh*, pp. 56-87; (India, Rajputana Agency), *Rajputana and Ajmer: List of Ruling Princes, Chiefs and Leading Personages*,

6th ed. (Calcutta, 1932), pp. 9-23; and Alwar (Rajputana), *The Alwar State Administration Report, 1938-39* (Alwar, 1939), Appendix II. While the Alwar jagir estates were not subjected to a regular land settlement until the 1920s useful data can be gleaned from M.F. O'Dwyer, *Final Report on the Alwar State Settlement (1900-1901)* (Lahore, 1901), and M.F. O'Dwyer, *Assessment Report of Tahsils Tijara, Bahror, Mandawar, Rajgarh and Kathumbar, Alwar State (1898-99)* (Calcutta, 1905). Also quite valuable are the *vanshavalis*, the traditional genealogical accounts, of the Kachhawaha Rajputs. One manuscript has been edited (not without flaws) by Ratnawat as *Kachhawan ri vanshavali*. More useful for Alwar and the Narukas, however, are the versions of the Kachhawaha and Naruka *vanshavalis* preserved in the records of the Alwar State Historical Department, Rajasthan State Archives, Bikaner, the most valuable files are: 16/214 'Jagirdaron ki vanshavali', 7/12 and 8/12 'Kachhawaha vanshavali' pts. 1 and 2, 1/158 'Jagiron ke halat ka mukammil rajistar', and 13/256 'Jagir bandobast'.

58. Tikkiwal, *Jaipur and the Later Mughals*, pp. 144-6; Sarkar, *Fall of the Mughal Empire*, 3: 118-19; and Gehelot, *Rajputane ka Itihas*, 3: 258.
59. Sharma, *History of Jaipur*, p. 194.
60. Sharma, *Jaipur*, p. 194; Tikkiwal, pp. 146-7; and Sarkar, 3: 119-20.
61. Tikkiwal, pp. 147-52; Sarkar, 3: 120-1; Sharma, *Jaipur*, pp. 190-1; and Tod, *Annals and Antiquities*, 3: 1362-3.
62. Sarkar, 3: 125-31, 233.
63. Sharma, *Jaipur*, pp. 196-7; and Tikkiwal, pp. 156-62.
64. R.K. Saxena, *Maratha Relations with the Major States of Rajputana (1761-1818 A.D.)* (Delhi, 1973), pp. 97-130; Sharma, *Jaipur*, pp. 198-9; Tikkiwal, pp. 164-78; and Anil Chandra Banerjee, *Rajput Studies* (Calcutta, 1944), pp. 205-6.
65. Sharma, *Jaipur*, p. 199; and Tikkiwal, pp. 178-9.
66. Sukhumar Bhattacharyya, *The Rajput States and the East India Company from the Close of the 18th Century to 1820* (Delhi, 1927), p. 23.
67. [Lyall], 'The Rajput States of India', p. 172. A slightly revised version in Lyall, *Asiatic Studies*, pp. 207-8.
68. Fox, *Kin, Clan, Raj and Rule*, p. 80.
69. Fox, *Kin, Clan, Raj and Rule*, pp. 91-7.
70. These and other population figures here cited are drawn from '1891 census'.
71. Ibid.; and Powlett, *Gazetteer*, p. 17.
72. Of the Chauhans *kul* almost all (89 per cent) were of the Chauhan *sakh*, with the Deoras recorded as the second largest. Jadon Rajputs come in as a close fourth, with 9.7 per cent of Alwar's Rajputs, mainly of the *sakham* of Tuar, Jadon, and Bhatti.
73. It is impossible to determine the distribution between Lalawat Narukas and the other *khampam*.

74. On this important broadening of participatory government beyond the narrow ruling lineage, especially to the merchant communities, see the comments by H.H. Mayurdhwajsinhji of Dhrangadhra in Charles Allen and Sharada Dwivedi, *Lives of the Indian Princes* (London, 1984), p. 63.
75. Throughout, information on jagirs has generally been drawn from: Alwar, *Jagir History;* and Alwar, *Alwar State Administration Report*, Appendix II. For figures on areas and land usage patterns, see: Powlett, *Gazetteer*, pp. 188-90; O'Dwyer, *Assessment Report of Kishangarh, Ramgarh, Govindgarh and Lachmangarh*; O'Dwyer, *Assessment Report of Tahsils Tijara, Bahror, Mandawar, Rajgarh and Katumbar*; O'Dwyer, *Assessment Report of Nimrana Estate*; and O'Dwyer, *Final Report on the Alwar State Settlement*.
76. As has been indicated already, the responsibility of the jagirdar was not simply to supply horses, but also the riders and logistical support for both. When an obligation is expressed in terms of 'horses', it should be taken to imply this unit.
77. This question requires extensive examination; see Edward S. Haynes, 'Land Use, Natural Resources, and the Rajput State, 1780-1980', unpublished paper presented to the Conference on Conservation of the Environment and Culture in Rajasthan (the 1st International Conference on Rajasthan), University of Rajasthan, Jaipur, December 1987.
78. Powlett, *Gazetteer*, p. 94.
79. India (Republic), Rajasthan, *Report of the State Land Commission for Rajasthan* (Jaipur, 1959), p. 7.
80. Powlett, *Gazetteer*, pp. 14-15; India, Foreign Department, *Chiefs and Leading Families of Rajputana* (Calcutta: Superintendent of Government Printing, India, 1894), p. 82; and Lyall, *Asiatic Studies*, p. 218.
81. Powlett, *Gazetteer*, pp. 122-3.
82. Alwar (Rajputana), *Thikana Jaoli* (Allahabad, 1925), pp. 6-7.
83. See, for example, Alwar (Rajputana), *Thikana Garhi* (Allahabad, 1925), pp. 3-4.
84. Powlett, *Gazetteer*, pp. 122-3.
85. Powlett, *Gazetteer*, pp. 122-3. Jaoli—for example—was not universally accepted as a *jagir* by the other Naruka families, although it claimed such status; see Alwar (Rajputana), *Thikana Jaoli* (Allahabad, 1925), pp. 6-7.
86. John T. Platts, *A Dictionary of Urdu, Classical Hindi and English* (Oxford, 1968), p. 511; cf. *The Compact Edition of the Oxford English Dictionary* (Oxford, 1971), 1: 724.
87. See Henry Yule and A.C. Burnell, *Hobson-Jobson: A Glossary of Colloquial Anglo-Indian Words and Phrases, and of Kindred Terms, Etymological, Historical, Geographical and Discursive*, new edn., ed. William Crooke (rpt.

edn.; Delhi, 1968, p. 311; and H.H. Wilson, *A Glossary of Judicial and Revenue Terms of Useful Words Occurring in Official Documents relating to the Administration of the Government of India . . .* (London, 1855; rpt. edn., Delhi, 1968), p. 125.

88. John B. Wolf, 'The Cult of the King', in *Louis XIV: A Profile,* ed. John B. Wolf (New York, 1972), p. 136.
89. Dasharatha Sharma, *Lectures on Rajput History and Culture* (*Raghunath Prasad Nopany Lectures,* 1966) (Delhi, 1970), pp. 109-17. The larger issue of earlier Rajput statecraft comprises, today, an important lacuna in our emerging understanding of preindustrial statecraft in South Asia. An important and challenging contribution to this emerging understanding has been offered by Kolff, 'The Rajput of Ancient and Medieval North India'. Nevertheless, the durbar of Mughal usage was the dominant informing ceremonial for Rajput usages, and the imperial symbols and institutions became the pattern also of Rajput States.
90. The best surveys of Mughal ceremonials are given by Mohd. Azher Ansari in his 'Court Ceremonial of the Great Mughals', *Islamic Culture* 35 (July 1961): 183-97, and 'Some Aspects of Social Life at the Court of the Great Mughals', *Islamic Culture* 36 (July 1962): 182-95, and Bernard S. Cohn, 'The Mughal, Court Rituals, and the Theory of Authority in the 16th and 17th Centuries', privately circulated draft, 1977.
91. Tupper, *Our Indian Protectorate,* pp. 361-2.
92. Unfortunately, sources are not at present available to examine this aspect of political mobilization in Alwar. It would be a logical progression from this study to examine the participation of Meos and other peasant groups in Alwar political and economic changes in the nineteenth and twentieth centuries.
93. India, Foreign Department, *A Collection of Treaties, Engagements and Sanads: Relating to India and Neighbouring Countries,* vol. 3, *The Treaties & c. Relating to the States of Rajputana,* 6 vols., comp. C.U. Aitcheson (Calcutta, 1932), pp. 400-1. See also A.C. Banerjee, *The Rajput States and the East India Company,* p. 411.
94. India, Foreign Department, *Treaties, Engagements, and Sanads,* 3: 401-2; and Powlett, *Gazetteer,* pp. 19-20.
95. K.N. Panikkar, *British Diplomacy in North India: A Study of the Delhi Residency, 1803-1857* (Delhi, 1968), pp. 44-5; and Bhattacharyya, *Rajput States and East India Company,* pp. 80-1.
96. India, Foreign Department, *Treaties, Engagements and Sanads,* 3: 402. See also: Panikkar, *British Diplomacy,* p. 47; and Sudarshan Chandra Maheshwary, 'British Relations with the States of Rajputana (1815-1835)' (Ph.D. dissertation, University of Rajasthan; Jaipur, 1963), pp. 51-2.

97. Panikkar, *British Diplomacy*, pp. 45-57; and Powlett, *Gazetteer*, p. 20.
98. India, Foreign Department, *Report on the Political Administration of the Rajpootana States, 1871-72*, No. C in *Selections from the Records of the Government of India, Foreign Department* (Calcutta, 1872), p. 17; Powlett, *Gazetteer*, p. 20; and Gehelot, *Rajputane ka Itihas*, 3: 268-9.
99. K.N. Panikkar, *British Diplomacy*, p. 47 and Maheshwary, 'British Relations', pp. 51-2.
100. Maheshwary, 'British Relations', pp. 181-7 and 'Bhanswar to Ajmere: Lt. Col. A. Lockett's Narrative of a journey from Bhuswar in Bhurtpore territory to a part in the North-West States (Ajmere), April-June 1831', Foreign Department Miscellaneous Series, National Archives of India, Delhi, No. 272, pp. 27-8.
101. [Lyall], 'Rajput States', p. 194. The 'ephemeral' label was, of course, an imperial necessity. For a useful overview of Lyall's important place in both imperial administration and historiography, see Roger Owen, 'Imperial Policy and Theories of Social Change: Sir Alfred Lyall in India', in *Anthropology & the Colonial Encounter*, ed. Talal Asad (London, 1973), pp. 223-43.

Maharaja Krisnacandra, Hinduism, and Kingship in the Contact Zone of Bengal

DAVID L. CURLEY

NADIYA WAS a little Hindu kingdom in Bengal, ruled by a line of Brahman kings who became zamindars under the Mughals, but lost much of their zamindari under the British. Nadiya was located along the eastern bank of the Hughli river, and at its peak extended from Plassey in the north to the shifting islands and mangrove swamps of the Sundarbans in the south. Its name was derived from the ancient centre of Sanskritic education, Navadvīpa, but like all Hindu zamindars of Mughal Bengal, the Nadiya rajas also studied Persian, and became familiar with Persian court culture. Nadiya also was in the heart of a contact zone with Europeans, a zone which ran north and south between European factories and settlements along the Hughli river. Parganas belonging to Nadiya were near neighbours of the English settlement at Calcutta; the road north from Calcutta to the English factories of Kasimbazar and Maldah went through Nadiya; and the silk-weaving centre of Santipur in Nadiya supplied fine *mulmul* for the European trade.

Long before the English began to rule territory in Bengal, relations between them and the Nadiya rulers involved calculations of mutual interest. In 1697 Ramkrisna, then Raja of Nadiya, deposited Rs. 48,000 in Calcutta with the English East India Company, while Bengal was disturbed by the anti-Mughal rebellion of Sobha Singh. He was 'unwilling to be knowne to the Government to have mony as is the Custome of all the Rajahs and Jimmidars [zamindars] of the Country to keep their Riches private . . .' and accepted interest of only 7.5 per cent.[1] The same man is said to have accepted a temporary garrison of English trained soldiers.

Relations between Nadiya rulers and the Mughal nawab became more uncertain in the mid-eighteenth century, and the presence of the English, more important. I will use works of art patronized by the Nadiya rajas in that century to explore their self-representation. In particular, I will examine family histories and temple architecture, to argue that during the chaotic middle decades of the eighteenth century, Maharaja Krisnacandra (1710-82) constructed a more unitary and inclusive meaning for 'Hinduism' to support his novel claim to a more independent sovereignty in Nadiya, as new threats and opportunities opened before him.

In those times sovereignty had to be defended and maintained. The Nadiya rajas' symbolic 'constitutions' of sovereignty could not by themselves create an independent kingdom. By attending to how Krisnacandra identified and solved problems of religious identity and kingship, we also can begin to see strengths and weaknesses, both in his cultivation of historical knowledge, and in his practice of politics.

The First and Second Foundings of Nadiya

Apparently written immediately after his ascension to the Nadiya throne in 1728, the *Kṣitīśavaṃśāvalīcaritaṃ* is a Sanskrit genealogy and history of the forebears of Maharaja Krisnacandra of Nadiya.[2] It describes the successes and failures of the Nadiya kings in terms of an uneasy combination of Sanskritic and Mughal roles and principles of legitimacy.

We may note, first, that this Brahman lineage had two founders. The first, Battanarayaṇa, was one of five Brahmans invited from Kanyakubja to Vanga by the legendary Hindu sovereign Adisura to perform a *homa* sacrifice of the flesh of a vulture, whose inauspicious appearance at his palace otherwise promised a future of misfortune; and in the Brahmans' success despite the utter strangeness of the task thus set them, we can read the superiority of their Vedic learning. In return Adisura settled the Brahmans in his own city, where they lived for one year. Desiring that Battanarayana continue to reside, Adisura then offered him a gift of some villages, but Bhattanarayana declined to demean himself by accepting any additional gifts, and instead offered to purchase the villages. Thereafter he and his descendants 'enjoyed' these villages 'exempt from taxation' for eleven generations, or 322 years.[3]

Unfortunately, Mahmud of Ghazna, 'coming from the land of the *mlecchas*', vanquished the 'lord of Delhi' at the same time that four brothers in the twelfth generation disputed the kingdom among themselves. One secured recognition from the sultan, and thus an advantage over his brothers, by offering to pay taxes.[4] Thus matters continued for another five generations and 167 years, bringing us to the time of Emperor Akbar (one must appreciate the schematic nature of this history), when Raja Kasinath lost his life, and the lineage its royal possessions, for daring to slay one of Akbar's royal elephants.[5]

This almost brings us to history more properly speaking, and to the second founder of the lineage, a grandson of Kasinath, who at the age of eleven joined the service of an unnamed Muslim 'minister' sent by the sultan of Delhi. This grandson, Durgadas, 'in a short while became adept in the meaning of all the Persian *śāstra*', so pleasing his employer that he was appointed to serve in the *qanungo daftar* (land registrar's office) of the sarkar of Satgaon, and given the title *majmuahdār* (temporary revenue accountant) and a new name, Bhavananda.[6] By learning Persian, and by entering directly into the Mughal land revenue bureaucracy, Bhavananda secured revenue-collecting rights to a few villages (but not to his patrimonial kingdom), and changed part of the royal culture of his lineage. Descendants are described as 'saluting' Mughal rulers 'with the customary ceremonies' and as being honoured, in return, 'with gracious and friendly conversations'—all according to Persian courtly culture.[7] When Bishop Heber visited Nadiya in 1824, he found the grandson of Maharaja Krisnacandra dwelling in one room of the ruins of his ancestor's palace. Nevertheless, after the Bishop's rank in English society had been ascertained, he was entertained in this man's 'court', and for his audience with the Nadiya raja the Bishop was supplied an interpreter, 'since in strict conformity with court etiquette, the conversation passed in Persian'.[8]

A crucial change in Bhavananda's fortunes is said to have occurred somewhat later. Raja Man Singh of Amber had been sent by the emperor to conquer Pratapaditya of Yasohar, the most powerful of twelve 'kings enjoying their kingdoms exempt from taxation' in Bengal. Bhavananda supplied Man Singh with transport and food for his army when they were caught in a week-long rainstorm, guided him to Yasohar, a kingdom neighbouring Nadiya to the east, and at the crux of the battle, advised renewed attack, which met with success. In return, Man Singh took Bhavananda back to Delhi, told Emperor Jahangir about his assistance, and secured for him a sworn and signed document (i.e. a *sanad*) granting him a 'kingdom' in the fourteen parganas originally held by his ancestors. The Nadiya genealogy emphasizes the honour conferred by Emperor Jahangir's signature on this document.[9]

In short, the two founders of this royal Brahman lineage mastered two kinds of learning, Vedic and Persian, and defined two ways of relating to their respective sovereigns. Bhattanarayana 'enjoyed' his villages outright, and did not receive gifts from or pay taxes to, the Hindu king Adisura. Bhavananda's position was far inferior. In fact, if this genealogy has a single lesson, it is that from Bhavananda on, failure to collect, account for and pay the stipulated revenue demand resulted in imprisonment.

It is necessary, however, to criticize this 'history' of Bhavananda. A second *sanad* from Jahangir also has been preserved by the family. According to it, Bhavananda in fact did not become a raja. Instead he became a pargana chaudhuri and *qanungo* in the local land revenue system, with the duty to present an 'account of the receipts and arrears of the revenue' (*jamā-wākil-bākī*) for all his parganas, to protect the weak from the strong, and to 'accomplish the weal and prevent the injury of the whole region by whatever means'.[10] Since Bhavananda already had been employed as *qanungo* at Satgaon supervising the record keeping of pargana *qanungos* under his authority, it seems reasonable that his position as one of the latter was in some way achieved through the former office.[11] One argument for this supposition is that the original *sanad*, now largely unreadable, is dated 1606, six years before the conquest of Pratapaditya in 1612.

Second, Pratapaditya was not defeated by Man Singh (who served as nawab of Bengal under Akbar during most of the period from 1589 to the latter's final illness in 1605). If Bhavananda really confirmed his position by assisting in the defeat of Pratapaditya, he must have helped not Akbar's Hindu general, courtier, and brother-in-law and nawab, but a Muslim, one Giyas Khan, sent by Nawab Islam Khan in 1612 to bring Pratapaditya to submission. (Although the Nadiya family's second *sanad* from Jahangir to Bhavananda, is dated 1613, it does not refer to Pratapaditya's defeat.[12]) What are the consequences of so retelling the family's history? Potentially embarrassing events are elided in this history, and it minimizes what may have been Bhavananda's shrewdness in promoting himself by means of his bureaucratic position at Saptagram, and in materially assisting a Muslim general against a powerful, local Hindu king.

Conflicting Principles of Legitimacy

Perhaps an ideal balance between the roles of Sanskritic king and Mughal zamindar may be taken from the life of Bhavananda's grandson Raghava (r. *c.* 1633-84). Retaining undivided possession of the kingdom by Mughal custom, he gave his brothers monthly funds for their maintenance. He also regularly paid the taxes due to the 'Yavana king', and so became the latter's 'faithful servant' (*viśvāsapātra*).[13] He built a huge tank, and a temple to Śiva on one bank (the Rāghaveśvara temple at Dighnagar, dated 1669) for the dedication of which he invited a 'great assembly' of learned Brahmans from all over India, and 'kings, princes and ministers from various regions' besides. For the dedication of this tank and the *Śiva-liṅga* he is said to have spent Rs. 3,00,000.[14]

It is easy to note cultural tensions between Sanskritic and Persian cultural forms. Raghava's son, Rudra Ray (r. *c.* 1684-91), refused to take the drum upon his shoulder as part of the ceremony of receiving *khil'at,* and when attending the sultan he insisted on wearing an unsewn dhoti beneath his court robe instead of sewn pants. 'Brahmans devoted to true conduct', he said, 'wear such a garment as mine; but by sewn garments they incur a fault.'[15] Rudra Ray remained in the nawab's good graces by his lavish distribution of bribes and presents. Comparing himself to a famous revenue official, he once acknowledged that, 'as wealth is the root of this qanungo's mastery of office (*karmādhykaṣatā*), so also it is the root of my kingdom'.[16]

Rudra Ray was responsible for constructing the family's palace and grounds at Krisnanagar. For this purpose he brought a Muslim builder from the provincial capital, Jahangirnagar (Dhaka), and secured permission from the nawab to use battlements (*kangura*) in the design, and to fly banners and beat kettledrums. The grounds included a gatehouse, a room 'suitable for the playing of musical instruments' (*naqqar khana*), a three-storied public audience hall into which one could drive elephants, horses and conveyances, elephant and horse stables, and an *antapur* 'like a palace of the goddess'.[17] Another detail gives us a glimpse of a possible source of his evident prosperity: he also built a high road from Krisnanagar to Santipur, which already was an important silk weaving centre for the Dutch.[18]

In the next generation, Ramcandra, who contested with his younger half-brother for the throne in the years 1691-4, was a powerful wrestler and prodigious eater, and won the affection of the faujdar of Hughli for his heroic qualities. But he neglected daily rites and worship, 'was adverse to good conversation with learned Brahmans', and did not follow his father's advice, for which reasons Rudra Ray gave the kingdom to his half-brother.[19] Other descendants also had to balance the contradictory requirements of king and Mughal zamindar. Ramkrisna (r. 1694-1705), half brother of Ramcandra, was a friend of Aurangzeb's grandson, Nawab Azim ush-Shan, entertained the Jagat Seth, was on good terms with the 'Chief of the *mlecchas* from the South' at Calcutta, from whom he received 2,500 skilled 'soldiers' (*choldār*) 'to use as he pleased', but died in prison of smallpox, having failed to pay Nawab Jafar Khan the taxes due.[20] Krisnacandra's father, Raghuram, proved his heroism in battle for Nawab Murshid Quli Khan, and thereby redeemed his father from prison, but he himself subsequently was confined at Murshidabad for failure to pay the taxes still owed. Even though imprisoned for debts to the nawab, he continued to distribute land to Brahmans;[21] indeed, this single act reveals the fundamental contradiction in his several roles. Nadiya's zamindar-kings in this account had distinct roles, one Mughal and one Sanskritic. In many ways the two were opposed to each other, but neither could be eliminated. Therefore, in this narrative the succeeding possessors of the Nadiya throne, their actions and passions, their successes and failures, are all arranged in a single field, like iron filings around a bi-polar magnet.

The Maratha Incursions

We now may turn to the life of Maharaja Krisnacandra, and to two remarkable works of art composed with his patronage a few years before Clive's victory at Plassey, 23 June 1757. These works of art are the *Anandāmaṅgala* by Bharatcandra Ray, first performed in 1751-2, and the Rājarājeśvara temple at Sibnibas, dedicated in 1754. I will argue that these two works fundamentally change the 'field' of kingship in Nadiya, by means of a unitary understanding of 'Hinduism' and a concomitant assertion of Hindu 'inclusivism'. I also will argue that both have as their occasion the almost annual Maratha incursions of 1742-50, and both preface Krisncandra's assertion of independent sovereignty.

Bharatcandra's poem begins with the death of Nawab Shuja-ud-din Khan on 13 March 1739, and the succession of his son, Sarfaraz, to the position of nawab of Bengal, Bihar and Orissa. Alivardi, deputy nawab of Bihar under the father, staged a revolt, defeated and killed the son in battle, and made himself nawab in April 1740. In Bharatcandra's narrative he then led his armies into Bhubaneswar 'in pomp and ceremony' and over this sacred place, Śiva's place in the world, 'the tyrant Mughal practiced tyranny'. To punish him, Śiva called upon the 'king' of the 'Bargis'; thus, 'for that sin the three *subas* came to be like hell'. Neither Nadiya nor Krisnacandra escaped ensuing difficulties.[22]

We can add that relatives and partisans of the slain Nawab Sarfaraz invited Raghuji Bhonsle, the Maratha chief of Nagpur, to invade Bengal, while Alivardi was campaigning in Orissa in 1742. Raghuji sent his general Bhaskar Ram in command of 20,000 cavalry to collect the *cauth* from Bengal. They surprised and surrounded Alivardi in the neighbourhood of Barddhaman town, and while Alivardi and his army fought their way back to Katwah, the Marathas looted the countryside, including parts of Nadiya. For a day they even entered the capital, Murshidabad, where they extracted Rs. 3,00,000 from the treasury of the nawab's banker Jagat Seth Fatehcand. Against all expectations the Marathas did not retire during the rainy season, and were not driven out until the following October. This first invasion was remembered for Maratha atrocities on Bengali men, women and children, and it is what Bharatcandra describes as a kind of 'hell'.[23]

I return to Bharatcandra's account. Some time during or shortly after the first invasion of 1742, Krisnacandra was imprisoned at Murshidabad for failure to pay Alivardi an extraordinary cess of Rs. 12,00,000. While in prison he worshipped the goddess. She took the form of Annapurna, who assures gods and humans their supply of food, and commanded him in a dream to establish her worship annually on the eighth night of the bright fortnight of *Caitra.* She also told him to command his court poet Bharatcandra to compose her 'auspicious song', for which she would reveal the narrative. This song the raja should make known publicly. Finally, Bharatcandra concludes, according to this very command Krisnacandra worshipped Annapurna and 'crossed over that difficulty'.[24] Some time after 1742 the raja relocated his capital about 12 miles east of Krisnanagar, at a fortified place he called Sibnibas, where he apparently escaped Maratha raids. Alivardi and Raghuji finally agreed to a truce in 1750, by which Alivardi ceded all the surplus revenues of Orissa, and promised to pay Rs. 12,00,000 annually as the *cauth* of Bengal.

To the ruler of Nadiya as to everyone, the Marathas must have revealed Alivardi's weaknesses, even as Alivardi increased his financial demands. The Marathas themselves, however, seem to have offered plunder and rapine as the only alternative. Could Maharaja Krisnacandra still define himself in relation to both of the roles of his position, Sanskritic king and Mughal zamindar, as hitherto imagined and practised by the Nadiya lineage? In this situation, Bharatcandra retold the story of its second founder, Bhavananda.

Unitary Hinduism

Before examining this story, we must briefly describe the unitary Hinduism advocated by Bharatcandra's poem in a previous section that describes the re-education of the great seer Vyasa. Vyasa, we are told, was a fanatic Vaiṣṇava. Together with his disciples he wandered from place to place, carrying with him loads and loads of books and almanacs, and engaging in various discussions on the sacred texts and their commentaries.[25] By chance one day he met a party of naked Śaiva ascetics led by Saunaka. The two leaders debated the merits of their respective deities, and came thus to Kāśī, where Vyasa denounced Śiva in his own city. For this impertinence he was struck dumb, until Viṣṇu himself taught Vyasa Śiva's greatness, at which point Vyasa became as fanatic a Śaiva as he had been a Vaiṣṇava, and recited yet another Purāṇa, the *Kāśī Khaṇḍa.*[26] The consequence is that Vyasa had to be taught by Annapurna herself that 'Hari, Hara and Bidhi (Viṣṇu, Śiva and Brahmā) are my body. The one who worships them without distinction is the judicious (*dhīra*) devotee.'[27]

In 1776 Krisnacandra built a temple to Hari-Hara at Amghata, on the inscription to which we find this same doctrine expressed. Distinguishing Murari (Viṣṇu) and Tripurahara (Śiva) is called 'the wrong notion of the foolish', and the temple's syncretic god, Hari-Hara, is identified as the 'nondual Supreme Reality' (*Advaita Brahman*).[28] The unitary theology of Bharatcandra's poem was Krisnacandra's own theology. We will see that it seems to have been attractive because it composed differences within Hinduism so as to present a united defence against challenges from non-Hindus.

Jahangir's Conversion and Hindu 'Inclusivism'

Bharatcandra alters in many ways the account of the *Kṣitīśa-vaṃśāvalīcaritaṃ.* First, the storm which halted Man Siṃha's army and during which Bhavananda's supplies of food were critical for the army's well-being, becomes an act of the goddess, Annapurna, who supplies gods and humans with food thereby secure wider worship. 'If you give sorrow with happiness,' her attendant Padmā advises, 'then you will receive pujā.'[28] Second,

Bhavananda worships Annapurna, and teaches Man Siṃha to do so, and because of her grace the army can be fed (true, with Bhavananda's own supplies), the storm passes, and the conquest of Pratapaditya proceeds. Third, the contrast between Bhavananda and Pratapaditya is elaborated and the latter's military resistance to the Mughal conquest is given a sacerdotal dimension. Whereas Bhavananda worships the gracious, pacific, and food-granting deity Annapurna, Pratapaditya worships Kali. (We should note that Bharatcandra himself tells us that Krisnacandra also worshipped Kali.[30]) Third, Man Siṃha requests from Emperor Jahangir a kingdom for Bhavananda, not because the latter fed the general's armies from his own stores, but because he worshipped Annapurna, and thereby secured her assistance. Finally, and understandably, the emperor expresses his opposition to so reward an infidel Brahman; he must be 'converted' before he will do so. The result of these interventions is that the poem brings the Mughal emperor within the field of Annapurna's authority, so that the Mughal *sanad* to Bhavananda may be derived, ultimately, from the goddess herself.

Jahangir's 'conversion' proceeds in two stages. The first is a debate with Bhavananda about the relative merits of Islam and Hinduism, by which the superiority of a Hindu 'inclusivism' is established,[31] although the emperor remains intransigent. The second is a conclusive display of Annapurna's *māyā*, as a result of which the emperor asks Bhavananda to direct him also in appropriate acts of worship.

We may consider a few of the claims advanced in this debate, first in the rhetoric of Jahangir. Hindus worship 'ghosts', a fraud perpetrated by Satan; really tailless monkeys eat the food offerings to these ghosts. The Hindu sacred texts, too, are false, the deceptions of Satan. Hindu men shave their beards, a sign of God's light. Hindus sacrifice goats, saying that God has eaten them, but the meat is not *hālāl*, and the taking of life therefore is unlawful. Hindus make a fault of accepting drinking water from others, to say nothing of cooked rice, but do not heed the *qazi* and the Prophet's deputy (*nāyeb*, the Islamic ruler). Hindu widows may not remarry, and the flower that blooms in them every month is wasted for want of seed, a great sin. Hindus make idols of clay, wood, and stone, and give them a soul; can something formed by a man and given a soul by a man really save that man? Hindus do not keep concubines, calling it the sin of adultery; God seems to have created them for suffering. (In *sālāṭ*) human servants (of God) should touch the ground with their heads as a sign of worship; for by an act of mercy the Merciful (God), has given them responsibility [lit., *diyāche māthā*, caused them to 'give' (place a burden upon) their heads]. Failing to understand this, Hindus greet everyone they serve by touching the ground with their heads. Brahmans compose lying books and teach people to be *kafirs*. Jahangir's desire is to give this and every Brahman he meets, not a *sanad*, but a *sunnat* (circumcision).[32]

Bhavananda's strategy in response is to deny that Hindus worship a different being than Muslims: 'As there is one Lord (*īśvar*) of Hindus, Muslims and all souls and living creatures, so there are not two creeds (*mat*).' The fundamental unity of religions he proposes, based on worshipping the one 'Lord', has the crucial feature that it gives priority to Hinduism: 'For what creed is there in the Qur'ān that is not in the Purāṇas? But consider, Hindus are prior and Muslims later.'[33] The proposed identity of the deity worshipped by Hindu and Muslim is the Formless Lord (*nirākār īśvar*)—who nevertheless can be known only through his 'enformed' (*sākār*) manifestations. Thus to the crucial charge of idolatry, Bhavananda replies:

> Look, according to both the Purāṇas and the Qur'ān, everything—clay, wood, stone, and so forth—is the Lord. One who forms an image and worships sees the Formless Lord enformed. But one who thinks of the Formless one without thinking of him as enformed is like someone who throws away the gold and then ties up the knot in the end of her *sāri*. . . . Thinking of the goddess Hindus put vermilion on trees, but what good is done by *nāmāz* in an empty room?[34]

From the rhetorically superior position of this Hindu inclusivism, Bhavananda then can respond, in a language as stereotypical as Jahangir's, to the other charges and make counter accusations against some of the beliefs and practices of Islam. A widow who remarries is like a cow that leaves one bull for another. If the Veda, Purāṇa, and Āgama are the deceptions of Satan, why should one fear to call the Koran also a deception of Satan? If piercing a boy's ears (to initiate a Hindu boy) is hoodwinking and knavery, circumcision is a terrible knavery. Hindus are not conscious of distinctions when thinking of what is beyond distinctions (*abhed*), so they touch their heads to the ground before everyone they serve, for the Lord is in all the forms of the cosmos. In the form of the sun the Lord rises in the east. Facing east to worship, Hindus obtain the sunrise of knowledge—but Muslims say *nāmāz* facing west. A Brahman who knows the Ultimate Reality (*brahmajñānī brāhmaṇ*) is the deputy (*nāyeb*) of Brahmā; such a one neither heeds prohibitions against nor incurs faults of commensal eating and drinking.[35]

This last defence upholds the Tantric adept's immunity to commensal restrictions. He truly knows that the same Lord is worshipped by all creeds. Is not the claim implied that Bhavananda and Krisnacandra were such adepts? In comparison with Muslims, Europeans too are non-sectarian and rule-free: 'They neither pierce their ears nor practice circumcision, have no cleansing rituals; and eat whatever they get. Saying the Lord exists is their only duty.'[36]

Comparing this debate to the roles of Nadiya kings in the *Kṣitīśavaṃśāvalīcaritaṃ*, one must note first that at issue is not the competing roles of king and zamindar, but the truth and 'merit' of Hinduism and Islam as systems of thought and practice. Second, the essential unity of different Hindu sects and of their particular deities is assumed throughout Bhavananda's response, as it earlier was assumed in the narrative of Vyasa's re-education. Third, Hinduism in this debate is given a position of supremacy to Islam, even though the 'Lord' ultimately worshipped by Hindus and Muslims is the same. Finally, in this narrative Bhavananda's agency has been circumscribed even more narrowly than in the *Kṣitīśavaṃśāvalīcaritaṃ*, so that he regains his kingdom only by means of sacerdotal knowledge, not by any other virtues.

When the emperor cannot be persuaded by reason and debate, Annapurna herself must intervene with a direct demonstration of her transforming power. By *māyā* she and all the gods recreate on a cosmic scale Jahangir's own court, with the goddess herself as emperor. This cosmic Mughal court then makes Bhavananda a raja. Then the goddess forms countless smaller replicas of Jahangir and makes these replicas beg forgiveness of Bhavananda. Here we have an explicit representation of the relation between the Mughal emperor and Annapurna's authority: the Mughal seems to be a speck of planetary dust caught within the gravitational field of the goddess, entirely dependent upon her even while he imagines his own independence of her. But in the following acts of her drama the goddess shows us that she herself cannot be imagined as a sun; she is not stable or unitary. She multiplies her images in ways more and more novel and contrary until the emperor 'wants to praise the enchantment, but no speech comes from his mouth'.[37]

Raja Krisnacandra's Temple at Sibnibas

Bharatcandra himself suggests that the unitary and encompassing understanding of Hinduism, so displayed by Annapurna, would be given architectural and liturgical expression at Raja Krisnacandra's refuge at Sibnibas. His poem concludes with a 'prophecy' of the goddess, foretelling the lives of the Nadiya kings (up to Krisnacandra she seems to follow the account of the *Kṣitīśavaṃśāvalīcaritaṃ*). About the poet's patron Krisnacandra, her 'prophecy' continues:

> At Kāśī he will build the flight of steps to Jñāna Vāpī. He will reveal the temple [*mandir*] and icon [*bigraha*] of the form [*mūrti*] of Brahmaṇyadeva and reside there, making it Śib'nibās [Śiva's residence, the word suggests a second Kāśī]. There he will reveal the worship of my image [*pratimā*].[38]

Her 'prophecy' then recapitulates the account of the Maratha incursions, and of the poet's own commission.

Jñanā Vāpī is the 'Well of Wisdom' to which pilgrims come 'to sip the waters and take a vow of intention (*saṃkalpa*)' before undertaking pilgrimages in and around Varanasi.[39] This well is associated with the introduction of Annapurna's worship in Varanasi from Kamakhya in Assam, so construction at this site continued the Krisnacandra's service to the goddess of food.[40] The raja's construction took place in the context of Aurangzeb's destruction of the old Viśvanātha (Śiva) temple immediately north of the well, in 1669, and the building of a mosque on the same site. The present temple of Viśvanātha was not built until 1777, by the Maratha queen, Rani Ahilyabai of Indore.[41] Krisnacandra's piety and self-assertion in building the flight of steps at Jñāna Vāpī would have been more conspicuous in his own time than it is now.

There are three large temples at Sibnibas: a Rām-Sitā temple built by his first wife and a Śiva temple built by his second wife, both in 1762; and the large Rājarājeśvara temple built by Krisnacandra himself in 1754.[42] The date of this last temple, completed about two years after Bharatcandra's poem, and the fact that it alone was built by Raja Krisnacandra himself, identify it and its deity as the poem's 'temple', 'icon', and 'form' of 'Brahmayadeva' by which Sibnibas became 'Śiva's residence', a second Kāśī. The inscription of this temple reads:

King Śrīyuta Kṛṣṇacandra, the crest-jewel among rulers, who, indeed, is born in Bharata like a Celestial Wish-fulfilling tree and a conqueror of the Guardians of the Quarters, having erected a temple whose tower touches the moon, in this learned town, installed Śambhu in the Śaka year 1676.[43]

For the form of this temple one finds few precedents among eighteenth-century brick temples of Mughal Bengal (see Plate 1). It is a tall, octagonal structure surmounted by an elongated, eight-sided *chālā* roof.[44] The east, south, and west facades have doorways set into cusped, pointed-arched entrances, and similar cusped pointed-arched niches are set into the remaining five facades. Above them two rows of rounded arched niches complete the decoration of each facade. There is no terracotta relief sculpture, nor any other figurative decoration, a feature which sets this temple apart from any of its predecessors built by the Nadiya raja. At each of the eight corners engaged columns rise just above the peak of the curved cornices between them. Hindu observers have not failed to notice the similarity to the *minara*, or more precisely, to engaged turrets and columns found in many mosques built at Dhaka and Murshidabad.[45] The characteristic spire-like roof of a Śiva temple, however, towers above all

Plate 1: Left to right: The Rājarājeśvara Temple, 1754; the Mahārājeśvara Temple, 1762; and the Rām-Sītā-Lakṣmaṇ Temple, 1762, at Sibnibas.

Islamicate elements that ornament the facades. From the outside, this seems to be an exact visual representation of the Hindu 'inclusivism' for which Bhavananda had argued in Bharatcandra's poem.

Within, the temple has a high, domed ceiling carried on squinches which appear almost to correspond in height to the exterior cornices. Rows of arched niches in each interior facade approximately replicate the exterior design. The high, spacious interior easily accommodates a very large *Śiva-liṅga* carved of black stone, 9 ft high and over 21 ft in circumference at the *pīṭha.*[46] Only the *liṅga* indicates the 'informed presence of the formless Lord' of Bharatcandra's poem. The *liṅga* carries a separate inscription, which tells us that just as Śiva came to be known as Rāmeśvara (Rāma's Lord) after being worshipped by Rama, so he became Rājarājeśvara (Lord of the King of Kings) because of being established by Śrī Krisnacandra, the Brahman, doer of many good deeds, a king of kings on earth, which very title has been bestowed on Krisnacandra by Śiva himself.[47] Raja Krisnacandra's claim to being a 'king of kings' by the grace of Śiva (not by Mughal *sanad*), accompanies the Hindu 'inclusivism' announced by his court poet Bharatcandra, and apparently replicated in the design of his great Rājarājeśvara temple at Sibnibas.

Krisnacandra's Vājapeya Sacrifice

Was the title 'king of kings' a claim to independent sovereignty? The title, or rather, an augmented version of it, first was acknowledged not by any mughal authority, but by an assembly of Brahmans, who the raja invited, to accomplish and witness an *agnihotra* and his royal, Vedic *vājapeya* sacrifice, performed jointly sometime after Bharatcandra's composition was completed (in 1752), and the Rājarājeśvara temple dedicated (1754), but before Alivardi's death in 1756. The Vedic sacrifices seem not to have been contemplated in 1752, for there is no mention of them in the 'prophecy' which concludes Bharatcandra's poem. Use of the *vājapeya* to secure recognition of, and in fact to augment, Krisnacandra's new title, seems to have been an improvisation. What inspired it?

The absence of information on the date of this event is perhaps our most important clue. In 1754, because of complex and violent events in Dhaka, Rajballabh, a Vaidya by *jāti*, who had achieved both wealth and prominence in the nawabi administration of Dhaka, was promoted by his patron, Nawazish Muhammad, as the latter attempted to 'raise money and amass troops' for a war of succession against Siraj ud-Daulah, should Alivardi die.[48] The same year Rajballabh dedicated a small Śiva temple at Srikhanda in Barddhaman. (Srikhanda itself, the birthplace of Caitanya's Vaidya follower Narahari, was a centre of Vaiṣṇava worship and Vaidya prestige, about 40 miles west of Sibnibas.[49]) On the dedicatory inscription of this temple Rajballabh recorded an extraordinary claim: that he had performed the *agniṣṭoma*, *vājapeya* and other Vedic sacrifices.[50]

Two further details bring into focus the relation between Rajballabh and Krisnacandra. As a Vaidya, Rajballabh could not have found Brahmans to officiate at Vedic sacrifices without already having secured recognition of his right to claim Vaiṣya rather than Śudra status, and to wear the sacred thread. This he did 'at great cost' on behalf of all Vaidyas, by assembling 'Brahman Pandits from different parts of India', who eventually rendered the decision Rajballabh desired. Brahmans from Navadvīpa participated in this decision, and were invited to the sacrifice itself. There is a doubtful tradition that Krisnacandra opposed this decision, and thereafter refused to admit to his court Vaidyas who wore the sacred thread.[51] In short, Krisnacandra seems to have arranged for his own *agnihotra* and *vājapeya* sacrifices after Rajballabh's, in order to imitate (and so to counter?) this act of royal self-assertion by a man who was only a Vaidya, but who, because of his status as a high official in the nawabi administration, was for more powerful than Krisnacandra.

A retrospective biography of Krisnacandra, written by Rajiblocan Mukhopadhyay and first published in 1805, gives the only account of Krisnacandra's *agnihotra* and *vājapeya* sacrifices, but describes few details. The former is a simple, twice-daily milk offering which emphasizes food and hospitality. It is interesting that a *kṣatriya* should not perform it, because he 'eats impure food, plunders and kills'.[52] Similar features of the *vājapeya* probably recommended it to Krisnacandra. Said first to have been performed by Bṛhaspati, it is 'the Brahman's own sacrifice'. It produces 'overlordship' (*saṃrāja),* and a claim is made that it is superior to the *rājasūya,* by which the Kshatriya becomes a king.[53] Second, one who offers the *vājapeya* is repeatedly said to win 'food', a substance analogically extended to include wealth, the earth, wheat, cattle, and peasants, 'for peasants are food for the *rājan*'.[54] The theme of control over 'food' that creates kingship, links the *vājapeya* to Annapurna, and Krisnacandra to his forebear Bhavananda.

The central act of the *vājapeya* is a ritual chariot race. By 'winning' it the royal sacrificer wins *soma,* food of the gods. It is followed by an ascent of the king and his queen to a symbolically constituted 'heaven'. They return immediately, the king having won the 'power', 'manhood', 'intelligence', and 'energies' of the gods, whereupon he is seated upon a throne and acclaimed as king by the Brahman priests.[55]

Rajiblocan retrospectively narrates only that the sacrifices were chosen, and their requirements were ascertained by learned Brahmans; that learned Brahmans were invited from all countries to witness the rite; and that immense expenditure (Rs. 2 million) was required for the rites and for lavish presents subsequently distributed to the Brahman priests and to invited guests. Having accomplished these rites, Krisnacandra was given by the assembled Brahmas the title: *agnihotrī-vājapeyī-śrīman-mahārāja-rājendra,* the prosperous, Indra-like king of great kings, who performed the *agnihotra* and *vājapeya* sacrifices.[56] Krisnacandra's claim to sovereignty was not just acknowledged by the Brahmans assembled for this royal Vedic sacrifice; it was in some sense accomplished by the sacrifice. By patronizing Bharatcandra's revisionary poem, by building the great Rājarājeśvara temple at Sibnibas, and by performing the *agnihotra* and *vājapeya* sacrifices, Krisnacandra made himself an independent sovereign, whose authority derived from Annapurna or Śiva or the Vedic sacrifice itself, not from a *sanad* of the Mughal emperor. One notes in the first and last of these acts of self-definition a consistent denigration of the martial prowess of *kṣatriyas,* a prowess which both his father and grandfather had cultivated.

Rajiblocan uses Krisnacandra's sacrifice to preface his account of the raja's relations with the English. In summary, he writes that Krisnacandra performed the Vedic sacrifices, and then secured the assistance of the English at Plassey, in order to take kingship away from the Mughal nawabs, who he believed always had oppressed Hindus. The English chief, in return for the raja's help, awarded him the title 'Maharaja Rajendra Bahadur', thus validating the award of the same title by the Brahmans who had witnessed his Vedic sacrifice.[57] Every element of this narrative must be questioned.

Krisnacandra and Plassey

Was Maharaja Krisnacandra content to reinscribe the nature of Hinduism and the nature of kingship in relation to Mughal authority in text, temple architecture and ritual, or did he also try to act politically in accordance with what he had redefined? Published English records are almost silent about him in the months leading up to Plassey, but there is one mention of him, in a letter from Roger Drake, Jr. (the leader who had abandoned Calcutta in 1756) to Clive, dated 3 May 1757. Drake reported that the raja had given 'one of my emissaries from Muxadavad' information about 'discontent among the Nawab's officers'. Drake, apparently continuing to convey news from Krisnacandra, wrote in particular that Mir Jafar, 'on being ordered to hold himself in readiness', complained that Nawab Siraj ud-Daulah 'had ruined his country, was destroying all mercantile affairs', and that he, Mir Jafar, would 'lift [his] hand against him'. His letter concluded: 'Kissenchund the Nudea Rajah has been long discontented and used ill by the Nabob.'[58] Drake plainly supposed a conspiracy against the nawab in which Krisnacandra participated, and for which Mir Jafar would supply military force. Of course, a conspiracy could not have been news to Clive. Ten days prior, on 24 April, Mir Jafar had sent a secret proposal to Watts that he would join the English in opposing the nawab and in setting another person on the throne; and on 26 April, Watts advised Clive to 'lay aside all appearance of war while we concert of measures with the principal jumidars' (*jamādār*, subaltern officer), and in the meantime to withdraw the Company's goods and servants from subordinate factories.[59]

Rajiblocan's retrospective account of Krisnacandra's life, written fifty years later, gives an extraordinary version of the conspiracy, in which the raja served as the principal advisor both to the British and to the Indian conspirators. This narrative can only be described as a 'fanciful story' that betrays 'little or no knowledge of the actual events' and 'mainly inspired by the desire to represent Krisnacandra as the main instrument in effecting the great revolution in Bengal'.[60] Nevertheless, Drake's letter proves that Rajiblocan's account was not completely without factual basis. Before Alivardi's death Krisnacandra had tried to project his sovereignty as independent of Mughal authority. It is not surprising to find him in a very small role in the conspiracy which led up to Plassey. Of course, the British themselves were interested in conspiring 'only with those persons round the Nawab, who might be of some use to them by virtue of the position they held in the Durbar'.[61] They had no use for, and took no further notice of the raja.

Again, what did the raja do to act in accord with the world he had imagined? For it may be one thing to 'constitute' a 'world' by poetic text, novel temple architecture, and lavish revival of Vedic ritual, but yet another to succeed in remaking one's part of the world by human labour, work, and action. If Rajiblocan can be trusted (but possibly he cannot), Krisnacandra spent Plassey itself in hiding at Sibnibas, worried about what would happen to his life and *jāti* if the nawab were not defeated.[62]

English Hegemony

Within a year, the penetration of the English into the interior of Bengal began to cause Krisnacandra problems, as the English or their appointees alternately supervised or themselves managed collection of revenues in Nadiya.[63] In January 1758 Nawab Mir Jafar, unable to meet the schedule of payments to the English, assigned them the revenues of the zamindaris of Barddhaman and Nadiya and of the faujdar of Hughli. Luke Scrafton, then the Company's Resident at the durbar, was put in charge of managing the collection of these revenues. Receiving little cooperation from Krisnacandra, Scrafton in July sent a party of 20 sepoys to Nadiya, and threatened the raja's son, Sibcandra, with arrest. Scrafton reported to the Calcutta Council:

> As the chief cause of the balance [due] is the Raja's extravagance, it therefore appears to me as the necessary step to send a trusty person into his country, to collect his revenues for him, allowing him only Rs. 10,000 per annum, or whatever your honor, etc., may think proper for his expenses. . . .[64]

It is a tribute to Krisnacandra's adroitness that for ten years thereafter he retained management of revenue collection of his zamindari in his own hands.

At first Krisnacandra seems to have relied on alliances with Nandkumar, and with Amircand and his heirs; that is, with Indians directly involved in the conspiracy before Plassey, people who could have been presumed to have influence with the British.[65] Later he relied as well on appropriate expressions of loyalty and good wishes.[66]

In the conspiracy of 1760 by which Mir Jafar resigned and was replaced by Mir Qasim, Nadiya again escaped coming under direct British management of the revenues; its place was taken by the more lucrative prize of Chittagong, which Mir Qasim gave the British as one price of their support.[67] Late in 1760 Krisnacandra appears to have resisted paying revenues to Mir Qasim's administration. In December the Ray-i-rayan asked the British for assistance:

> It is now two months the zemindar of Nuddea has put us off by saying first that his Dasharrah holidays were coming on, and afterwards that his Dewally holidays were at hand, and now he has complained to you that his wife is sick . . . therefore I beg you will write to the zemindar to proceed speedily to this city [Murshidabad] with the money for the two months revenues which he has not paid.[68]

The following February Krisnacandra complained to the British that his son had been 'carried away' to Murshidabad, no doubt as security for payment of revenue arrears.[69] In the summer months of 1761, one notes a continuous record of default, both to Mir Qasim and to the English.[70]

Rajiblocan elides Krisnacandra's efforts to avoid paying the full revenue demand. He also does not mention two crucial, subsequent events. Sometime during this period Krisnacandra was able to keep in his control enough revenue to resume his programme of temple construction at Sibnibas. Simultaneously, as English affronts to Nawab Mir Qasim's honour increased, and their claims to private trading privileges threatened all integrity of his administration, the nawab, pushed toward a break with them, and inveterately suspicious of disloyalty, set spies upon his leading zamindars.[71] By the beginning of 1763 both Krisnacandra and his son Sibcandra had been identified as supporters of the English and were being held prisoner.

The Mahārājeśvara and Rām-Sitā-Lakṣmaṇ Temples and Krisnacandra's Imprisonment

In 1762 Krisnacandra's two wives dedicated two new, large temples at Sibnibas to the east of the Rājarājeśvara temple. The middle temple, dedicated by Krisnacandra's second wife, is a four-sided Śiva temple with a tall *cār-chālā* roof. It simplifies but repeats design elements of the Rājarājeśvara temple. The dedicatory inscription on the base of the *liṅga* installed in this temple also cleverly repeats Krisnacandra's title obtained at the *vājapeya* sacrifice: *srīmān adhigatya rājati mahārāj-ādi-rājendratāṃ*, 'to that prosperous one who, having attained the status of "Rājendra" preceded by "Mahārāja", shines forth'.[72]

The Rām-Sītā-Lakṣmaṇ temple dedicated by Krisnacandra's first wife (Plate 2) is more remarkable for many reasons. It is architecturally more ambitious than the Rājarājeśvara temple of 1754. Furthermore, it employs both design elements and techniques of construction that suggest a deliberate search for novelty. It consists of a square central tower, surmounted by a bell-shaped, *cār-chālā* roof, and surrounded by a verandah. Interior arches allow entry from the verandah to the central tower, where the images are kept. When Bishop Heber visited, a Brahman guide called his attention to the use of a 'vault', sprung between each exterior wall of the verandah and the corresponding wall of the interior tower, to roof each side of the verandah,

Plate 2: The Rām-Sītā-Lakṣmaṇ Temple, 1762, at Sibnibas.

and Heber added: '. . . the Brahmin made me observe, with visible pride, the whole roof was "pucka" or brick and "belathee" or foreign'.[73] Comparing this temple to its neighbours, however, one most notices the absence of curved cornices. The long straight cornices of the verandah, the linear slope of the verandah roof, and the square tower and its straight cornices all together present a rectilinear framework unmistakably *belathee* (if not English) in inspiration. The temple's rectilinear design is softened by the ornaments of its facades. These include Islamicate elements like those of the Śiva temples: the arches of the verandah, and the arched niches of the tower facades. Curves in the brickwork on each tower facade above the arched niches are offset by straight lines above them, which repeat the lines of the cornices. Above all is the graceful, bell-shaped roof of the tower.

Can we attempt to compare this temple with that of Rājarājeśvara temple built eight years earlier? If representing a new 'inclusivism' were Krisnacandra's purpose, one designed to demonstrate Hinduism's capacity to subsume the English, the temple would appear to fail. In general, 'foreign' elements of its design threaten to overwhelm the Rām-Sītā-Lakṣmaṇ temple's visual identity as a Hindu temple. Perhaps instead the raja desired from Englishmen of his day the kind of enthusiastic response his descendants received from Bishop Heber, and sought therefore an English architecture, as his forebear once had imported a Muslim builder from Dhaka to design the palace at Krisnanagar. In any case, I think, with this temple Krisnacandra publicly signed himself as an associate (and supporter?) of the English power—at the same time, of course, that he avoided paying them the full revenue demand.

Krisnacandra himself may already have been arrested by Mir Qasim for his identification with the cause of the English when these latter temples at Sibnibas were dedicated. He stopped writing to the Calcutta Council in February 1761, and they to him the following June.[74] In April 1763 he and his son certainly were taken from prison in Murshidabad to Mir Qasim's fort at Monghyr, and held there with the Jagat Seths, Rajballabh, and with some other leading zamindars whom Mir Qasim suspected of treachery.[75] Both father and son escaped the execution of prisoners which followed the loss of Monghyr to Major Adams on 19 July 1763.[76] Did they remain captives? Apparently both father and son were unable to return to Murshidabad until the following February;[77] there Mir Jafar, restored to the position of nawab, also kept them in confinement until May 1764, when the English ordered them released.[78]

Denouement

Victory at the Battle of Buksar in 1764 and getting the office of diwan for Bengal, Bihar and Orissa the following year made the English East India Company masters of Bengal in all but name. In 1767 they carefully arranged for Krisnacandra to receive a title from Shah Alam II, the puppet Mughal emperor. For them the title was a formality. It preserved a certain fiction of the continuity of Mughal authority. For Krisnacandra it seems not to have been meaningless, for the title he chose to receive, Maharaja Rajendra Bahadur, echoes that given him more than a decade earlier by the assembly of Brahmans who had witnessed his *vājapeya* sacrifice. Of course, his new title had nothing to do with participation in the conspiracy before Plassey.[79]

Collection of the revenues of Nadiya seems to have remained in Krisnacandra's hands until 1769-70, when they were offered in 'farm' to a number of speculating Calcutta merchants. On this occasion Governor Harry Verelst wrote tendentiously:

> *Nadia.* The Rajah having behaved very ill in retaining a large sum from his malguzarry [revenue assessment], and (if the general voice is to be credited) having neglected the good of his country, and distressed the ryotts, we are of opinion the most eligible method to be pursued for the security of our employers and the welfare of the ryotts of these districts, would be to deprive the Rajah of power, and let the country out to farm for three years.[80]

As the rains failed in 1769, these Calcutta merchants also defaulted, and collection of revenues in Nadiya reverted to the maharaja's control during the famine year of 1769-70. He was no more successful than the merchants had been, and the Nadiya revenues again were farmed out, this time for a period of five years, in 1771. Apparently, the maharaja himself successfully bid on at least some of his own zamindari, for in 1776 we find Krisnacandra so far in arrears that his lands were to be sold at auction.[81] In 1777 Philip Francis visited him at Sibnibas, and 'saw an immense place in ruins, and the Prince of the Country, a venerable old Man, lodged in one Corner of it in a State of Beggary and Misery, not to be believed'.[82] Since Krisnacandra already had moved his residence from Sibnibas in 1774, and built a new home closer to Navadvipa, no doubt this is what Krisnacandra meant Francis to see.

Despite the military and political supremacy demonstrated by the British since 1764, and closer to home, despite the auctioning of rights to manage some of his lands, Krisnacandra again had claimed the title *mahārāja-rājendra* in his last temple, the Hari-Hara temple at Amghata. The dedicatory inscription of this temple explicitly records his accomplishment of the *vājapeya* sacrifice.[83] This temple was dedicated after 1774, when Krisnacandra had transferred management of what remained of his zamindari to his son, Sibcandra, and abandoned Sibnibas for a new home at Gangabas, in order better to pursue *mokṣa*.[84] The temple itself is a small room surrounded by a simple, open portico carried on square pillars; it has none of the grandeur of the temples at Sibnibas. Above it rise two equal, pyramidal *cār-chālā* roofs, symbolizing, like the *mūrti* of Hari-Hara within, the unity of Śiva and Viṣṇu. The dedicatory inscription celebrates Krisnacandra's intent to 'destroy the wrong notion of the foolish who were sinking into a sense of difference' between the two deities. The architectural form of the temple and its dedicatory inscription both suggest that Krisnacandra was withdrawing from an understanding that Hindu inclusivism could subsume Islam. Nor was he any longer able or willing to use elements of a European architectural style to identify himself with the English. Having retired to pursue *mokṣa,* he gave new emphasis to the unity of competing Hindu sects in a single structure of divine truth, which unity his court poet Bharatcandra long ago had asserted. He also for the first time asserted his own religious authority, not only as a king who once had performed the *vājapeya* sacrifice, but also as one who was 'given to pious deeds according to the instructions of the Sāstras and the Vedas'.[85]

Conclusion

Krisnacandra's forebears had a bi-polar model of rulership. On the one hand they were zamindars in the Mughal system of authority, office-holders whose rights were given by *sanad* of the emperor, and depended on their collecting, accounting for, and paying the stipulated revenue demand. On the other hand, they also were rajas, little Hindu kings, whose authority was constituted by acts of redistribution: giving revenue-free land to Brahmans and other worthy recipients, building splendid temples and palaces, and performing ritual celebrations with lavish generosity. Ideally, they mediated between two worlds, cultivating both Sanskrit and Persian courtly culture, for example, or developing the martial arts expected of a noble in Mughal society, without losing their taste or ability to converse with learned Brahmans.

The chaotic and destructive Maratha incursions of 1742-50, and the weakness of Nawab Alivardi which they revealed, suggested to Krisnacandra the possibility of a different model of kingship. In Bharatcandra's *Anandāmaṅgal,* performed in 1751-2, and in the great Rājarājeśvara temple at Sibnibas he patronized works of art which redefine both Hinduism and kingship. Both represent a superior capacity of Hindu 'inclusivism' to subsume and make relative the inferior truths of Islam. Both explicitly represent Krisnacandra's kingship as the gift of the one supreme deity, in the form of either Annapurna or Śiva, to a deserving devotee, either Bhavananda or Krisnacandra himself. Bharatcandra's poem asserts that Jahangir granted a *sanad* to Krisnacandra's forebear Bhavananda only because of the direct intervention of the goddess and only after learning to worship her. Krisnacandra's dedicatory inscription on the *liṅga* of the Rājarājeśvara temple suggests a claim to independence for it asserts that the title *rājarāja* was authorized by Śiva himself, because of Krisnacandra's devotion. Performance of the *vājapeya* sacrifice further constituted that independence, winning for Krisnacandra *saṃrāja,* 'overlordship', and the augmented title, *mahārāja-rājendra,* 'the Indra-like king of great kings', from the assembly of Brahmans who witnessed the sacrifice.

What may 'independence' have meant to Krisnacandra? We must at once recognize its qualified nature. Krisnacandra, like most other Bengali zamindars of the eighteenth century, did not try to develop a military capacity able to compete with the new armies of drilled foot soldiers and rapid-firing artillery.[86] In fact, compared to his father and grandfather, he seems to have withdrawn from military pursuits. We can recognize 'independence', nevertheless, in his limited participation in the conspiracy before Plassey to unseat Siraj ud-Daulah, and in his continual efforts thereafter to avoid paying the full revenue demand, both to the English, and to the nawabs they put on the throne at Murshidabad. 'Independence', that is to say, is written in the repeated complaints of the raja's 'duplicity' and 'bad character'.

Krisnacandra's practice of politics with respect to those who could exercise coercive power over him was ambiguous, devious, and adroit. In comparison, the performances and works of art by which he constituted a claim to independent authority seem relatively simple. Based on a unitary understanding of Hinduism, they assert, in various ways, the sacred, royal authority of a Brahman who knows ultimate reality, and who has divinely given powers over 'food': wealth, taxes and peasants.

In the practice of history, both by Krisnacandra's poet and by his descendants who wrote about him, we note a similar erasure of complexity. Bharatcandra's history of Bhavananda, by its emphasis on the actions of Annapurna, reduced Bhavananda's similarly adroit and ambiguous role, with respect to the Mughals, to one of providing correct sacerdotal knowledge. Again, in Rajiblocan's retrospective account of Krisnacandra's relations with the English, his ambiguous record of alliance, duplicity and contestation is replaced by one of constant loyalty and service.

To note coherence in most of the raja's self-representations is not to say that he simply reproduced pre-existing understandings of Hindu kingship. Creativity and novelty mark Bharatcandra's poem as they mark the great Rājarājeśvara temple. Nor do all of the self-representations repeat the same themes. His careful attention to the requirements of the Vedic *vājapeya* sacrifice, and his implicit claim, as a Tantric adept, to immunity from faults of commensality; or again, his worship, perhaps at different times, of Śiva, Annapurna, Kālī and Hari-Hara, need further investigation; but they indicate Krisnacandra's ability to re-imagine the sacred basis of his authority. Nowhere is this creativity more evident or more problematic than in the Rām-Sītā-Lakṣmaṇ temple of 1762. By employing elements of a foreign, European architecture, does it reassert and extend Hindu 'inclusivism' to them, or does it instead acknowledge the alliance with (and dependence on) the English? Events foreclosed this ambiguity; upon his break with the English Nawab Mir Qasim identified Krisnacandra as a traitor.

Pressure from the English pushed Krisnacandra towards a final redefinition of his authority. He seems to have tried to preserve his authority with respect to the 'religious' life of Hindus. He certainly withdrew from the cares and responsibilities of ordinary life to pursue *mokṣa*. He withdrew also from attempts to represent Hindu 'inclusivism' in temple architecture; one sees in the modest temple at Amghata neither Islamicate nor European elements of design. At the same time he gave new emphasis to the unitary supreme being of Hinduism, and to his own pious deeds and exemplary fidelity to Śāstras and Vedas.

NOTES

1. Chutanutte Diary and Consultations, 1 April 1697; in India Records Series, Old Fort William in Bengal, 2 vols., ed. C.R. Wilson (London, 1906) 1: 21-2. For the notion of 'contact zone', see Mary Pratt, *Imperial Eyes: Travel Writing and Transculturation* (London, 1992), pp. 6-7.
2. *Kiṣitīśavaṃśāvalīcaritaṃ* (apparently composed in 1728), in *Kiṣitīśvamśāvalicarita,* Mohit Rāy sampādita (Kalikātā, 1986). Hereafter Rāy's edition of this Sanskrit history is cited as *KVC.* (In addition to re-editing the Sanskrit text Ray has supplied a Bengali translation, and has edited and included two nineteenth century Bengali biographies of Raja Krisnacandra.) The nineteenth century translation by W. Pertsch, *Kiṣitīśavaṃśāvalīcaritaṃ, A Chronicle of the Family of Raja Krishnachandra of Navadvīpa, Bengal* (Berlin, 1852), is unreliable.
3. *KVC,* pp. 197-9; Bengali translation, pp. 239-41.
4. *KVC,* pp. 200-1; Bengali translation, p. 243.
5. *KVC,* pp. 202; Bengali translation, pp. 244-5.
6. *KVC,* pp. 203-4; Bengali translation, p. 246.
7. See the exemplary audience of Ramkrisna with Muhammad Azimuddin, *KVC,* p. 228; Bengali translation, p. 270.

8. Reginald Heber, D.D., Lord Bishop of Calcutta, *Narrative of a Journey through the Upper Provinces of India, from Calcutta to Bombay, 1824-25,* 3 vols. (London, 1828), 1: 123, 125.
9. *KVC,* pp. 204, 207; Bengali translation, pp. 246, 250.
10. The first *sanad* has become largely unreadable. The family's remaining *sanads* were translated into Bengali by Kārtikey Candra Rāy, *Pariśiṣṭa* (appendix), *Kṣitīṣavamśāvalicarita* (1st published 1875), edited and republished in *Kṣitīṣavamśāvalicarita,* Mohit Rāy sampādita, p. 143.
11. Ratnalekha Ray, *Change in Bengal Agrarian Society* (Delhi, 1979), pp. 27-8.
12. Kārtikey Candra Rāy, *Pariśiṣṭa,* p. 143; Alok'kumār Cakrabartī, *Mahārājā Kriṣnacandra o Tatkālīn Baṅgasamāj* (Kalikātā, 1989), p. 4.
13. *KVC,* p. 211; Bengali translation, p. 254.
14. *KVC,* p. 212; Bengali translation, p. 255.
15. *KVC,* p. 217; Bengali translation, p. 259.
16. *KVC,* p. 216; Bengali translation, p. 258.
17. *KVC,* pp. 214, 216-17; Bengali translation, pp. 256, 259.
18. Om Prakash, *The Dutch East India Company and the Economy of Bengal, 1630-1720* (Princeton, 1985), p. 61.
19. *KVC,* pp. 218, 222; Bengali translation, pp. 260, 264.
20. *KVC,* pp. 228-30; Bengali translation, pp. 270-2.
21. *KVC,* pp. 230-3; Bengali translation, pp. 272-4.
22. *Bhārat'candra Granthābalī, sampādak Brajendranāth Bandyopādhyāy o Sajanīkānta Dās, dvitiya saṃskaraṇ* (Kalikātā, BS 1357), p. 11. Hereafter this work is cited as *BCG.*
23. Kalikinkar Datta, *Alivardi and his Times,* 2nd edn. (Calcutta, 1963), pp. 45-94; John McLane, *Land and Local Kingship in Eighteenth-century Bengal* (Cambridge, 1993), pp. 161-71.
24. James Grant mentions 'extraordinary temporary exactions' levied by Alivardi in 1743-50 from the 'principal zemindars, such as those of Rajeshahy, Dinagepoor, and Nuddeah, whose jurisdictions, situated for the most part to the east of the Ganges [i.e. the Bhagirathi-Hughli], were not liable to be ravaged' by the Marathas. See, James Grant, 'Historical and Comparative Analysis of the Finances of Bengal', in Walter K. Firminger, ed., *Affairs of the East India Company* (Being the Fifth Report from the Select Committee of the House of Commons, 28 July 1812), 3 vols. (rpt. edn., Delhi, 1984; 1st published 1917-18), 2: 216-20.
25. *BCG,* p. 90.
26. *BCG,* p. 100.
27. *BCG,* p. 133.
28. A.K. Bhattacharyya, *A Corpus of Dedicatory Inscriptions from Temples of West Bengal* (Calcutta, 1982), No. 100, pp. 164-6.
29. *BCG,* p. 291.

30. *BCG*, p. 12: 'In the breast of the moon, blackness [*kālī*] is only a stain, but in the heart of Krisnacandra Kālī is always luminous.'
31. I take this term from William Halbfass, *India and Europe* (Albany, 1988), pp. 403-18.
32. *BCG*, pp. 305-6.
33. *BCG*, p. 307.
34. *BCG*, p. 307.
35. *BCG*, pp. 307-8.
36. *BCG*, p. 308.
37. *BCG*, pp. 316-19.
38. *BCG*, pp. 348-9.
39. Diana L. Eck, *Banaras: City of Light* (Princeton, 1983), pp. 125-9.
40. Eck, p. 162.
41. A.S. Altekar, *Benares and Sarnath: Past and Present*, 2nd edn. (Benares, 1947), pp. 22-4.
42. The site is described in *Nādīyā Jelār Purākīrti*, tathya-saṃkalan o granthanā Mohit Rāy, sampādanā Amiyakumār Bandyopādhyāy o Sudhīrañjan Dāś (Pūrta Bibhāg, Paścim'bṅga Sar'kār, 1975), pp. 98-100. I am grateful to Mohit Ray and his family for hospitality in Krisnanagar in September 1994, and for helping me visit Sibnibas, the *rājāṛi* at Krisnanagar, the Hari-Hara temple at Amghātā, and Rāghava Rāy's Rāghaveśvara temple at Dighnagar.
43. A.K. Bhattacharyya, No. 80, pp. 141-2.
44. David McCutchion, *Late Medieval Temples of Bengal* (Calcutta, 1972), p. 60, H(2) (c), and Plate 103. Interesting comparisons can be made to the simpler Naldanga Ganeśa and Śiva temples, H(2) (a), and to the much more complex temple built by Rani Bhavānī *c.* 1755, which has an inverted lotus dome and a verandah surrounding the entire structure; p. 61, H(6) (a), and Plate 94. The Naldanga Śiva temple, a nineteenth century structure, is illustrated in *Brick Temples of Bengal: from the Archives of David McCutchion*, ed. George Michell (Princeton, 1983), Plate 106.
45. *Nadīyā Jelār Purākīrti*, p. 99. An interesting comparison can be made to the 'slender engaged columns' flanking the entrance bay of the mosque attached to the tomb of Nawab Shuja al-Din, built in 1743-4 by Nawab Alivardi at Murshidabad, 'a feature seen in many mosques of Dhaka'. See Catherine Asher, 'Inventory of Key Monuments', *The Islamic Heritage of Bengal*, ed. George Michell (Paris, 1984), p. 100.
46. *Nadīyā Jelār Purākīrti*, p. 99; A.K. Bhattacharyya, Plate LXXXV.
47. A.K. Bhattacharyya, p. 10; No. 81, p. 143.
48. R.C. Majumdar, *Maharaja Rajballabh* (Calcutta, 1947), pp. 5-9.
49. Binay Ghoṣ, *Paścim'baṅger Smskṛiti* (Kalikātā, 1957), pp. 286-8.
50. Majumdar, p. 90.
51. Dineś'candra Sen, *Bihat Baṅga*, 2 khaṇḍa (Kalikātā, 1993, 1st published 1341 [1934/35]) 2: 1002-3; Alok'kumār Chakrabartī, p. 217. In

formulating this line of argument I have been helped by the comments of Professor Binoy Chaudhuri and Rajat Kanta Ray.

52. J.C. Heesterman, *The Broken World of Sacrifice* (Chicago, 1993), pp. 210-12.
53. *Satapatha-Brāhmaṇa* 5.1.1.11-13.
54. *Satapatha Brāhmaṇa* 5.1.2.9; 5.1.3.3,10; 5.1.4.4; 5.2.1.16, 24 and *passim.* See also Brian K. Smith, *Classifying the Universe* (Oxford, 1994), pp. 98-9.
55. *Satapatha-Brāhmaṇa* 5.1.5 and 5.2.1.
56. Rājiblocan Mukhopādhyāy, *Śrī Mahārāja Kṛiṣṇacandrarāyasya Caritraṃ* (Londonmahānagare cāpā haila, 1811; in the British Library), pp. 27-9. This biography also has been included in *Kṣitīśabamśābalīcarita,* Mohit Rāy sampādita, pp. 309ff.; but I have not had access to a complete copy.
57. Rajiblocan Mukhopadhyay, pp. 33-77.
58. S.C. Hill, *Bengal in 1756-57,* 3 vols. (rpt. edn., Delhi, 1985; 1st published 1905), 2: 375-6.
59. Subhas Chandra Mukhopadhyay, *British Residents at the Darbar of the Bengal Nawabs at Murshidabad (1757-1772)* (Delhi, n.d. [1988]), pp. 127-9.
60. R.C. Majumdar, p. 42.
61. R.C. Majumdar, p. 39.
62. Rajiblocan Mukhopadhyay, pp. 69-70.
63. Ranjit Sen, *Metamorphosis of the Bengal Polity (1700-1793)* (Calcutta, 1987), pp. 130-1.
64. Public Consultations, 24 July 1758, in Rev. James Long, *Selections from the Unpublished Records of Government,* 2nd edn., ed. Mahadeveprasad Saha (Calcutta, 1973), p. 195.
65. Scrafton was replaced by Nandkumar as supervisor of collections for Nadiya, Barddhaman and Hughli in August 1758. A few months later, Amircand and his heirs are reported as being 'security' for the Nadiya collections, so that Krisnacandra could resume their management. See Letter from Clive and Becher to the Court of Directors, dated 31 December 1758, *Fort William-India House Correspondence,* vol. 2., ed. H.N. Sinha (Delhi, 1957) p. 79. Nandkumar was dismissed in 1760 for 'mismanagement' of the collections, and Krisnacandra remained on sufficiently good terms with Nandkumar that he married his daughter to the latter's son in 1765. See A.M. Khan, *The Transition in Bengal, 1765-1775* (Cambridge, 1969), pp. 28, 77.
66. Imperial Record Department, *Calendar of Persian Correspondence,* 3 vols. (Calcutta, 1911), vol. 1, p. 21, No. 327, dated 11 Aug. 1760, letter to Vansittart offering congratulations on his appointment, with a *nazar,* for the first of many examples.
67. A.M. Khan, pp. 34-5.
68. Long, p. 310, No. 522.
69. *Calendar of Persian Correspondence,* 1: 54, 55, Nos. 868, 874.

70. *Calendar of Persian Correspondence,* 1, p. 100, No. 1176, letter to Krisnacandra dated 24 May 1761; No. 1177, letter to Mir Abu-l-Qasim (Collector of Nadiya revenues under Mir Qasim), dated 24 May 1761; No. 1178, letter to the Rāy-i-rāyān, dated 25 May 1761, and p. 156, No. 1277, letter to the Rāy-i-rāyān, dated 26 July 1761.
71. Ghulam Husayn Khan Tabataba'i, *A Translation of the Sëir Mutaqherin, or View of Modern Times,* 4 vols., trans. Haji Mustapha (rpt. ed., Lahore, n.d. [1975], 1st published 1789), 2: 426-32.
72. A.K. Bhattacharyya, No. 94, p. 157.
73. Heber, 1: 120-1.
74. The last letter received from Krisnacandra was written to congratulate them on the fall of Pondicherry, dated 15 February 1761. See *Calendar of Persian Correspondence,* 1: 62, No. 928. The last letter to him was written in June to complain of non-payment of an assignment of his revenues to the English. See p. 107, No. 1222.
75. Ghulam Hussain Salim, *Riyāz-us-Salātīn: A History of Bengal,* trans. Abdus Salam (rpt. edn., Delhi, 1975; 1st published 1903), pp. 394-5; Kārtikey Candra Rāy, p. 80.
76. Kārtikey Candra Rāy, pp. 81-2.
77. *Calendar of Persian Correspondence,* 1:281, No. 2045, from Raja Krisnacandra, dated 2 Feb. 1764, advising that he and his son have arrived safe in Murshidabad.
78. Letter in the Persian Department to Mir Jafar, dated 11 May 1764, in Long, p. 513, No. 772.
79. Krisnacandra's letter thanking the Governor for his receipt of the new title is dated 9 March 1767; see *Calendar of Persian Correspondence,* 2:44, No. 154. Compare Rajiblocan, pp. 76-7; Kārtikey Candra Rāy, p. 79.
80. Secret Committee Consultations, 30 June 1769, quoted in W.K. Firminger, *Historical Introduction to the Bengal Portion of the Fifth Report* (rpt. edn., Calcutta, 1962; 1st published 1917), p. 187 (original pagination, clxxxi).
81. Firminger, p. 313 (cccxv).
82. Journal entry 15 May 1777, quoted by Ranajit Guha, *A Rule of Property for Bengal* (Paris, 1963), p. 121, fn. 142.
83. A.K. Bhattacharyya, No. 100, pp. 164-6.
84. A.K. Bhattacharyya prefers 1688 Saka (1766) as an interpretation of the line encoding the date. See No. 100, pp. 164-5, fn. 7. Kārtikey Candra Rāy explicitly states that Krisnacandra built a new residence at Gangabas a little before the end of 1774, and thereafter he also built the temple in which he installed the *deva-mūrti* of Hari-Hara. See p. 91.
85. A.K. Bhattacharyya, No. 100, p. 164.
86. McLane, pp. 43-4.

Jagirdari in the Eighteenth Century: A Case Study of Two Afghan Families of Western Awadh

IQBAL HUSAIN

THE JAGIR SYSTEM, by which the nobles of the Mughal empire received virtually all of their income, was a crucial institution. Its basic element was the right to claim and collect the land-revenue and other taxes due to the empire.[1] the right in ordinary *tankhwah* jagirs was temporary and subject to transfer.[2] But a number of jagirdars also received permanent *in'ām altamgha* jagirs. As Jahangir explained in the *Tuzuk,* this form of jagir assignment was instituted to permit nobles to have certain places where they could lodge their families permanently[3] and presumably build houses and gardens, in the secure knowledge that they would always hold the jagir of the locality. It seems, however, that the *in'ām altamgha* holders subsequently increased their possessions around their jagirs through the purchase of zamindaris. The descendants of such jagir holders enjoyed a dual position as jagirdar as well as zamindars in the eighteenth century.

In this paper, an attempt is made to study the history of two Afghan jagirdar families holding *in'ām altamgha* in Shahabad[4] and Shamsabad[5] in what is now western UP.

The *Ain* in its account of twelve *subas* does not refer to the Afghan as dominant in parganas Pali and Shamsabad. However, by the close of the seventeenth century, a hundred years later, Afghans had emerged as jagirdars and zamindars not only in these parganas but also in the adjoining parganas of Kant and Patiyali.

The rise of Afghan jagirdars in the parganas of Shahabad and

Shamsabad had its roots in the local Rajput magnates' chronic refractoriness in the region. To counter it, Afghan generals were assigned jagirs in the area. Significantly parts of the jagirs were assigned in *in'ām altamgha* in seditious areas where Rajput resistance has been severe. The Afghan jagirdars then tried to increase their power and income by acquiring nominal zamindari rights as well, mainly through purchase. Diler Khan Ruhela, for example, extended his zamindari around his *in'ām altamgha* jagir villages by this means. Originally he received an *in'ām altamgha* of 6,00,000 *dams* from thirty-seven villages in *tappa*[6] pargana Pali (sarkar Khairabad, *suba* Awadh) through a farman of Emperor Aurangzeb dated 22 April 1662.[7] This grant was in addition to an earlier jagir of 26,00,000 *dams* in *tankhwah* (salary) from the same pargana.[8] Diler Khan is said to have purchased zamindari rights in a number of villages,[9] in parganas Kant, Pali, Sandila[10] and Sandi.[11]

Diler Khan died in 1683 and his jagir and zamindari were inherited by five of his sons, Kamaluddin Khan,[12] Fath Ma'mur Khan,[13] Chand Khan, Allah De Khan and Dildar Khan. It is not clear that the inheritance was allowed according to Islamic law or customary law. Adherence to the Islamic law of inheritance, however, seems unlikely as Kamaluddin Khan, the eldest son, is noted to have been in possession of a larger number of *in'ām altamgha* jagirs and zamindari villages.[14] Kamaluddin Khan also increased his zamindari possession through purchases. Moreover, he secured an additional *in'ām altamgha* grant of twenty-six villages from Aurangzeb in February 1687, on the condition that the villages mentioned in the grant were not to be assigned to any one else so long as a single member of Kamaluddin's family survived.[15] The evidence of the documents reproduced in the Urdu history *Nama-i Muzaffari* indicates that being the eldest son of Diler Khan, Kamaluddin Khan gave thirteen villages to each of his brothers which included some villages which were parts of the *altamgha* grants.[16] Kamaluddin Khan died in 1712-13, leaving about 1,500 villages to his heirs. Sardar Khan, his eldest son, inherited his properties.[18]

The jagirdars of the Mughal empire had modelled their household administration on the pattern of the imperial palace. They usually maintained separate departments to look after different parts of the household. One or other loyal servant would gain the confidence of the jagirdar and be honoured in many ways, including land grants.

An excellent example of this is Muhammad Mubarak, who by dint of merit rose from a petty position to the post of deputy (*naib*) of the jagirdar Muhammad Sardar Khan. Muhammad Sardar Khan apparently voluntarily transferred zamindari rights of villages, Isa Nagar and Kundrah (pargana Saroman Nagar[19]), to Muhammad Mubarak.[20] Muhammad Mubarak in the meantime also obtained zamindari rights to villages Sarai Ranak, Jamra,[21] and Sarbhanpur. It may be pointed out that the last three villages had been originally assigned to Diler Khan in *in'ām altamgha* jagir; but this jagir also now changed hands.

There is no evidence that imperial permission was any longer needed or obtained by the early eighteenth century for such transfers. Muhammad Mubarak also seems to have obtained zamindari rights of villages Ganga Mau and Sarai Salih, but his grandson, Namdar Khan, sold these villages to Chaudhari Hem Nath of Pali for Rs. 2,000.[22] Thus the zamindari of these villages was transferred to another family altogether. Muhammad Sardar Khan also gave village Tarerpuranpur in zamindari to Pir Muhammad, a house servant, in 1709-10.[23] Numerous other examples of the transfer of zamindari rights out of the area of *altamgha* grants to persons of the non-jagirdar family can also be cited.

These illustrations are only a few examples of how Mughal jagirdars were dividing their jagirs, and slowly helping the growth of new class of eighteenth-century zamindars in rural areas.

To return to our narrative: Sardar Khan was succeeded by his son, Sher Andaz Khan, in 1737-8. He was succeeded in turn by his son, Aizaz Khan, in 1172 *Hijri*/1758-9.[24] By this time, the family seems to have lost much of its control due to the increasing power of the nawabs of Awadh. Apparently, Aizaz Khan maintained good relations with the Awadh rulers, but after the fall of Ruhela power in 1774, the Afghans were demoralized and Aizaz Khan's position also suffered.[25] A copy of a *sanad* dated 25 *Safar* 1204 *Hijri*/1789-90 reproduced in the *Nama-i Muzaffari*, refers to the assignment of twenty villages in *mua'fi* to Mohan Lal, chakladar of Shahabad by Aizaz Khan, a transaction which is of great interest itself.[26] An *altamgha* jagir could be described as a *mua'fi* from the point of view of administration, since the revenue remained with the holder. What Aizaz Khan was now transferring was essentially his *altamgha* jagir. Second, the transfer shows his subservience or subjugation to the rapacity, or at least authority, of revenue agents of the Awadh administration. The chakladar concerned was the brother of Raja Hulas Rai, diwan of Awadh's ruler, Asaf ud-Daula.[27] Among the villages so assigned in *mua'fi* to Mohan Lal include Sarai Ranak, Manjgawan, Nagla Toho (or Nagla Lotho) and Rasulpur,[28] which had originally been assigned to Diler Khan in 1662 by Aurangzeb.[29] It will thus be seen that within 132 years of the *altamgha* grant a number of villages were transferred in *mua'fi*, enabling a new element in the rural society to exercise both the revenue and zamindari rights at the direct cost of the previously established family.

Aizaz Khan died in 1796/7, leaving no male heir to succeed him. The jagir and zamindari villages were inherited by his two widows in equal shares, through a confirmatory deed from Asaf ud-Daula's court.[30] Within the next few years the jagir and zamindari of the widows of Aizaz Khan were transferred to their sons-in-law.[31]

As mentioned earlier, Fath Ma'mur Khan[32] had received thirteen villages, including Udharanpur,[33] from his brother, Kamaluddin Khan. After his death in 1684 Murtaza Khan and Mustafa Khan, his sons, inherited equal shares in Jagir and zamindari.[34] Murtaza Khan died in 1748. He had, however, during his lifetime divided his jagir and zamindari villages among his sons. Angpur, Kharseli,[35] Yasinpur, Kachura,[36] and Haibatpur were given to Muhammad Raushan Khan. The remaining part of the jagir and zamindari villages were shared equally among Bahramand Khan, Hidayat Khan, Khair Andesh Khan, and Salih Muhammad Khan. The jagir and zamindari villages of Raushan Khan were resumed by Safdar Jang; but upon a petition, the *altamgha* jagir was restored in 1748. After the death of Raushan Khan, internal feuds led to the decline of the family, which eventually lost control over the zamindari.[37] The jagir broke up, and the old zamindars (Rajputs) regained their possessions through purchases from the Afghans.[38]

Chand Khan, the third son of Diler Khan, was given Harai

with another twelve villages, including Parera, by Kamaluddin Khan. One of the documents preserved in *Nama-i Muzaffari* shows him assigning a land grant in *mua'fi* to Shah Ismail, son of Shah Baqi, in 1717.[39] This leads one to infer that Chand Khan did not lag behind the others in assigning grants to persons from his jagir and zamindari.

Diler Khan's fourth son, Allah Dad, alias Allah De Khan,[40] was also the recipient of thirteen villages, including Naurozpur, from Kamaluddin Khan. Since Allah Dad Khan had no heirs, his zamindari villages—Naurozpur, Jaitpur and Suhagpur in pargana Pali—were inherited by his nephew Mohammad Ali Khan in accordance with his wishes.[41]

Dildar Khan, the fifth son of Diler Khan, was given thirteen villages, including Basitnagar,[42] by Kamaluddin Khan.[43] Basitnagar does not appear in the list of *altamgha* jagirs assigned to Diler Khan and Kamaluddin Khan; we may assume that it was purchased by Diler Khan in zamindari. Dildar Khan was succeeded by his grandson, Sa'adat Khan, who served as a tahsildar of Sara[44] during the rule of Asaf ud-Daula.[45] Sa'adat Khan managed to increase the number of villages to forty through purchases, mortgages, and other well-known means. He emerged as ta'aluqdar of Sa'adatnagar.[46] By 1823 the property held by his heirs had dwindled to twenty-three villages. The revenue of the pargana was farmed out to a Kashmiri Brahman who held it till 1856. At the annexation of Awadh, these villages were settled upon the old Hindu proprietors.[47] However, at the regular settlement it was restored to Husain Ali Khan, and the family retained the zamindari of Basitnagar and the adjoining villages till 1917.[48]

The origin of Afghan jagirdari in pargana Shamsabad has a similar history to that of Shahabad. The Rajput zamindars of Mainpuri, Rampur, Thatiyaon, and Khemsipur, combining together, had defied imperial authority during the reign of Jahangir.[50] As a reward for suppressing the revolt, in 1629 the jagir of Mau, held by Rashid Khan Ansari, was converted to an *in'ām altamgha* by Shah Jahan.[51] The grant included his sons.[52] It seems that Rashid Khan also brought under his zamindari a large part of the adjoining areas. A *hasb-ul hukm* of 1795 confers 600 bighas of land upon one Iradatullah Khan, son of Kale Khan

Raushani, the grandson of Rashid Khan Ansari, in village Ruhela, pargana Shamsabad. The *hasb-ul hukm* carries endorsements to the effect that the grant had been in *mua'fi* (revenue free) with the family since a long time past, in accordance with the earlier *farmans* and *sanads* issued by previous emperors, including Shah Alam I.[53] The heirs of Rashid Khan Ansari could not retain their *in'ām altamgha* jagirs due to the rise of the Bangash nawabs of Farrukhabad in the first half of the eighteenth century. Documentary evidence obtained from Shahabad reveals an interesting case of zamindari transfer from one of the descendants of Rashid Khan Ansari to one of the Afghan settlers in the pargana. A *hiba nama* (voluntary gift letter) dated 16 July 1768 records that Musammat Saliha Banu, widow of Haqdad Khan, and Musammat Sanadu, widow of Raushandad Khan (sons of Haqdad Khan) *Khanazads*,[54] transferred the zamindari rights of the share amounting to fourteen *biswas* and fifteen *biswansis* of village Chilsari, pargana Shamsabad, to Muhammad Khan Afridi. On the surface, the document seems to be a routine case of gift or *hiba*[55] a largely recognized practice in Muslim law. But another document of 16 July 1768 (the same date of the *hiba nama*) shows Musammat Saliha Bano and Sanadu selling the zamindari rights of the same share of fourteen *biswas* and fifteen *biswansis* in village Chilsari to the same Muhammad Khan Afridi for a consideration of Rs. 600. This creates the suspicion that there was some element of both force and fraud in the transaction. Musammat Saliha Banu and Sanadu are styled in both the documents as the widows of Haqdad Khan and Raushandad Khan. In both the documents their husbands are referred to as *Khanazads*, a term which the descendant of Rashid Khan Ansari generally used to emphasize their association with the Mughal court. This example shows how the earlier jagirdar families were losing their positions under the pressure of the newly emerging and rowdy arms of the Bangash Afghans of Shamsabad during the eighteenth century.[57]

It may be seen that the *altamgha* jagir holders were compelled to relinquish their possessions by a new rising class that gradually supplemented them, taking advantage of their close alliance with the nawabs of Farrukhabad.

From the study of these two *in'ām altamgha* jagirs one is tempted to deduce that the descendants of the original assignees could not retain their jagirs in the eighteenth century even when there were no outright resumptions by post-Mughal regimes. In the case of Diler Khan's *altamgha* jagirs, the element of pressure from Awadhi officials, as well as division and sub-division of the jagir and zamindari among family and non-family members, appear to be the major factors of decline. The decline and decay of the family of Rashid Khan Ansari, however, was entirely attributable to the rise of the Bangash nawabs,[58] under whom a new class of Afghan settlers were encouraged to edge out the older jagir-holding families.

The process of disintegration or survival of the jagir was apparently cushioned for the holders by the fact that the jagir-holding families tended to acquire zamindari rights in the localities of their jagirs. It is not clear whether the tendency was also visible among jagirdars other than the Afghans in the eighteenth century. It would be interesting if the matter could be investigated on the basis of local records, so that the question of what happened to the jagirdar class in the eighteenth century is adequately answered.

NOTES

1. Irfan Habib, *The Agrarian System of Mughal India* (Bombay: Peoples Publishing House, 1963), pp. 257, 318-19 (hereafter cited as *Agrarian System*).
2. Satish Chandra, *Parties and Politics at the Mughal Court 1707-1740* (Aligarh, 1959), Introduction, pp. xxi-xxv; *Agrarian System*, p. 260.
3. *Tuzuk-i Jahangiri*, ed. Sir Syed Ahmad Khan (1865, p. 10).
4. It was a part of pargana Pali when the *Ain* was compiled. It was constituted a separate pargana in 1745. See Muzaffar Husain, *Nama-i Muzaffari* (hereafter quoted as *N.M.* I) (Lucknow, 1917), pp. 174-9; Nevill, *Hardoi District Gazetteer*, p. 271.
5. An old pargana listed in Abul Fazl, *Ain-i Akbari* (Lucknow), vol. II, p. 87.
6. The author of *N.M.* I reads it as *patta* Shahabad *urf* Angai. In the *zimn* he reads it *tah.* Shahabad, see *N.M.* I, pp. 175-9.
7. *N.M.* I, pp. 174-5.
8. Ibid.
9. The author of *N.M.* I, p. 277, claims that Bahadur Khan Ruhela and Diler Khan Ruhela purchased 3,000 villages in zamindari.

10. Nearly midway between Lucknow and Hardoi at a distance of 34 miles south-east of Hardoi and 32 miles north of Lucknow. *Hardoi District Gazetteer*, p. 225.
11. Sandi stands 13 miles from Hardoi, 35 miles from Sandila and 25 miles from Farrukhabad. *Hardoi District Gazetteer*, p. 242.
12. An Alamgiri noble who rendered valuable service to the empire even after 1707. For career and achievements see, Samsam-ud Daula, *Maasir-ul Umara* (Calcutta, 1891), vol. II, pp. 504-5; *N.M.* I, pp. 237-92.
13. *Maasir-ul Umara*, II, p. 505.
14. *N.M.* II, pp. 21-2.
15. Aurangzeb's *farman, N.M.* I, pp. 284-8.
16. *N.M.* I, p. 278.
17. *N.M.* I, pp. 316-17.
18. *N.M.* I, pp. 309-11.
19. This is now a small pargana lying to the south of Shahabad, between Pali on the west and Bawana and Sara North on the east. *Hardoi District Gazetteer*, p. 263.
20. *N.M.* I, pp. 309-11.
21. Records as a village, pargana Shahabad. It was held by the Afghans until the early twentieth century. *Hardoi District Gazetteer*, p. 271.
22. *N.M.* I, pp. 311-12.
23. *N.M.* I, pp. 311. In another case, Sardar Khan gave village Bihdasi, pargana Pali in zamindari to Muhammad Ja'afar on 28 September 1732. *N.M.* I, pp. 315-16.
24. *N.M.*, I, p. 318.
25. The Awadh rulers followed a vigorous policy of resumption of zamindari and *madad-i ma'ash* grants from the very beginning of their rule. For resumption of Afghan jagirs, zamindars and *madad-i ma'ash* grants see *N.M.* I, p. 356; *Hardoi District Gazetteer,* pp. 239, 273; Azad Bilgrami, *Maasir-ul Kiram,* vol. I, p. 222 refers to Sa'adat Khan's orders for general resumption of land grants, causing large-scale destruction to the landholding families. Also see Qazi Sharif-ul Hasan Bilgrami, *Tarikh-i khitta-i pak Bilgram*, Aligarh, Ms, pp. 193, 196.
26. *N.M.* I, pp. 320-1.
27. For his life and career see *N.M.* II, pp. 14-20.
28. Now in pargana Kalyan Mal, tahsil Sandila, *Hardoi District Gazetteer,* p. 210.
29. *N.M.* I, pp. 174-9.
30. *N.M.* I, p. 321.
31. Ibid.
32. Fath Mumur Khan had served the Mughal empire with distinction. He held a *mansab* of 1,000 *zat* and 1,200 *sawar.* See Athar Ali, *The Mughal*

Nobility under Aurangzeb (Delhi, 1968), Appendix II, p. 260. The author of *N.M.* I, pp. 322-8, says that Fath Mamur Khan rose to the high *mansab* of 3,000/3,000.

33. Now a large village on the main road from Hardoi to Shahjahanpur at a distance of 4 miles from Shahabad. *Hardoi District Gazetteer*, p. 275.
34. *N.M.* I, pp. 330-3; *Hardoi District Gazetteer*, p. 272.
35. It is also a large village in pargana Sara, South district, Hardoi, 11 miles north of Hardoi and 2 miles west of the road to Pihani. *Hardoi District Gazetteer*, p. 110.
36. Kachura was recorded as village in pargana Shahabad, Hardoi, when the District Gazetteer was compiled. *Hardoi District Gazetteer*, p. 110.
37. *N.M.* I, pp. 327-8; *Hardoi District Gazetteer*, p. 272.
38. *N.M.* I, pp. 330-3; *Hardoi District Gazetteer*, p. 272.
39. *Hardoi District Gazetteer*, p. 272.
40. *N.M.* I, pp. 337-8.
41. *N.M.* I, p. 339.
42. A village in pargana Shahabad. *Hardoi District Gazetteer*, p. 109.
43. *N.M.* I, p. 278.
44. A pargana—now divided into two—Sara North and Sara South, in 1866. *Hardoi District Gazetteer*, pp. 258-60.
45. *N.M.* I, p. 343; *Hardoi District Gazetteer*, p. 88, mentions him as son of Dildar Khan.
46. *Hardoi District Gazetteer*, pp. 88-9, 260.
47. *Hardoi District Gazetteer*, p. 260.
48. *Hardoi District Gazetteer*, pp. 89, 260; *N.M.* I, pp. 358-9.
49. For the antiquity and history of this see *Farrukhabad District Gazetteer*, p. 82.
50. Cf. *Mukhtasar halat-i tarikhi Nawab Rashid Khan*, transcript, Research Library, Department of History, AMU, Aligarh, pp. 10-12.
51. *Shamsabad Documents*, No. 2, Research Library, Department of History, AMU, Aligarh.
52. The *farman* carries the word *in'ām ba ism-e Rashid Khan ma'i farzandan* (gift in favour of Rashid Khan including his sons).
53. *Qaimganj Documents*, No. 2, photocopies with Professor Iqtidar Alam Khan, Department of History, AMU, Aligarh.
54. A term generally used by the Mughal nobles.
55. *Hiba* in Muslim Law is normally an oral and not written transaction. But *hiba* documents were prepared. See *Nama-i Mazaffari*, I, p. 312, for two *hiba* documents.
56. *Qaimganj Documents*, No. 2.
57. *Farrukhabad District Gazetteer*, pp. 82-3, refers to the new zamindars in Shamsabad. The author of *Mukhtasar halat-i tarikhi Nawab Rashid*

Khan, pp. 16-17, alleges that Qaim Khan and Ahmad Khan Bangash encouraged Afghans to settle in Mau Rashidabad and the adjoining areas. They incited the Afghans to eject the *Khanazads* who were thus turned out from the pargana altogether. Also see *Farrukhabad District Gazetteer*, pp. 82-3.

58. *Farrukhabad District Gazetteer*, p. 241.

Was there a Crisis in Mid-Eighteenth Century Bengal?

SUSHIL CHAUDHURY

IN RECENT YEARS several noted historians have propounded the thesis that there was a 'crisis' in Bengal in the mid-eighteenth century which ultimately brought in the British. Earlier the 'crisis' was seen only in Bengal's body-politic but is now being that this was the case in the economic sphere too. The 'crisis' in Bengal politics is explained with emphasis on the breakdown of the 'new class alliance' of military aristocrats, merchant-bankers and zamindars which sustained the nawabi regime from Murshid Quli to Alivardi Khan. As an indication of the economic 'crisis', it has been pointed out that prior to Plassey (1757), economic conditions deteriorated, trade and industry languished, merchants were impoverished, prices of different commodities sky-rocketed, and the exports of the English Company declined—all presumably because of the disastrous impact of the Maratha incursions in the 1740s. The aim of this paper is to examine this thesis in the light of new evidence found in European and Indian archives.

*Subsequent to the presentation of this paper in the workshop at Charlottesville, Virginia, in October 1994, my book *From Prosperity to Decline: Eighteenth Century Bengal* came out in 1995 (Manohar, Delhi) wherein I have incorporated most of the material used in the article. But the main thrust of this paper has not been discussed in detail in the book. I am grateful to the Maison des Sciences de l'Homme, Paris for their support during the preparation of this paper.

'Crisis' in the Body-politic?

Of late, historians are keen on explaining the origin of the Anglo-Nawabi conflict in 1756/7 (which resulted in the Plassey revolution and the British conquest of Bengal) in terms of one broad generalization, namely, the breakdown of the alliance among military aristocrats, merchant-bankers, and zamindars that underpinned the nawabi regime from Murshid Quli till Alivardi Khan. Near-contemporaneous Persian chronicles written mostly at the behest or under the patronage of British 'masters' came in handy, and a selective use of European sources helped build the general thesis that with the accession of the young Nawab Siraj ud-Daulah (April 1756) the 'class alliance' broke down and everything began to fall apart, and that the British had to intervene almost in a fit of 'absent-mindedness' in order to avert the 'crisis' in Bengal's body politic. Hence the obvious conclusion is that Plassey should be explained as the consummation of an internal crisis arising out of the alienation of the dominant ruling class by the nawab which inevitably brought in the British. The actual role of the British in the Plassey conspiracy against the nawab is thus conveniently lost in the maze of 'theorization' and the young nawab remains the villain of the piece. To use the age-old cliche, this is nothing but old wine in new bottles—the ghost of S.C. Hill (1905) is very much alive beneath the facade of the broad generalization.[1]

There is little doubt that the appointment of Murshid Quli as the diwan of Bengal heralded a new era in the history of Bengal. Not only did it witness the setting up of a new pattern of provincial administration, but it convulsed the entire Bengal polity as well. Murshid Quli, a man of proven ability, was sent to the province with specific instructions to try to increase the revenue. But the process of increasing revenue collection led to significant changes in the landholding and political structure of Bengal resulting as they did in the 'formation of a new, regional group'. These changes can be described as the emergence of big zamindaris with a consequent decline in the total number of zamindaris, the increasing importance of larger zamindaris in the political system of the province, the enhancement in the power of the moneylender and banking class.[2]

The Mughal mansabdars who were the most dominant ruling group earlier become less powerful in the changed circumstances because they no longer found support or assistance from the centre. Hence they compromised to share power with local elements. The various socio-economic groups which so far remained subdued now got an opportunity to assert themselves. One of these groups, especially the bigger and stronger zamindars who emerged as a result of Murshid Quli's revenue reorganization, became much more powerful in the new set-up. As the demands of revenue increased, so did the power of the zamindars. In fact, the history of the large zamindars shows that Murshid Quli made it a policy to increase the power of the loyal and big zamindars. They also became partners in the new ruling group. Similarly, the merchant-bankers who began to play a significant role in the administrative and revenue reform of Murshid Quli were drawn into the new ruling councils. Thus, a new power-bloc was created in Bengal in the first half of the eighteenth century.

Yet it would not be correct to view the new ruling alliance as a bureaucratic superstructure or as a solid bloc. It was a group of different people with divergent interests who came close to rally round the nawab to enhance their own interests. In the particular setting of Bengal politics, their policy was directed towards strengthening his position on the one hand and their personal interests on the other. The nawab on his part needed the help of the insulated Mughal mansabdars, the landed magnates, and the merchant-bankers to run the administrative machinery and generate economic resources. Murshid Quli found a group of people from various sections looking at him at the head of the administration as their sole benefactor. He and his successors utilized the services of this group to fill a vacuum created in the peculiar circumstances of the early eighteenth century. A pyramid-type structure was evolved in Bengal with the nawab at the apex and the members of the ruling alliance deriving their power from him.

Moreover, there was no conscious attempt on the part of the government to share power with the various groups so as to forge a 'partnership'. The emergence of the big zamindars was the result of Murshid Quli's prime concern—revenue reforms. The merchant-banking class came into prominence because of the administrative reorganization and the fostering of trade and commerce. The Mughal mansabdars were rendered less powerful as a consequence of the decline of the central authority. The relationship between the government these segmented groups had more of a personal character, but no institutional basis.[3] It was an arrangement in which new vistas of glory were open to efficient and successful adventurers by meeting the increased state demand. At the same time the state became assured of the help and support of those who received the benefit of it. The most striking example of the personalized character of the alliance was the house of Jagat Seths. Starting as a mere usurer, the house, by developing a personal relationship with the government became the 'direct beneficiary' and built up the richest banking house in Bengal.

Since the relationship in the new alliance was based on personal vested interests, the prime concern of the various groups was to protect and promote their own interests, even if that meant a change in alignments. This is well illustrated throughout the first half of the eighteenth century. After Murshid Quli's death, according to his wishes his grandson, Sarfaraj Khan, became nawab. But when Sarfaraj's father, Shujauddin, then deputy governor of Orissa, wanted the *masnad* (throne) for himself, the former gave into the pleading of Murshid Quli's widow,[4] and there was no scope for any intervention by the new ruling groups. Even the great banker, Jagat Seth, reported the English factors, was not very sure in the beginning of his position in the changed circumstances.[5] That the new alliance was purely based on personal relationships is demonstrated by the fact that the two adventurer brothers, Haji Ahmed and Alivardi Khan, who were to play crucial roles in Bengal politics later on, were appointed to high posts by Shujauddin as they were his personal friends.[6] Neither belonged to the important mansabdar or zamindar groups when they were inducted into the administrative machinery.

Thus the new alliance was not a monolith. It showed definite cracks under stress. When Sarfaraj became nawab after Shujauddin's death, he wanted to give promotions and mansabs to his father's old officers. But the triumvirate of Haji Ahmed, Chand (diwan) and Jagat Seth, whom he allowed to continue to act as councillors according to his father's last instructions, opposed the move. Thus, a rift was created in the court. It was the personal intrigues of the triumvirate which brought about the revolution of 1740 in favour of Alivardi Khan. The personal ambition and conspiracy of a few persons resulted only in the deposition of Nawab Sarfaraj Khan, not either the latter's inefficiency and corruption so much nor the new ruling group's concerted effort. The author of *Riyaz* writes: 'This Revolution in the Government threw the City (Murshidabad—the capital) as well as the Army and the people of Bengal, into a general and deep convulsion.'[7] Even in the battle of Giria where Sarfaraj died fighting, quite a sizeable group of important mansabdars and zamindars like Ghaus Khan, Mir Sharafuddin, Mir Muhammed Bakir Khan, Bijay Singh, and Raja Ghandarab Singh fought on the side of Sarfaraj, while another group joined Alivardi's army, thus clearly indicating the division in the mansabdar-zamindar alliance on personal and other considerations.[8] That personal ambition was the driving force, with little regard for cohesion, is clearly reflected in Mir Jafar's (the commander-in chief) conspiracy to assassinate Nawab Alivardi Khan in 1747.[9]

Thus the suggestion even in recent studies that the alienation of the dominant ruling class by the new and young Nawab Siraj ud-Daulah (1756-7) broke down the new 'class alliance' and led to the subsequent political crisis resulting in the British conquest is not tenable. The so-called 'class alliance' was in fact an exigent arrangement at a personal level and had no institutional base, and hence quite fragile. Moreover, there was nothing unusual about this political situation in the mid-eighteenth century. With every succession question since the death of Murshid Quli (1728-9), the ruling clique was divided; so it was in 1756-7. Though a dominant group with the active support of the British opposed the succession of Siraj ud-Daulah, there was another group including merchant princes, zamindars, and military aristocrats, who supported the young nawab. This was the pattern in (1728-9) as also in 1739-40. So Plassey can hardly be explained as the consummation of an internal political crisis in Bengal in 1756-7.

Economic 'Crisis'?

It should be made clear that no one actually speaks of economic 'crisis' as such in the mid-eighteenth century Bengal.[10] But if one reads carefully some of the latest authorities,[11] one would find that there are explicit and positive hints on this point. The 'crisis' is seen in deteriorating economic conditions, a decline of trade and industry, the impoverishment of merchants, soaring prices of different commodities, and the decline in the exports of the English Company in the period prior to Plassey. For all this, it is generally presumed, the Maratha invasions of the 1740s (which, it is argued, had disastrous effects on the Bengal economy) were mainly responsible.

But let us first examine whether the Maratha invasions were as disastrous in their impact on the economy as most historians would have us believe. There is no denying the fact that they resulted in serious dislocation in the economy of some areas of Bengal, but the impact has been greatly exaggerated. The Marathas caused destruction generally along the line of their march, leaving the remaining part of the country more or less unaffected. Even in the affected areas, as Richard Becher, a Company official present in Bengal during the period, pointed out, the Marathas were obliged to return home at the approach of the rainy season, and the inhabitants were again safe till the following January. So they immediately went back to work, and arranged to raise and sell their crops before the next year's impending invasion.[12] That the country was not that much impoverished is proved by the fact that the zamindars paid Alivardi Rs. 10 million at one time and Rs. 5 million at another, besides their annual revenue, to enable him to meet the increased military expenditure.[13] The argument that many merchants in Bengal 'were crippled by losses and exactions' following the Maratha invasions, and that as a result of this both the English and the Dutch Companies increasingly turned to direct dealings with the artisans, is not tenable. As we have shown elsewhere,[14] the Dutch Company made such and experiment for a few years only from 1747 to 1749 in view of the 'bankruptcy' of several merchants in a particular *aurung* but reverted to contracts with *dadni* merchants from 1750. The change over in the English

Company's investment pattern from the *dadni* to the *gomasta* system in 1753 was not because of any decline of Bengal merchants, but was actually the result of the Fort William Council's attempt to resolve its commercial crisis concerning private trade by cutting out the *dadni* merchants.[15]

Again, historians rely too much on contemporary Bengali literature and Persian chronicles to corroborate the disastrous effects of the Maratha invasions. That these are mostly exaggerated accounts is clear from the very nature of the evidence. For example, the poet Gangaram wrote 'rice, pulses, *dal* of all sorts, oil, ghee, flour, sugar, salt began to be sold at one rupee per seer. . . . All of them from the lowest to the highest, including the Nawab himself, had to subsist on boiled roots of banana trees.'[16] It is simply absurd that rice, oil, ghee, sugar, salt were all sold at Re. 1 per *seer*. Equally unbelievable is the assertion that even the nawab subsisted on roots of banana. Even making allowance for poetic license, the above can hardly be evidence of the impact of the Maratha invasions. The author of *Riyaz* refers to human beings living on banana roots to avert death by starvation. But if even true, this was description mostly of Burdwan city when its granaries were burnt down and the supply of imported grains was completely cut off by the Marathas for a short while.[17] Another Bengali poet, Bharatchandra, gives an account of Malini shopping in Burdwan but the prices she paid for different articles, said to be 'abnormal', cannot be compared with earlier prices (for lack of precise data) to see if they were really so.[18] The simple fact that the total value of the investments of the major European Companies, especially the English and the Dutch, as also the export by Asian merchants, was hardly affected during or after the Maratha incursions is sufficient proof that the invasions had really no long-term disastrous effects on the overall economy of Bengal.[19]

That trade and industry were not seriously affected by the Maratha inroads is evident from the level of European and Asian exports in the mid-eighteenth century. The English Company's exports to Europe reached its zenith in the first quinquennial period of the 1740s. As a matter of fact, English exports from Bengal had increased substantially from the early 1730s. Though there was a slight decline in the average annual value of the English exports between 1750 and 1755 , it can be asserted that the average annual value of the English exports did not show any marked decline over the period from 1730 to 1755 , which is evident from Table 1. It is important to note that the slight decrease in the average annual value of the English exports in the first half of the 1750s was balanced (as far as Bengal is concerned) by the increase in the value of the Dutch exports during this period. So there is no reason to believe that the decline in the English exports was due to any economic 'crisis' in Bengal.

Dutch exports in the 1720s declined to some extent but picked up from the early 1730s. As a matter of fact, the value of Dutch exports shows a steady increase throughout the period from the early 1730s to the middle of the 1750s. It is interesting to note that the Dutch, who lagged far behind the English in the early 1730s, almost caught up with them in early 1750s. Of course, Dutch exports included those to different parts of Asia as well. Table 2 will bear the point out.

As far as Asian exports are concerned, they were quite substantial even in the mid-eighteenth century. Perhaps the total value of Asian textile exports could have been in the range of Rs. 9 million to Rs. 10 million.[20] That this is not an overestimation can be established with reference to indirect evidence and assumptions. If the share percentage of the textiles exported by the Dutch and English from Dhaka ranged between 5 and 10 per cent in the early 1750s, the share of Dhaka textiles in Asian exports

TABLE 1: QUINQUENNIAL TOTAL AND AVERAGE ANNUAL VALUE OF ENGLISH EXPORTS, 1730-55

Years	Total	Average	Florins
1730-1 to 1734-5	£ 2,117,689	£ 423,538	*f*. 5,082,453
1740-1 to 1744-5	£ 2,401,785	£ 480,357	*f*. 5,764,284
1750-1 to 1754-5	£ 2,033,244	£ 406,649	*f*. 4,879,785

Source and note: Computed from K.N. Chaudhuri, *Trading World*, pp. 509-10, with a one-year lag.

TABLE 2: QUINQUENNIAL TOTAL AND AVERAGE ANNUAL VALUE OF ENGLISH AND DUTCH EXPORTS, 1730-55

(*in Florins*)

	English	Dutch	
Years	Average Annual Value of Exports to Europe	Average Annual Value of Exports to Europe	Average Annual Value of Total Exports (Europe and Asia)
1730-1-1734-5	5,082,453	2,020,460	3,489,567
1740-1-1744-5	5,764,284	2,390,558	3,475,770
1750-1-1754-5	4,879,785	3,417,306	4,480,104

Source and note: Dutch exports compiled and computed from export invoices in VOC records. The figures for English exports calculated with one-year lag from K.N. Chaudhuri, *Trading World,* pp. 510-11. The rate of conversion used is £ 1= *f.* 12.

could be assumed to have been no more than 10 per cent.[21] In the estimate of the textiles exported from Dhaka in 1747, the value exclusively for Asian export is mentioned as Rs. 1.15 million[22] which means that the total value of the Asian textile export from Bengal could have been around Rs. 11.5 million.

We are on much stronger ground so far as the Asian export of silk is concerned. The total of silk exports by Asians can be computed from W. Aldersey's report as is given in Table 3.

Adding up the value of silk exports by Asians (Rs. 4.8 million

TABLE 3: QUINQUENNIAL TOTAL OF SILK EXPORT BY ASIANS, 1749-58

Years	Total (mds.)	Average (mds.)	Average (lb.)	Total Value (Rs.)	Total Value (Rs.)
1749-53	99,016	19,803	14,85,240	2,77,24,365	55,44,873
1754-8	74,692	14,938	11,20,380	2,09,13,345	41,82,669

Source: B.P.C., Range 1, vol. 44, Annex to Consult., 19 June 1769.

on an average) with that of textiles (between Rs. 9 million and 10 million), the total value of Asian exports of textiles and raw silk could have been at least Rs. 13 million to Rs. 14 million a year, leaving aside minor exports like sugar, opium and grains.

As regards the decline of Bengal merchants, there is ample evidence to show that there was actually none. The Setts and Basaks were still the leading and dominant merchant families of Calcutta in the 1750s, while Hari Krishan Roy was the influential Dutch broker at Chinsurah. The most important thing one has to remember in this connection is that despite all wars, depredations and troubles, the credit market in Bengal was not at all destroyed, largely owing to the great financial resources of the Jagat Seths. There is evidence that this banking house used to extensively finance Asian as well as European trade in Bengal. The financial solvency of the Jagat Seths was never in question, even in the 1750s. The house used to finance the *dadni* merchants of Calcutta.[23] Moreover, when merchants princes like Umichand and Khwaja Wazid were still operating in full swing and playing a dominant role in Bengal's commercial life, with their extensive trade connections with Calcutta merchants, the thesis of the general decline of the Bengal merchants becomes wholly untenable.[24]

As regards the contention that the decline of the Bengal merchants in the early 1750s forced the East India Company to change its investment pattern from the *dadni* to the *gomasta* system,[25] it can be safely asserted that there was really no decline of the merchants in Bengal, and that the change in the investment system was due to other considerations. The prominent merchant families of Calcutta, the Setts and Basaks, and the Katmas of Kasimbazar were still prominent and quite substantial merchants in the early 1750s. Moreover, merchant princes like the Jagat Seths, Umichand, and Khwaja Wazid saw their heyday during these years. So long as these merchant princes were there, Bengal's credit market was as strong as ever, and there was no paucity of capital for the smaller merchants to thrive in their won trade. The fact of the matter was that the *dadni* merchants refused to contract for investment in 1753 except absolutely on their own terms. In view of the uncertainty of trade in the troubled times, they rejected the Company's terms that the *dadni* should not exceed 30 per cent as opposed to 85 per cent earlier that the contract should be made on 'old musters' which were prepared in normal times that a penalty of 10 per cent would be levied on any deficiency of supply[26] which the merchants thought, not without some justification, were extremely unreasonable. On the other hand, as the private trade of the Company's servants was dwindling in the early 1750s, they saw an opportunity in the introduction of the *gomasta* system to augment their private trade interest.

As to the question of price trends there has been complete unanimity among historians that from 1720 to 1760, especially from the early 1740s, prices of commodities show 'a fairly sustained and market increase', 'particularly strong for raw silk and Bengal textiles', as also for rice.[27] With the help of such sophisticated devices as the 'weighted moving-average' of price series the histogram, and the assessment of polynomial and linear trend of prices of several commodities, these authorities conclude that 'the general synchronic trends are clearly visible' and that there was a gradual rise in prices over the period as a whole.[28] But the general emphasis so far has been on the 'sharp increase' in prices from around the 1740s.

Even assuming for the sake of argument that the prices of export goods such as textiles and raw silk registered a rise over the period under review, it may be argued that 'such a sectorial rise might only reflect a failure of the supply of these goods to increase as fast as the demand for them, and may not necessarily indicate a general price rise in the economy'.[29] In order to prove the latter, we have to look for movements in the price of the so-called wage-goods. The most important among these are staple food items like rice and wheat. But at the present state of our knowledge, such an exercise is fraught with the danger of a wide margin of error because of the lack of precise information on the numerous varieties of staple food items, especially rice. One suspects that such an attempt might only lead to extremely erratic behaviour of the prices of provisions, as has been demonstrated in a recent study of Bengal prices on similar lines for the period 1650 to 1720.[30]

Even so, in order to determine whether there was any sharp rise in prices in general one should look into the prices of major food grains, especially rice, the staple food of Bengal, and not at the prices of major export commodities like textiles and raw silk where the demand for such goods on the part of Asian and European merchants might have resulted in such a rise. But as even the latest studies emphasize this aspect to prove a general rise in prices and as 'evidence of sustained and marked increased in prices',[31] let us examine how far, or if at all, the prices of these commodities show a secular upward trend during the period under review. One has to take into account here that even earlier authorities pointed out a 'sharp increase' in the prices of textiles and raw silk, and asserted that between 1738 and 1754 these increased by no less than 30 per cent.[32] The latest study on the period, quoting earlier authorities, also arrived at the same conclusion.[33]

The sole basis of that conclusion regarding the steep rise in the price of textiles is a complete misreading (and out of context too) of an entry in the Bengal Public Consultations under December 1752.[34] The particular consultation refers to a letter from Dacca of 4 December 1752 wherein the Dacca factors were trying to answer allegations from Calcutta regarding the bad quality of their textiles, pointing out that the sample of 1738 was not 'fit standard for judging' the quality of cloth sent fro Dacca in the former year. The reasons for the badness of the quality of cloth, as the Dacca factors wrote, were:[35]

as the Copass [*kapas* or cotton] or country cotton has not been for *the two years past* under 9 or 10 rupees and the price of rice at the same time very dear, whereas in 1738 the Coppas did not exceed Rs. 2 or Rs. 2-8 and the rice very cheap, mostly 2 maunds 20 seer to 3 maunds for a rupee to which may be added which is well known to all the purchasers of cloth that the prices of all sorts of cloths have risen *near 30 per cent*, some more, since the year 1738, and that they now labour there and has done so *for these two years past* under the inconvenience of a French factory continually emulating the Hon'ble Company's trade and have advanced the price to all cloth both coarse and fine and obliged them to be less severe with their dellols in prizing their cloth. . . .

Clearly, this is a desperate bid on the part of the Dacca

factors—scrupulousness not being their strong point, true also of other Company servants working in India at that time—to justify the poor quality of the cloth and hence the emphasis on a 30 per cent increase in its price between 1738 and 1752. As the 'muster' (sample) of 1738 had been the standard, so 1738 becomes the target date and for no other reason. Moreover, if one carefully examines the above passage, one cannot miss the stress on 'these two years past' which signifies that the quality of cloth had deteriorated in *those* years and not really for the whole of the period from 1738 to 1752. There is the specific reference to 'near 30 per cent' increase in the price of cloth during the period but, if at all true, that applies only to Dacca, and not all of Bengal. Besides, one can rightly suspect the validity of evidence produced in self-defense against allegations of malpractice. One who has gone through the Company records carefully can hardly fail to observe that throughout the period, whenever an allegation was made regarding bad investments, the factors always answered in the same vein—that it was because of the high price of staples like rice and cotton, competition from other Asian and/or European merchants, and the general increase in the price of export commodities. One should accept such 'evidence' or 'excuses' with caution.

However, the fact remains that a distinguished authority has demonstrated with diagrams, polynomial and linear trends, as also time series, that 'a fairly sustained and marked increase (in prices) is particularly strong for raw silk and textiles' during the period under review.[36] How can one reconcile this with the fact, as we shall see shortly, that the increase in prices of these two main export commodities was not particularly spectacular. The answer is not far to seek. The weighted average, diagrams polynomial and linear trend, etc., do not take into account the most crucial factors which determined the price of either textiles or raw silk. There were numerous varieties of textiles and even within the same category (e.g. muslins of fine calicoes), there were different types (e.g. in muslin, there were *khasas, mulmuls,* etc.) and the price of each type (e.g. *khasa*) depended on size, quality, and the *aurung* in which it was produced, which will be evident in the Table 4.

TABLE 4: DUTCH COMPANY'S CONTRACT WITH MERCHANTS FOR TEXTILES, 24 JUNE 1752

Name of Piece-goods	No. of Pieces	Length (co.) x Breadth (co.)	Price per Piece (Rs. as.)
Khasa	3,000	40 x 3	14.11
Khasa	840	40 x 2⅜	12.11
Khasa Jagannatpur	6,000	40 x 2¼	10.13
Khasa Hendial with gold head	2,000	40 x 2¼	11.6
Khasa Jagannatpur	2,000	40 x 2	9.8
Khasa Hendial	2,000	40 x 2	9.8
Khasa Jagannatpur	2,960	40 x 2⅘	8.7
Khasa Jagannatpur	1,200	40 x 2½	7.6
Khasa fine Hendial with gold head	500	40 x 3	18.15
Khasa fine Hendial with gold head	1,500	40 x 2¼	14.3
Khasa Nadona	1,000	40 x 2¼	7.2
Khasa Nadona	2,000	25 x 2¼	4.6
Khasa Bourang	4,000	38 x 1⅞	6.10
Mulmul fine	200	40 x 3	17.10
Mulmul fine	300	40 x 2¼	13.11
Mulmul fine Haripal	100	40 x 2¼	12.4
Mulmul fine Haripal	350	40 x 1¾	10.4
Mulmul fine Haripal	50	40 x 1⅓	8.13
Mulmul (assorted)	1,000	40 x 3	14.11
Mulmul (assorted)	400	40 x 2⅝	12.11
Mulmul (assorted)	4,500	40 x 2¼	10.12
Mulmul (assorted)	500	40 x 1¾	8.7
Mulmul (assorted)	1,200	40 x 2	9.8
Mulmul (assorted)	400	40 x 1½	6.12
Mulmul ordinary	4,000	40 x 2¼	7.6
Mulmul ordinary	1,200	40 x 2	6.12

Source: VOC 2821, HB, 20 Feb. 1753, ff. 91-5, Contract, dt. 24 June 1752.

The same was the case with raw silk, the price of which depended on the particular variety (e.g. 'Gujarat', Kumarkhali), fineness and racolta (*band*—Indian term for the harvest).[37] If all these factors are not taken into consideration in working out the cost price, the results are bound to be misleading. Just by deflating the total cost price by the total amount exported to find out per unit cost price does not reveal the real picture as has happened in this case.[38] Hence even with the scientific tools of analysis used by K.N. Chaudhuri, the results—showing a secular upward trend—can hardly be taken for granted.

For a precise study of the movement of textile prices, one has to take into account how many pieces of a particular type of cloth, of what length and width, of which *aurung* and of what quality were exported at what total price—from which alone one can get the exact picture of price movements. To give an illustration, if we are looking into the price of *khasa*, just taking into account the number of exported and their total price, to find the unit price, could be quite erroneous. We have to know whether the *khasa* was ordinary, fine or superfine, whether its measurement was 40 *co.* x 3 *co.*,[39] 40 *co.* x 2¾ *co.*, or 40 *co.* x 2¼ *co.*, and whether it was produced in Jagannatpur or Cogmaria or Orrua (i.e. the *aurung* in which it was produced). The price of *khasa* will depend on all these factors, and hence we have to take all these variables into consideration. This is almost an impossible task as in all the export invoices, whether of the Dutch or the English Company, what is given is the total number of *khasas* exported, and the total cost price. There is no mention of size, quality, or *aurung*. Again, if the unit price of the textiles in a particular year is arrived at just by dividing the total cost price by the total number of pieces exported without taking into account the composition of different categories such as muslins, fine calico or ordinary calicos (which varied over the period in the total textile export) then too the picture of price movement could be distorted. Thus the steady upward trend in K.N. Chaudhuri's time series can be explained by the fact that while the share of the more expensive category of textiles, muslins, and silk piece-goods steadily increased in the first quinquennial period of 1740s and 1750s, that of the cheapest variety, ordinary calicos, remained the same,[40] and not because of any real increase in the price of textiles. That the unit price of textiles could vary widely depending on the category of textiles and place of procurement is amply clear from the unit price of the textiles exported by the Dutch Company in 1753-4 for which such breakdowns are available. Thus the unit price of textiles sent from Patna, mostly ordinary calicos, worked out at *f.* 613; from Dacca, mostly muslins and fine calicos, *f.* 20.04; from Hughli, mostly medium quality, *f.* 9.6; and from Kasimbazar, silk piece-goods and ordinary calicos, *f.* 7.85.[41]

The only accurate evidence of price movement in textiles is the contract the Companies entered into with the *dadni* merchants for supply of goods every year. In these contracts we find the particular details of the size, quality and the *aurung* of each type of cloth which are absolutely essential for a proper scrutiny of the movement of price of textiles. Until and unless we know these details of the variables, nothing definitive can be said about price movement. As is well known, the prices were arrived at after days' of bargaining and wrangling between the Company and its merchants. When the Companies tried to pay lower prices for cloth delivered by the merchants, it was mainly on grounds of inferior quality, and the original contract price was never altered.

So let us see what are the general trends, as revealed in these contracts over the period for which we select six years, namely, 1732, 1741, 1744, 1751, 1752 and 1754. These particular years are chosen for such an analysis because 1732 was a normal year without political disturbance or natural calamity, 1741 was the year just prior to the Maratha invasions, and 1744 was the year when the impact of these incursions could be expected to be reflected in the price movement. The Maratha invasions stopped in 1751; 1752 was the year immediately after the peace with the Marathas, while 1754 was the first normal year after the famine of 1752. A such these years would give us a broad spectrum of the period with its ups and downs, whether political or economic. For our present analysis, we take up the Dutch contracts for these six years to see how prices moved in the two main types of muslins, *khasas* and *mulmuls* which were the staples in the export list of the Europeans (Table 5).[42]

It is evident from Table 5 that between 1734 and 1754 there was no increase in the price of twenty different types of *khasas* and *mulmuls* that were noted in the list of contract, except for *khasa* Nadona which seems to be, from its price, a medium or low quality fabric. What is extremely significant, as is apparent

TABLE 5: CONTRACT PRICE OF *KHASAS* AND *MULMULS* 1732-54 (SELECT YEARS), DUTCH COMPANY

		1732	1741	1744	1751	1752	1754
Textile type	Measure (in *covid*)	Price (Rs. as.)	Price (Rs. as.)	Price (Rs. as.)	Price (Rs. as.)	Price (Rs. as.)	Price (Rs. as.)
Khasa ordn.	40 x 3	15.00	15.00	15.00	14.11	14.11	14.11
Khasa fine	40 x 3	18.00	x	x	x	x	x
Khasa ordn.	40 x 2⅝	13.00	13.00	13.00	12.11	12.11	12.11
Khasa ordn.	40 x 2¼	11.00	11.00	11.00	x	10.13	10.13
Khasa ordn.	40 x 2½	x	x	x	10.13	x	x
Khasa ordn.	40 x 2	9.12	8.00	9.12	9.8	9.8	9.8
Khasa ordn.	40 x 1¾	8.10	7.00	8.10	8.7	8.7	8.7
Khasa ordn.	40 x 1½	7.8	x	7.8	7.6	7.6	7.6
Khasa Nadona	25 x 2¼	3.14	3.14	3.14	4.6	4.6	4.6
Mulmul ordn.	40 x 3	15.00	15.00	15.00	x	x	14.11
Mulmul fine	40 x 3	18.00	18.00	x	17.10	17.10	17.10
Mulmul ordn.	40 x 2⅝	13.00	13.00	13.00	12.11	12.11	x
Mulmul ordn.	40 x 2¼	11.00	11.00	11.00	10.12	10.12	10.12
Mulmul fine	40 x 2¼	14.00	14.00	14.00	13.11	13.11	13.11
Mulmul ordn.	40 x 2	9.12	9.12	9.12	9.8	9.8	9.8
Mulmul ordn.	40 x 1¾	8.10	8.10	8.10	8.7	8.7	x
Mulmul ordn.	40 x 1¾	10.8	x	x	10.4	10.4	10.5
Mulmul ordn.	40 x 1½	x	7.00	7.00	x	6.14	6.14
Mulmul fine	40 x 1½	x	9.00	x	8.13	8.13	8.13
Mulmul ordn.	40 x 1¼	7	x	x	6.14	x	x

Source: Contracts with Merchants, VOC 2241, ff. 649-61; VOC 2537, ff. 1427-8; VOC 2629, f. 218; VOC 2783, ff. 236-7, VOC 2821, ff. 91-5; VOC 2840, ff. 715-16.

from this Table is that the price of all the different *khasas* and *mulmuls* (except *khasa* Nadona) actually went down in the period 1751-4 from the level between 1732 and 1744. In other words, the prices of *khasas* and *mulmuls* in the period from 1732-54 will negate the thesis of a 'fairly marked and sustained' increase in the prices of textiles in general during the period.

But one might argue that *khasas* and *mulmuls* were finer varieties of calicos, and perhaps the price rise was reflected in not-so-fine and medium types of textiles. So let us see how the prices moved in these varieties during the years under consideration. In Table 6 we note the contract prices for several types of textiles coarser than muslins and which were prominent in the export list of the Dutch Company.

The price trend that emerges from Table 6 is undoubtedly different from the one in Table 5. Of the six types of coarse textiles, the prices of four rose by 10 to 20 per cent while the price of two others actually show a downward trend. Though it is difficult to explain such mixed trends, one possible explanation could be that most of these piece-goods were produced in the areas around Hughli, which was one of the worst affected by the Maratha raids. Secondly, the competition among the buyers, whether Asians or Europeans, was more severe for the coarser varieties than for finer muslins. But then we cannot explain, at the present state of our knowledge, the slide in the prices of the two types of ginghams. Still what is notable from the prices of the coarser types of textiles is that there is hardly anything which can be termed 'a marked and sustained increase' in prices over the period.

So far as the price of coarsest textiles is concerned, no clear picture emerges from the Dutch contracts (Table 7). Though at the first glance it seems that the prices went up considerably, it is extremely difficult to measure the rise because the measurement of textiles by the Dutch varied over these years, and there is no

TABLE 6: CONTRACT PRICES OF COARSER TEXTILES 1732-54 (SELECT YEARS), DUTCH COMPANY

		1732	1741	1744	1751	1752	1754
Textile type	Measure (in *covid*)	Price (Rs. as.)	Price (Rs. as.)	Price (Rs. as.)	Price (Rs. as.)	Price (Rs. as.)	Price (Rs. as.)
Sanoes	24 x 2	4.8	4.8	4.8	4.15	4.15	4.15
Kharadaries	18 x 2¼	4.00	4.00	4.00	4.3	4.8	4.8
Allabanies	24 x 3	4.12	4.12	x	5.7	5.12	5.12
Ginghams (plain)	18 x 2¼	3.8	3.8	3.8	3.7	3.7	3.7
Ginghams (check)	18 x 2¼	4.12	4.12	4.12	4.7	4.7	4.7

Source: Contracts with Merchants, VOC 2241, ff. 649-61; VOC 2537, ff. 1427-8; VOC 2629, f. 218; VOC 2783, ff. 236-7, VOC 2821, ff. 91-5; VOC 2840, ff. 715-16.

precise data how the price of any of the coarsest textiles of exactly the same length and width rose during the period (Table 7). Here it is important to note that in Bengal, the price of the same type of textile often jumped when the traditional measurement was even slightly altered—a fact which is borne at by numerous references in the Company records. Yet, it is possible that the price of the coarsest textiles went up to some extent though it is not obvious from Table 7. The explanation for this probable rise in the price of coarsest textiles is not obvious from Table 7. The explanation for this probable rise in the price of coarsest textiles is not far to seek. Most of these textiles were produced in Birbhum, Burdwan and Kasimbazar areas, which were the most heavily affected by the Maratha invasions. Besides, as we have shown elsewhere,[43] the keenest competition in the market was for this variety, which was the reason why the merchants were most reluctant to contract for these textiles which, as they alleged, brought them little or no profit while they were extremely eager to contract for finer varieties. Often the Companies had to impose the contract for these ordinary calicos on unwilling merchants.

TABLE 7: CONTRACT PRICES OF COARSEST AND CHEAPEST TEXTILES 1732-54 (SELECT YEARS), DUTCH COMPANY

		1732	1741	1744	1751	1752	1754
Textile type	Measure (in *covid*)	Price (Rs. as.) per *corge*	Price (Rs. as.) per *corge*	Price (Rs. as.) per *corge*	Price (Rs. as.) per *corge*	Price (Rs. as.) per *corge*	Price (Rs. as.) per *corge*
Garras	36 x 2½	x	x	x	84	84	84
Garras	30 x 2½	x	x	x	70	70	70
Garras	30 x 2½	45	48	x	x	x	x
Garras	24 x 2½	x	x	x	56	56	56
Guinees	75 x 2½	x	x	x	175	175	175
Guinees	75 x 2½	118	121.8	x	x	x	x
Salampuris	37½ x 2½	x	x	x	87.8	87.8	87.8
Salampuris	37½ x 2½	x	60.12	x	x	x	x

Source: As in Table 5 and VOC 2783, ff. 248-9; 2840, f. 680. Per *corge* means per 20. Generally the coarsest textiles were contracted per *corge*.

Thus prices of textiles do not show a 'sharp and marked increase' from an analysis of the English Company's contracts from 1730 to 1757.[44] Similarly it can be shown that the price of raw silk, fluctuated a lot during the period, does not show any secular upward trend.[45]

As pointed out earlier, rice is the most important food item, the price of which should be looked into to determine any precise price movement in Bengal during the period under review. But the main difficulty here is the varieties of rice, and their different prices (Table 8). So it is not a simple case of fine or coarse rice only; when the price of coarse rice can vary as widely as between 4 mds. 15 *seers* and 7 mds. 20 *seers* per rupee (the difference being about 71 per cent), there is a grave risk in taking the price of rice as an indicator of price movements, until and unless one can be absolutely sure of the exact quality. Otherwise the result could be extremely erratic and gravely misleading. Yet depending on such data and sometimes fragmentary at that, recent authorities made such assertions as 'Rice which was sold at 100 to 120 *seers* for a rupee in 1738, was being sold only 30 seers for a rupee' in the mid-1740s as evidence to show that 'production declined and prices soared' or that by the 1740s 'Bengal's advantages seemed to be disappearing'.[46] Basing his evidence on earlier authorities, the most recent authority affirms that 'between 1738 and 1754 it was thought that the price of rice in Calcutta had

TABLE 8: PRICE OF RICE 1729

Variety	*Mds.-Seers*	Per Rupee
Fine Rice: *Bansephool*		
1st sort	1-10	”
2nd sort	1-23	”
3rd sort	1-35	”
Coarse Rice: *Desna*	4-15	”
Coarse Rice: *Poorbie*	4-25	”
Coarse Rice: *Munsurah*	5-25	”
Coarse Rice: *Kurkashallee*	7-20	”

Source: Sixth Report (1782-3), Appendix 15.

risen by three or four times' and reiterates that 'local shortages' led to 'greatly increased food prices'.[47] But a close scrutiny of price of rice in Bengal shows no 'marked and sustained' increase during the period.[48]

Thus the thesis of the crisis in mid-eighteenth-century Bengal crumbles under close scrutiny. Indeed it was not because of any internal crisis in Bengal that the British had to intervene; it was because of the private trade interests of Company servants. This was the motivating force behind the conquest. The golden days of British private trade began to decline from the late 1730; it was facing a severe crisis in the late 1740s and early 1750s because of a substantial increase in French private trade.[49] So the destruction of the French, to prevent any possible Franco-Bengali alliance against the British, and the deposition of a nawab who was threatening to stop illegal private trade and misuse of *dastaks* by the British—both essential for rescuing the battered private trade fortunes of the British—became the main goal of the Company servants' subimperialism.[50]

NOTES

1. For this broad generalization, see P.J. Marshall, *Bengal—The British Bridgehead* (Cambridge, 1987), pp. 56, 63; Rajat Kanta Ray, 'Colonial Penetration and Initial Resistance', *Indian Historical Review,* vol. XII, Nos. 1-2, July 1985-Jan. 1986, pp. 4, 6, 7, 14. It should not be misconstrued that I am against any 'theorization' but my point is while doing so, one should not lose sight of the specific issues involved. Also, a recent study has pointed out (Munshi Mazibor Rahman, 'Nizamat in Bengal: A Study of its Rise, Growth and Decline, 1700-1757', unpublished M.Phil. thesis, JNU, 1988) that the new class alliance or 'compact' had more of a personal character to serve vested interests than any institutional basis and hence was bound to be short-lived. For Hill's views, see S.C. Hill, *Bengal in 1756-57* (London, 1905), vol. 1, p. lii.
2. P.B. Calkins, 'The Formation of a Regionally Oriented Ruling Group in Bengal', *Journal of Asian Studies* XXIX, 4, 1970, p. 800.
3. M. Mazibor Rahman, 'Nizamat in Bengal', unpublished M.Phil. thesis JNU, 1988.
4. Ghulam Husain Salim, *Riyaz-us-Salatin* (Calcutta, 1904), p. 288.

5. Bengal Public Consultations (henceforth BPC), Range 1, vol. 6, f. 490, 14 Aug. 1727.
6. *Riyaz*, pp. 294-5.
7. Ibid., p. 320.
8. Ibid., pp. 311, 314-15, 319-20.
9. K.K. Datta, *Alivardi and His Times* (Calcutta, 1952), p. 81.
10. Only P.J. Marshall spoke about the economic 'crisis' in a seminar (1988) in Calcutta.
11. For example, K.N. Chaudhuri, *The Trading World of Asia and the English East India Company* (Cambridge, 1978); P.J. Marshall, *East Indian Fortunes* (Oxford, 1976); *Bengal—The British Bridgehead.*
12. Richard Becher's letter to Governor Verelst, 24 May 1769, quoted in W.K. Firminger, *Fifth Report*, pp. 183-4.
13. Ibid.
14. See S. Chaudhury, 'Merchants, Companies and Rulers—Bengal in the Eighteenth Century', *Journal of the Economic and Social History of the Orient*, February 1988.
15. For details, see S. Chaudhury, *From Prosperity to Decline—Eighteenth Century Bengal* (Delhi, 1995), Chapter 5.
16. Gangaram, *Maharastrapurana*, lines 234-42.
17. *Riyaz*, p. 340.
18. Bharatchandra quoted in K.K. Datta, *Studies in the History of Bengal Suba* (Calcutta, 1936), p. 466.
19. For the value of Dutch and English exports, see Chapters 3, 7 and 8, and for Asian exports, Chapters 7 and 8 of S. Chaudhury, *From Prosperity to Decline.*
20. For detailed reasoning for this assumption, see S. Chaudhury, 'Asian Merchants and Companies in Bengal's Export Trade, circa 1700-1757', paper presented at the International Conference on 'Merchants, Companies and Trade—the Asian and European Scene, 16th-18th Century', Paris, 1990; in S. Chaudhury and M. Morineau (eds.), *Merchants, Companies and Trade* (Cambridge, 2000).
21. Though the markets for the European and Asian exports were different, the demands for the various categories of Bengal textiles in these markets were more or less the same. The detailed analysis of the percentage share of different categories of textiles exported by the Companies (see S. Chaudhury, 'Continuity or Change in the Eighteenth Century? Price Trends in Bengal, circa 1720-1757', *Calcutta Historical Journal*, vol. XV, Nos. 1-2, July 1990-June 1991, p. 24, Table 11) establishes that the bulk of the exports comprised ordinary, medium and fine cotton piece-goods. The demand in the Middle East and Central Asia which was the main area of Asian exports was also for the same varieties as will be apparent from the analysis of the Dutch textile export to the Persian Gulf region (see, S. Chaudhury, *From Prosperity*).

22. Leaving aside the amount sent for the emperor at Delhi, the breakdown of the value of the export is as follows: Upper Provinces Rs. 1,00,000, Pathans Rs. 1,50,000, Mughals for foreign consumption Rs. 4,00,000, Armenians to Basra, Mocha and Jeddah Rs. 5,00,000.
23. BPC, vol. 12, f. 263, 26 Sept. 1737; vol. 22, f. 345vo, Annex. to Consult., 26 Oct. 1749.
24. For details, see S. Chaudhury, *From Prosperity to Decline,* Chapter 5.
25. K.N. Chaudhuri, *Trading World,* pp. 311-12
26. BPC, Range 1, vol. 26, f. 164, Annex. to Consult., 7 June 1753.
27. For example, see K.K. Datta, *Bengal Suba,* pp. 463-9; Brijen K. Gupta, *Sirajuddaullah and the East India Company* (Leiden, 1962), p. 33; K.N. Chaudhuri, *Trading World,* pp. 99-108; P.J. Marshall, *East Indian Fortunes,* p. 35; *Bengal,* pp. 73, 142-3, 163-4, 170.
28. K.N. Chaudhuri, *Trading World,* pp. 99-108, 159.
29. Om Prakash, *Dutch East India Company and the Economy of Bengal* (Princeton, 1985), p. 250.
30. Ibid., pp. 251-3. K.N. Chaudhuri, however, shows with a histogram a steady increase in the price of rice during the period under review.
31. K.N. Chaudhuri, *Trading World,* p. 102; following him, P.J. Marshall, *Bengal,* p. 73. Chaudhuri depends on polynomial and linear trend of textile and silk prices (pp. 103-4, 107-8) which shows a 'strong and gradual' rise in prices but as we shall see the method followed is subject to a wide margin of error.
32. K.K. Datta, *Bengal Suba,* p. 464; Brijen K. Gupta, *Sirajuddaullah,* p. 73.
33. P.J. Marshall, *East Indian Fortunes,* p. 35; *Bengal,* p. 33.
34. BPC, vol. 26, f. 214, Consult., 11 Dec. 1752; *Bengal and Madras Papers,* vol. II, p. 34; James Long, *Selections from Unpublished Records* (Calcutta, rpt., 1973), p. 40, doc. no. 103.
35. All emphasis mine.
36. K.N. Chaudhuri, *Trading World,* pp. 100-8, 533-4, 544-5.
37. See S. Chaudhury, *From Prosperity,* Chapter 8.
38. K.N. Chaudhuri, *Trading World,* pp. 506, 546.
39. *co.* is *covid,* measuring 18 inches.
40. See S. Chaudhury, *From Prosperity,* Chapter 7, Table 7.7 and Figure 7.5.
41. Collected and computed from export invoices in VOC records, Verenighde Oost-Indische Compagnie (henceforth VOC), 2811, ff. 6vo-7, 20-20vo, 46-46vo, 99-99vo; 2821, ff. 635-6; 2840, ff. 39, 441-2.
42. For the wide variation in the price of the same type of textiles, e.g. *khasa* and *mulmul,* depending on size, quality and *aurung,* see Table 4.
43. See S. Chaudhury, *From Prosperity,* Chapter 7.
44. Ibid., Chapter 10.
45. Ibid.
46. Brijen K. Gupta, *Sirajuddaullah,* p. 33; P.J. Marshall, *East Indian Fortunes,* p. 35.

47. P.J. Marshall, *Bengal*, p. 73; *East Indian Fortunes*, p. 35.
48. See S. Chaudhury, *From Prosperity*, Chapter 10.
49. The Dutch shipping records in the VOC archives will bear this out.
50. See S. Chaudhury, 'Trade Bullion and Conquest—Bengal in the Eighteenth Century', Presidential Address, Medieval India Section, Indian History Congress, Golden Jubilee Session, 1989.

PART II

Material and Visual Evidence: Readings and Meanings

Symbolic and Structural Constraints on the Adoption of European-style Military Technologies in the Eighteenth Century

STEWART N. GORDON

When the introduction of a new technology causes stress in a society, it illuminates the complex, changing and often contradictory symbolical systems which surround and embed both the old and the new technologies. What we expect to find in such a situation are a series of micro-theatres in which 'efficiency' is not abstract; rather, real actors weigh and contest full or partial adoption of the technology against a variety of changes and their perceived costs. Moreover, this is a long historical process, and calls into question periodizations such as 'modern' and 'pre-modern' and generalized social science formulations like 'paradigm shifts'.

The Weaponry of the Mughal India

As a point of departure, let us consider the Mughal armies, from the time of Babur to Akbar. Plate 1 (*c.* 1586-7), from an *Akbarnama* manuscript, depicts such an army at the siege of Cambay.[1] Most obviously, this was an army of cavalry. Out of the Central Asian background, men (and women) learned to ride early in life. Most illustrations of the Mughals at war or on the hunt shows them on horseback. Babur, hearing of an opportunity for conquest more than 150 miles away, described the whirlwind of the next three days, as follows:

Off we hurried, that very hour,—it was sunset—without reflecting, without a moment's delay. . . . Through that night it was rushed without delaying anywhere, and on next day until at the Mid-day Prayer, halt was made. . . . There we cooled down our horses and gave them corn. We rode out again at beat of (twilight) drum and on through that night till shoot of dawn, and through the next day till sunset, and on through that night till, just before dawn, we were . . . [at] Marghinan.[2]

The Mughals successfully used an earlier revolution in Military technology, the horseback warfare of the Central Asian steppe nomads. Out of these grasslands, so productive for raising horses, had come the Huns, various Turkish bands, and the Mongols (under Ghenghis Khan and his successors) who invaded Europe, China, and the Levant.[3] Cavalry could travel vast distances, choose where and when to fight, and disengage in an orderly, rapid, strategic retreat.

In this tradition, the Mughals took horse grading and branding seriously. The top grade was a Turki horse, followed by Yabu, Tazi, and Jangalah. The first three were larger, stronger, breeds imported into India and the lowest category was smaller, locally bred horses.[4]

'Every man brings his own horse and offers himself to be inlisted [*sic*]. The horse, and not the man, is carefully examined; and according to the size and value of the beast, the master receives his pay.'[5] The downgrading of locally-bred horses was a result of how the Mughals defined warfare. Cavalry meant heavy cavalry. A trooper normally wore linen quilting and chain mail, a helmet, plus a breast plate, back plate, and two side plates, leg plates, arm plates, a neck piece, and gauntlets.

The principal weapon of this heavily armoured soldier on horseback was the bow and arrow. In the *Akbarnama* illustration we see the typical short, reverse-curve bow common to Persia and Central Asia (here, in Plate 2, in its bowcase, ready for use). Recent scientific experiments have shown that this bow delivers substantially more penetrating power than any but the largest and heaviest long-bows.[6] Often, it was made of composite materials, such as wood and horn, which made it even more powerful. Unlike the longbow, it can be used from horseback.

The swords in the *Akbarnama* illustration are curved swords, effective only for slashing from horseback. The curved sword appears in many depictions of the Mughal emperor, even when he was at leisure in his harem.[7] Along with swords and daggers, ornate quivers and horse trappings were routinely given to honour meritorious actions. Archery was a part of the daily round of responsibilities of the Mughal cavalry.[8]

And what of firearms? Consider the *Akbarnama* illustration again. We see a single matchlockman, and he hardly seems central to the battle. This is corroborated in Babur's memoirs, as well as the court chronicles of his successors, Humayun and Akbar. Matchlocks had serious problems; they were heavy, inaccurate, slow to load, and could not be used from horseback.[9] Even well into the seventeenth century, a cavalryman could get off six arrows in the time it took to fire a single shot from a matchlock.[10] Matchlocks were basically relegated to the infantry, indigenously-recruited units held in such low esteem that they were listed along with litter bearers, carpenters, woodcutters, and cotton carders in the military pay records.[11] The only campaigns in which honourable cavalry routinely used shoulder arms were in areas of difficult terrain, such as the riverine areas of eastern Bengal and the Himalayas.[12]

In yet another painting of the late sixteenth century, Plate 3, artillery is shown. The guns seem completely unintegrated into the swirl of cavalry charges; they are not even manned, as the battle flows beyond them.[13] Documentary sources supports this visual evidence that guns were slow to fire (on the order of a couple of times an hour), inaccurate, and far too heavy to move in support of cavalry movements.[14] For Babur, even the successful casting of a field piece was such a wonderful event that he spent several pages describing the process.[15] These early guns were, in fact, much more effective against forts than they were in battles on the plains; and this is why one often sees them portrayed in the paintings of the period.[16] Like the infantry, the artillery branch had little prestige or chance of advancement; it was mainly staffed by 'Portuguese, English, Dutch, Germans, and French; fugitives from Goa, and from the Dutch and English companies'.[17]

The optimal battle situation for such an army was on the plains, where the cavalry could manoeuvre, wheel, and charge. In the portrayal (Plate 4) of the Battle of Samugarh, 1658,[18] tactics being a division of the cavalry into 'wings' that look like circles, and there is a designated vanguard and reserve. Artillery was drawn up in front and usually opened the battle, but was still too heavy to move with the fighting of the remainder of the day. The main tactic was the massed charge (to the accompaniment of huge drums), using first bow and arrow, followed by hand-to-hand combat with sword. If the line weakened, the commander (watching from his elephant) sent in reserves. The battle was decided by the death, capture, or retreat of the commander, after which his army fled, leaving tents, baggage, reserve horses, the bazaar, and guns as loot for the winning side.

Paying Armies in India: Loot, Mansabdari, and Watan

For the early Mughal armies, as under Babur, loot was the most common source of payment for troopers. The choice of battle site was often dictated by the availability of nearby populated countryside to loot. From the nomadic background of the Mughals, we find the expected tension between the mobility and freedom of the conquering war band and the desire for stable ongoing revenue. Babur is especially poignant on this subject. 'It passed through my mind that to wander from mountain to mountain, homeless and houseless, without country or abiding place, had nothing to recommend it.'[19] Thus, whenever Babur held a region for even one agricultural season, he promptly allotted various sections and villages to his main leaders as their 'places', for their maintenance.

Within two generations, this simple allotment of 'place' had grown into the extraordinary, sophisticated system of service known as mansabdari. Research of the last two decades has given us a rich picture of the personnel and operations of this structure. In briefest summary, the highest officials of the Mughal empire were 'ranked'; their pay and status were tied to a number of 'horses' they commanded. Most could and did, in fact, command these troops, if only occasionally. Pay and status were public and courtly, and severed from long-term association with a particular area. Other well-known features of the system were the mixing of various ethnic groups and strong symbolic and emotional ties to the emperor.

I wish to argue that the mansabdari system was, in fact, extraordinary. As historians, our focus on it has neglected the ordinary, ongoing processes of military service in India, in which mansabdari was always 'embedded'. As Dirk Kolff suggests, at least as early as the fourteenth century, there were large groups of armed men seeking service, willing to move fairly long distances to find it; and there was a widely shared ethos of service.[20] Men and families sought military service for pay, booty, status, and honour—but principally as entrepreneurial activity. While Kolff emphasizes the migratory nature of military service, even his own data shows that men joined armies for the chance to establish hereditary rights to revenue by written appointment from the ruler they served.[21] They fought to get or enhance their *watan*, a word used across all of India (except the extreme south) to mean core familial rights to revenue, deeply tied to sense of place.

The *watan* process was equally familiar and expected among the Afghans whom Babur fought for control of the north Indian plains. Various Afghan clans and families were 'settled' in local areas, in which they controlled the flow of information and taxes to the centre.[22]

For a clearer understanding of this South Asian *watan* process, let us look briefly at the family records of the Manes of southern Maharashtra, who served the Bijapur sultans in the seventeenth century, and whose *watan* was the area around the town of Mhasvad.

A cluster of documents from 1666-7 shows the dependence of the Adil Shah government on the Manes for local military forces and their forces in larger campaigns.

April 1666

Sayyad Ilias Saya Khan, commander, pleased with the valour of Rataji Narsingrao Mane in repulsing the attack of Mirza Raja Jai Singh on Bijapur, recommended to Ali Adil Shah II [Sultan of Bijapur] that the *deshmukhi watan* of Kasbe Kaladhon be granted to Rataji Mane. So a *watan* sanad is issued.[23]

The accompanying papers refer to Rataji Mane as *deshmukh* and *sardeshmukh* (head of any and all *deshmukhs*) of both pargana

Man and the newly-granted town of Kaladhon, entitled to a share of the government revenue. He was further honoured with the grant of the *sardeshmukhi* of pargana Mangalavede for his services in the war against the Mughals, and one gold *hon* from each of ten villages. If we plot these new grants, a 'nested' pattern emerges. Kaladhon is about 20 miles south-west of Mhasvad, while Mangalavede is about 45 miles east. Both were probably adjacent to Mane headquarters in Man pargana. Of the ten villages giving Rataji one *hon* each year, seven were within 20-30 miles of Mhasvad.

Other papers of the same time illustrate the use of Ratajis troops closer to home.

> Ali Adil Shah II writes to Rataji that you have Kasegaon as mokassa (grant) for people working in the faraskhana (police) and the palki-bearers. These villages are troubled by Naiji Pandre, who has claimed that he has the mokassa grant and began collecting the revenue, by force. So, proceed immediately on receipt of the firman (order), with the necessary force and give stern warning to Punjaji Jamadar, who represents said Naiji Pandre. Expel him, and warn him not to come again. . . . Inform us accordingly.[24]

Two months later, in recognition of expelling Naiji Pandre from his district, Rataji Mane was rewarded with robes of honour from the Bijapur court. 'Wear it and be honoured; you have done good service.' In only three weeks, Rataji was ordered on another mission.

> Ali Adil Shah II writes that Narsoji and Yaswasnt Rao Mankoji have troubled the people of Malgaon, pargana Kagal [near Santwadi] and have taken shelter with the headman of Benur; recruiting infantry and cavalry, they have plundered Malgaon, collecting 209 cattle and bulls, also some goods. So, immediately on receipt of this letter, proceed to Malgaon. Give stern warning to both these men. Ask them to produce the cattle, bulls, and goods [and] bring them back to Malgaon; deliver them to the people, with the assistance of the muqqadam. Advise the people of Malgaon that they will be given protection, and that there will be no further trouble. . . . Also capture Narsoji and Yeshwant Rao. Send them here, with necessary guard. See that there will be no further complaints in this regard.[25]

Note that Malgaon is in the Konkan, more than 220 miles

from the family base in Mhasvad. In late June, during the monsoon, this would have meant a difficult journey down the Ghats of more than seven days. Whatever convoy took the prisoners to Bijapur would have been gone for several weeks.

In the next year, Rataji undertook two more tasks, using his troops to enforce the authority of Bijapur. At the request of Ali Adil Shah II, he drove one Kandoji out of a village that had been granted to him but had been resumed. He was also instructed to warn two Nimbalkar brothers that they should leave the territory as it belonged to Ali Adil Shah II, not Shivaji. Presumably, Rataji completed both tasks, because he was later rewarded with robes of honour.

The Manes were the most important source of troops in the countryside, probably more valuable than troops housed in the forts of the area. The Bijapur sultan used this armed local family and its troops to repel invaders, disarm rebels, and join other troops as main-force fighting units of the kingdom. We may recall the close ties between this loyal family and the Bijapur king, which included personal audiences, many letters, robes of honour, and most importantly, written contracts to local rights in the *watan* area around Mhasvad.

It hardly matters where one tracks similar family documents of men in military service in UP, Rajasthan, Bengal, Malwa, or Maharashtra, this is the dominant pattern. Let me suggest some examples. In Kolff's section on the Bhojpur Rajputs, the area where they fought and aspired to rulership, was a rather small region of present-day UP.[26] The pattern is similar for the Bundelas of Jhansi and Orcha.[27] In the Bengal campaigns (1612-28) witnessed by Mirza Nathan, dozens of local 'powers' both fought and allied with the Mughals in search of such rights and recognition.[28] Family histories of Rajasthan tell much the same story, as does Iqbal Husain's recent history of the Ruhela chiefs of UP.[29] Even those most associated with the Mughal empire, the Kachhwaha Rajputs, turned service into nested local rights as quickly and thoroughly as possible. Finally, the mansabdari system which appears so tidy and non-local in Mughal lists, looks far more ragged and local at the bottom. Sub-assignment down to individual villages was the pay of groups of relatives serving the mansabdar. The pattern of service in expectation of *watan* cuts across religious lines. In Malwa, for example, Bhopal's Afghans were pursuing *watan* in eastern Malwa in the same decades of the late seventeenth century as the Rajputs were establishing *watan* in western Malwa under direct patronage of the Mughal empire. Overall, many many times more fighting men could and did aspire to *watans* than the few thousand who were mansabdars.

I want to emphasize several features of this system. First, in any region, the number of families involved in this system was large. On the central plains of Malwa (roughly 120 miles by 150 miles), a Mughal heartland, more than eighty named, armed families possessed administrative functions similar to the Mores of Maharashtra. All had fortified houses. More than a dozen had significant stone forts. If we include the hill areas of eastern and western Malwa, the number probably doubles.[30]

Second, this system of local troops was deeply intertwined with the rhythm of the Indian agricultural year. The monsoon was the time of year for planting and harvesting; whether or not the local military family did it themselves, they had an intimate interest in the results. The end of monsoon and the Dussehra festival were the time for meeting, mustering, and campaigning. Though these troops were 'available' for campaigns, but primarily in their own areas. Kings knew this; if one tracks the activities of the More family for the sultan of Bijapur, they rarely travelled more than 50 miles from home.

Third, this whole system was defined by cavalry, men on horses. Pay at the beginning of campaign was called 'stirrup money'. The tradition of horse-mounted locally-based service was not at all a Central Asian or Turkic tradition. We have only to look at the hero stones of the tenth to thirteenth centuries from local areas of Karnataka, Maharashtra, or tribal areas of central India and Rajasthan, to see that the local hero and protector was mounted on horseback.[31] It was horse-mounted service (and its attendant *watan* rewards) which differentiated the family from the surrounding peasant cultivators. Virtually all the symbols of honour granted by kings to *watan*-holders were associated with the horse—especially *khillat*, but also horses, saddles, daggers, and standards.

Fourth, while the Mughal empire was in decline in the first half of the eighteenth century, this *watan* system was strengthening. During the seventeenth century, the ethos of horse service and the symbols had reached people never before associated with it. For example, in broad areas of tribal central India, Rajputs displaced local kings. The process so elegantly described by Surajit Sinha of tribal people aspiring (often successfully) to be Rajputs had begun.[32] Richard Eaton describes a similar process in Bengal, where it was bound up with Islam and the agricultural frontier. In Maharashtra, horse service in the Deccan sultanates had deeply changed the self-image of various castes into something known as 'Maratha'.

Fifth, this system could be scaled up or down, unit by cavalry unit, with little change of strategy or tactics. Small groups of cavalry were just as effective at what we would now call police operations against raiders or outlaws as they were in main force battles.

In summary, whereas both muskets and artillery were thoroughly embedded in an indigenous military system of symbols, practice, and honour well before the advent of the new European system, cavalry was the high-prestige, high-pay branch of military service. Local militarized families pledged cavalry service against lucrative shares of local government taxation. For rulers, such forces were the principal troops in the countryside performing police duties and joining main force armies. Symbols such as robes and swords were overwhelmingly associated with horse service. Some small evidence indicates that muskets were starting to be considered 'honourable', when carried by cavalry, who dismounted and fired.[33] Infantry, nevertheless, remained low-pay, low-prestige, and rarely decisive in battle.[34]

> The foot soldiers receive the smallest pay; and, to be sure, the musketeers cut a sorry figure at the best of times, which may be said to be when squatting on the ground, and resting their muskets on a kind of wooden fork. . . . Even then, they are terribly afraid of burning their eyes or their long beards, and above all lest some Dgen, or evil spirit, should cause the bursting of their musket.[35]

Artillery remained equally low-status, if somewhat higher pay. If we compare the placement of guns among the rocks in Plate 3 with placement at the vanguard in Plate 4, there had been solid progress in integrating the use of field guns in the sixty years which separate the two images. Mughal artillery was generally respected and feared by other Indian powers throughout the later seventeenth and into the eighteenth century. Indeed, some nobles of the seventeenth century were quite committed to the development of artillery. The best known of these was Mir Jumla, the nobleman from Bijapur who took up Mughal service when that state was annexed. Nevertheless, guns remained heavy and slow-firing, and of limited use on the mobile battlefield dominated by cavalry. Above all, like the infantry, there was no honour or hope of gaining local tax rights in artillery service.

The Military Revolution Reaches India

This is the military world into which the Europeans introduced their system of artillery and infantry in the middle of the eighteenth century. Let us briefly summarize the military revolution in Europe. After 1500, rapid developments occurred in metallurgy and gun casting, the crossbow and pike, and the musket, all responses to the dominance of heavy cavalry. Continual warfare spurred all manner of experiments in technology, strategy, and tactics. By the opening of the sixteenth century, massed firepower of infantry could more often than not prevail against massed heavy cavalry.[36] In the next century, musket and pikeman still got in each other's way and were occasionally overrun by heavy cavalry. With lighter guns came the technical solution: simply attach the pike to the gun as a bayonet. Sporadic firing gave way to organized firing on command. Drill, uniforms, officer training schools, and many other refinements came later as the system was introduced into India.

Plate 5, from an engraving of the early eighteenth century, shows all the features relevant to the introduction of this system.[37] Note the massed infantry at the centre of the battle. This massed firepower had the typical form seen from here: lines, five to six men deep, the front man firing and moving to the back to reload. Reloading was slow and cumbersome, though muskets got lighter and faster to load through the course of the eighteenth century.

Plate 1: 'Flight of Sultan Bahadur during Humayun's Campaign in Gujerat, 1535' from the *Akbarnama* manuscript.
Courtesy: Los Angeles County Museum of Art.

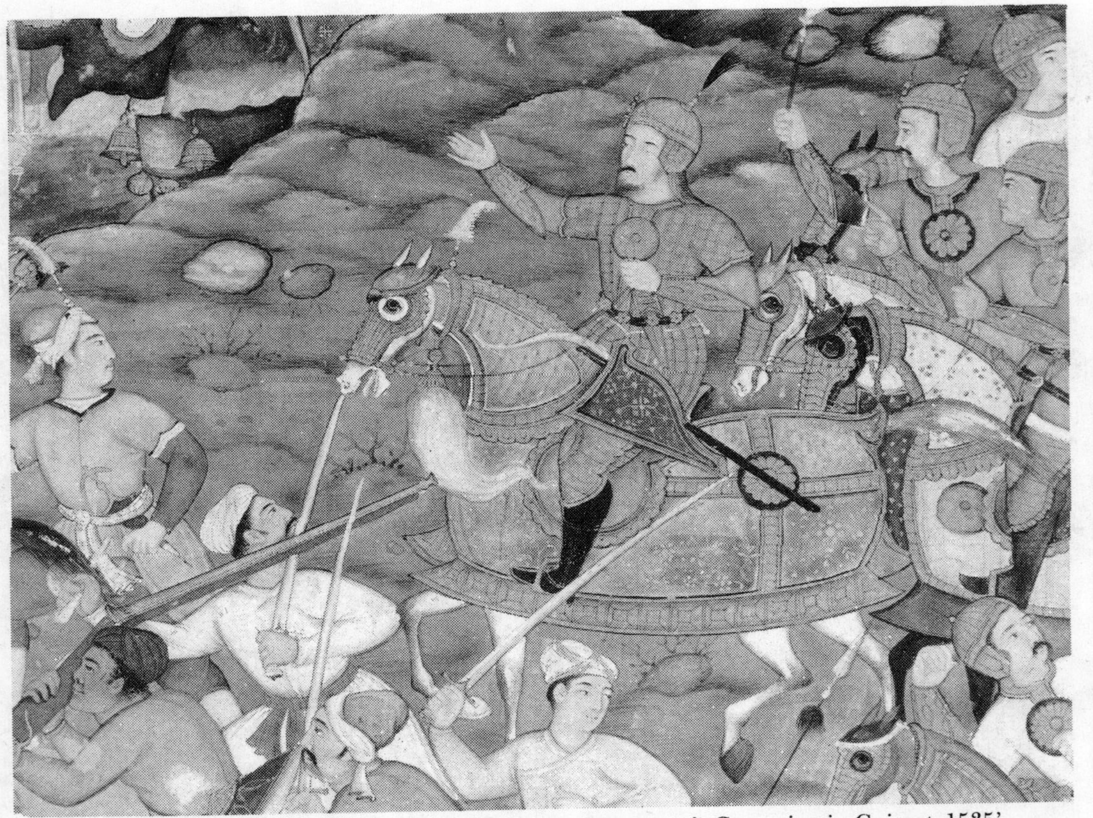

Plate 2: Detail of 'Flight of Sultan Bahadur during Humayun's Campaign in Gujerat, 1535'.

Plate 3: 'Aᶜzam Khan captures Fort Dharur' (fol. 91b).
Courtesy: Royal Library, Windsor Castle.

Plate 4: 'Battle of Samugarh' from Private Collection. Courtesy: The Harvard University Art Museums.

Plate 5: 'Battle of Torino' by Giovanni Huchtenberg. Courtesy: Fratelli Alinari Art Resource, Inc. NYC #89.1.

This massing of muskets was extremely lethal to cavalry. However, the range was short, at best no more than 80 yards. By mid-century, Fredrick the Great's army could sustain three rounds per minute per man. With this rate of fire, the lines thinned down to two to three men deep, and stretched out.

Everything depended on rate of fire, and, therefore, on the training, discipline, and command structure which clearly differentiated 'officers' from 'men'. By the period of our illustration, the European knightly code of honour, with its symbols associated with individual combat and heavy cavalry, had been almost entirely supplanted by a structure of honours and rewards (such as colours and insignia) for officers of infantry units.

Plate 5, unfortunately, does not show the static placement of artillery reflecting the heavy cumbersome guns of the early eighteenth century. Over the next fifty years, however, developments in artillery were quite rapid, especially under government standardization of bore, ball weight, and firing procedure at the Woolwich arsenal. The results were much lighter, more accurate field pieces, which could keep up with marching infantry. By mid-century, these light, rapidly-firing field pieces were placed at the ends of the lines of infantry, to fire at an angle down the opposing lines.

What about the role of cavalry? On level, open ground, cavalry was decimated trying to assault this infantry/artillery structure. We do not find cavalry at the centre of the battle, in our Plate 5. Cavalry, with superior mobility, was reduced to flanking actions, trying to ride around the ends of the lines and attack from the rear. Defensively, cavalry was often placed on the ends of the lines to prevent such flanking movement.

A well-trained infantry could manage without cavalry. When attacked by cavalry, they formed up into the famous square which as long as ammunition and discipline held was impervious to cavalry.

As is well known, this infantry/artillery system was introduced in India during the worldwide campaigns between the British and the French in the middle decades of the eighteenth century. Its strengths were apparent from Bussy's campaigns in the Carnatic and Maharashtra, British efforts in Bengal and Oudh, and the swift British capture of Surat. Trained musketeers, backed by artillery, could defeat much larger numbers of indigenous cavalry. The European command structure allowed the unit to carry on even if the leader were injured or killed. The unit could, if necessary, retreat in order.

Indian rulers were quickly became aware of the convincing demonstrations of effectiveness. For example, the Peshwa, when negotiating with the British envoy from Bombay in 1756, 'expressed a definite desire to have a body of English troops and artillery in the same manner as Mohomed Ali of Arcot had been favoured by Madras'.[38]

Rulers were equally aware that it was not only technology they wanted; it was a whole system, including uniforms and symbols, discipline and training, command structure and battle array. The knew that this knowledge was the provenance of foreigners. If the earliest response was to simply hire the whole system from either the English or the French, the second response was to hire Europeans who knew the system. Within a decade, some enthusiastic indigenous emulations of the new system emerged. Probably the best known is Mir Kasim in Bengal, who raised 25,000 infantry under Walter Reinhard and a regiment of gunners under Europeans. Unfortunately, much less is known about Ibrahim Gardi, who raised a similar unit in Hyderabad, based on the experience of serving with Bussy. (This unit was destroyed at the Third Battle of Panipat, 1761.)

Limitations of Technology Transfer

The responses of Indian rulers to the European military system ranged all the way from full adoption to complete rejection. Tipu Sultan's forces had uniforms, an officer corps, insignia, training manuals, and an order of battle comparable to any European infantry/artillery army of the day. No other Indian ruler went that far. For example, Mahadji Shinde's infantry battalions under De Boigne (aprox. 8,000 men) were mixed with 20,000 cavalry, raised by the older *watan* system. Hyderabad and Oudh simply hired European units and kept them separated from the rest of the army. But the Peshwa, failing at hiring European units, employed

Muslims trained in the new system. Still other rulers, such as Malhar Rao Holkar in the 1760s, developed only artillery and did not hire Europeans or attempt to raise European style infantry. Meanwhile the Bhonsles of Nagpur chose to ignore the new system completely and continued to recruit cavalry on the older *watan* system throughout the eighteenth century.[39]

Let me suggest that there were three reasons for this variety of response and that each individual response was in its way correct. First, along with the convincing shows of strength in the best of conditions, there were equally convincing demonstrations of the failures of the new infantry/artillery system. There were problems of scale. Small units of under 200 men (larger if unsupported by artillery) could not sustain a rate of fire necessary to stop a cavalry charge.

More serious were problems of terrain. In 1772, the British expeditionary force struggling up the Western Ghats was effectively attacked by Maratha cavalry. (Incidentally, the British were having similar problems with terrain in America, at the same time. Braddock's tight column was cut to pieces crossing the Monongahela Valley by French and Indians behind trees.[40]) More serious were problems of grain and ammunition supply. The new army could not survive by foraging. The two major defeats of the new armies in Maharashtra, Bussy's near Aurangabad in the 1750s and the British force in the early 1770s, resulted from the cutting off of supplies (tactics which had been relatively successful against the Mughals for a hundred years). Finally, as was broadly known in the eighteenth century, the new troops were cash-expensive. A campaign was as likely to stop because of lack of credit as any other reason.

Second was the problem of the bad fit between the infantry/artillery system and the expectations of honour and reward of a king's own nobles and military. Military service had a very specific dynamic and symbolic content. If we track, for example, the career of a Malhar Rao Holkar or a Mahadji Shinde from the 1720s, the accoutrements and rewards of horse service are obvious. Each started as a young trooper, mustering at the end of the monsoon, in a small contingent led by a relative. Through personal bravery and leadership, both received booty, the ceremonial ornate robes, daggers, horses, and trappings. They also received the real rewards of service, rights to the government's share of revenue; in this case, both received rights in a compact region of northern Maharashtra. Advancement was very rapid, and within a decade of service, both men were leading large contingents of cavalry, having received the revenue grants to support them mainly in southern Malwa.[41]

If we compare this cavalry-based scenario to the new infantry, such rapid advancement, such symbolic and material rewards were not possible for an ordinary infantry soldier; he was but a musket in a mass of firepower. There was no scope for individual bravery and initiative which might come to the notice of the king. Thus, the main effect of using these new forces was to sever the intimate relations of horse-based personal service, honour, legitimacy, and reward which bound together a king and service military families.

In the new infantry/artillery system, only officers could claim rights to the government's share of the revenue. Indeed, several Europeans, including De Boigne, Perron, and Walter Reinhard, gained large estates and rights to shares of taxes. It is no surprise that these officers were treated with suspicion and hostility by Indian nobles; they were upstarts and direct rivals.[42]

In states not adopting the European system, throughout the second half of the eighteenth century, new families rose from obscurity through service and advancement through the older cavalry-based *watan* system. For example, we have the Rastes and Patwardhans in southern Maharashtra, the Rajput states on the western rim of Malwa, and the Muslim state of Bhopal in eastern Madhya Pradesh.[43]

Conclusion

In the eighteenth century, a king experienced problems whichever military system he chose. He either cobbled nobles and local military families into an effective cavalry force by the *watan* system, or tried to find enough taxes and creditors to pay the wages of the new artillery/infantry units. Neither path was 'right' or 'wrong'. Each king, pretender or usurper, made his own judgement.

Real commitment to the new system meant jettisoning the older nobility. The Peshwa's newswriter at Shinde's court recog-nized this process when he wrote:

As for his army expenditure, the Maratha forces from the Deccan have been suffering appalling miseries which I am unable to describe in words. They are not able to pay off their debts even by selling their horses. A trooper hardly gets Rs. 10 a month; how can he live on this? Mahadji [Shinde] has spent tremendously on his new regiments of infantry, but his eminent Maratha assistants, who laid down their lives capturing Gohad and Gwalior, have suffered terrible destitution.[44]

Throughout the 1780s, Shinde dropped Marathas in favour of Muslims, Rajputs, and Gosains as fighting troops.[45]

Perhaps the best reason to adopt the new system, over religion and geopolitical factors, was the lack of legitimacy suffered by a ruler. Illegitimate heirs such as Shinde, usurpers such as Tipu, pretenders like Raghunath Rao, and women rulers such as Begum Samru, readily adopted the new forces predominantly against their own nobility and local militarized groups.

It is also noteworthy that the new forces were adopted only by larger terrirorial rulers. Rulers throughout India seemed well aware that only large states, with prospects of regular income, could afford to pay both European officers and the infantry. Perhaps smaller states were also aware that the new system was effective only on large scale, and that a long-term commitment to a substantial regular flow of cash required a tax-collecting and credit structure that they did not have.

Throughout the eighteenth century, there is little evidence that rulers developed new symbolic structures to tie infantry in bonds of legitimacy and loyalty. With the important exception of Tipu Sultan, rulers retained the same horse-based symbols and the same cavalry-based *watan* reward structure right through the British conquest of India.[46]

I wish to emphasize that eighteenth-century India was not some sort of Darwinian situation, with those states adopting the new system somehow forcing out 'conservatives' who retained the older cavalry system. If we track the survival of princely states into the nineteenth century, some of the military adaptive states like Shinde survived, some like Tipu did not. Likewise, hundreds of the smaller states based on cavalry and familial entrepreneurship survived as princely states in the nineteenth century. If anything, many more of the states based on cavalry survived because they threatened British colonial power less than larger states with infantry forces, such as Tipu's Mysore.

Finally, let us broaden the perspective to a similar eighteenth-century situation in another part of the world. Was the conservative intertwining of cavalry and honour, reward and kingship merely an Indian cultural trait? Certainly not. Consider the decimation of the Egyptian Mamluke heavy cavalry by Napoleon's trained infantry at the Battle of the Pyramids, in 1798. In spite of the intense exposure to European armies for nearly two centuries, Egypt's Khedive and his nobility had not been able to break the monopoly connecting heavy cavalry and honourable service, and the rewards of land revenue rights.[47]

NOTES

1. Los Angeles County Museum, M.78.9.6. Folio from an *Akbarnama* Manuscript: 'Flight of Sultan Bahadur during Humayan's Campaign in Gujerat, 1535', used by permission. The mailed cavalry are identical to those depicted in other *Akbarnama* paintings of this period, for example, Victoria and Albert Museum, Acc. No. 102/117, 'Daud Shah of Bengal is taken prisoner', published in Geeti Sen, *Paintings from the Akbar Nama: A Visual Chronicle of Mughal India* (Delhi, 1984).
2. *Baburnama*, trans. A.S. Beveridge (Delhi, rpt. 1989), pp. 99-100.
3. John Keegan, *A History of Warfare* (New York, 1993), pp. 182-206.
4. Rafi A. Alavi, 'New Light on Mughal Cavalry', in *Medieval India: A Miscellany*, 2 (Aligarh, 1972), pp. 73-4. See also William Irvine, *The Army of the Indian Moghals: Its Organization and Administration* (Delhi, rpt., 1962), p. 52.
5. Robert Orme, *Historical Fragments of the Mogul Empire* (London, 1805), p. 418.
6. Edward McEwen, Robert L. Miller, and Christopher A. Bergman, 'Early bow design and construction', *Scientific American* (June 1991), pp. 76-82.
7. Vishaka N. Desai, *Life at Court: Art for India's Rulers, 16th-19th Centuries* (Boston, 1985), Plate 71.
8. For other representations of this type of army in camp and in battle, see P. Pal, *Court Paintings of India, 16th-19th Centuries* (New York, 1983). Also, Michael Brand and Glenn D. Lowry, *Akbar's India: Art from the Mughal City of Victory* (New York, 1986).

9. Mughal paintings show these early shoulder arms in use from covered platforms mounted on the backs of elephants, but mainly in hunting.
10. Francois Bernier, *Travels in the Mogul Empire,* AD *1656-1668,* 2nd edn., revised by Vincent A. Smith (Delhi, rpt., 1989).
11. Irvine, *Army of the Indian Moghals,* p. 155.
12. The use of muskets in river warfare in Bengal is illustrated in a dispersed page from the Beatty Collection *Akbarnama* now in the Cincinnati Museum. See Ellen S. Smart and Daniel S. Walker, *The Pride of Princes: Indian Art of the Mughal Era in the Cincinnati Art Museum* (Cincinnati, 1985), Plate 7. Documentary evidence corroborating this portrayal is found throughout the many battles described by Mirza Nathan, who served in Bengal for twenty years in the reign of Jahangir. See *Baharistan-i-Ghaybi,* M.I. Borah (trans.) (Gauhati, 1936).
13. After G.N. Pant, *Mughal Weapons in the Baburnama* (Delhi), Plate 1.
14. For example, see the static arrangment of the artillery in 'A[c]zam Khan captures Fort Dharur' from the Royal Library, Windsor Castle (fol. 91b). Published in P. Pal, *Master Artists of the Imperial Mughal Court* (Bombay, 1991), p. 143.
15. *Baburnama,* 536-8, 547.
16. See, for example, the famous *Akbarnama* painting by Miskina and Paras of cannon being dragged up to the siege of Ranthambore, Victoria and Albert Acc. No. 72/117. Published, among other places, in Geeti Sen, *Paintings from the Akbar Nama: A Visual Chronicle of Mughal India* (Delhi, 1984).
17. Bernier, p. 217.
18. Harvard University Art Museums, 631.1983. 'Battle of Samugarh'. Used by permission.
19. *Baburnama,* 153.
20. Dirk H.A. Kolff: *Naukar, Rajput and Sepoy: The ethnohistory of the military labour market in Hindustan, 1450-1850* (Cambridge, 1990).
21. Ibid., 63-4.
22. See the early chapters of Rita Joshi, *The Afghan Nobility and the Mughals (1526-1707)* (Delhi, 1985).
23. *Tarabaikalin Kagadpatre,* D.A. Pawar (ed.) (Kolhapur, 1969), p. 124.
24. Ibid., p. 129.
25. Ibid., p. 130.
26. Kolff, pp. 90-110.
27. Bhagwan Das Gupta, *Life and Times of Chhatrasal Bundela* (Delhi, 1980).
28. *Bahristan.*
29. See Dilbagh Singh, *The State, Landlords and Peasants: Rajasthan in the 18th Century* (Columbia, 1990); Iqbal Husain, *The Rise and Decline of the Ruhela Chieftaincies in 18th Century India* (Oxford, 1994).

30. W.H. Tone, who travelled through Khandesh in the late eighteenth century, counted twenty forts in the course of a day's march. W.H. Tone, *Illustrations of Some Institutions of the Maratha People* (London, 1818), p. 9.
31. S. Settar and Gunther-D. Sontheimer, *Memorial Stones: a Study of their Origin, Significance and Variety* (Dharwad and Heidelberg, 1982).
32. Surajit Sinha, 'State formation and Rajput myth in tribal central India', *Man in India*, 42, 1 (Jan.-March 1962): 35-75.
33. This appears to be the case in two mid-eighteenth-century paintings, one from Central India and one from the Himalayan hills. See P. Pal, *Court Paintings of India, 16th-19th Centuries* (New York, 1983), Plate R.33. See also, B.N. Goswamy and Eberhard Fischer, *Pahari Masters: Court Painters of Northern India* (Zurich, 1992), Plate 97.
34. In looking at hundreds of images of Mughal and Deccan sultanate rulers, it seems striking that I have yet to see a ruler with a firearm either in a battle or a courtly setting. The only context in which royalty regularly used firearms seems to have been hunting; rulers were, however, proud of good marksmanship, and had their kills recorded in the official memoirs.
35. Bernier, p. 217.
36. Keegan, p. 337.
37. Turin Pinacoteca, A Painting by Giovanni Huchtenberg of the 'Battle of Torino', used by permission (Alinari 31397).
38. W.S. Desai, *Bombay and the Marathas up to 1774* (Delhi, 1970), p. 154.
39. In passing, note that none of our usual social science indicators , such as language, region, religion, caste, is a good predictor of who adopted the new system and who did not.
40. Contrary to this prevailing view, current research sponsored by the U.S. army on the relevant diaries and letters proves that in the decisive battle of this campaign the British decimated themselves through 'friendly fire', one of the best-documented cases on record.
41. Stewart N. Gordon, *The Marathas, 1600-1818*, The New Cambridge History of India (Cambridge, 1993), pp. 117-18.
42. C.B. Baillie Fraser, *Military Memoirs of Lt.Col. Skinner* (London, 1851), pp. 188-90.
43. The enormous overland horse trade which every observer noted in the seventeenth century, simply continued in the eighteenth, in the form of large annual horse fairs. See Stephen F. Dale, *Indian Merchants and Eurasian Trade, 1600-1750* (Cambridge, 1994), pp. 25-6.
44. Quoted in G.S. Sardesai, *Main Currents of Maratha History* (Bombay, rev. edn., 1949), p. 148.
45. The British Resident thought that Shinde was but little inconvenienced by the desertion of the unpaid Maratha troops and their leaders,

as others were readily available. See India Office Library, Bengal Political and Secret Proceedings, June-Sept. 1786, 476-80.

46. This intact structure of honour for cavalry service coupled with the actual replacement of such service by infantry in the states of central India was the background of the Pindari phenomenon of the early nineteenth century. See Baillie Fraser, pp. 84-6.
47. Keegan, pp. 36-9. A contemporary engraving of this battle is shown in the illustrations following page 143.

'Passionate Delineation and the Mainstream of Indian Painting': The Mughal Style and the Schools of Rajasthan

DANIEL J. EHNBOM

The history of Indian painting is cloudy. Perhaps one of the more difficult questions in this history is that of the extent and significance of 'Mughal influence' following the inception of that school (around 1560-5) during the reign of Akbar. It is a given that the Mughal style had a considerable impact on subsequent Indian painting, a given that I accept, though I might question the description and interpretation of that impact by colleagues in my field and elsewhere. As we begin to consider the matter in relation to eighteenth-century Indian painting in the former princely states of Bundi and Kota, a region known traditionally as Hadauti after the ruling Hada clan of Rajputs, it is necessary to go back into history and historiography. Coomaraswamy's *Rajput Painting* (1916) and Stchoukine's *La Peinture Indienne à l'Époque des Grands Moghols* (1929) are two major early works that helped to fashion our present understanding of Indian painting, though they are too little read today. No one has stated the differences between Rajput and Mughal painting more eloquently (nor in more extreme terms) than Coomaraswamy, and it is worth repeating his words here:

> It is no longer necessary to argue the distinction of Rajput from Mughal painting; for every addition to our knowledge makes it only more evident that there could scarcely exist two contemporary schools more diverse in temper. That the few Rajput paintings which formerly came to light

were confused with Mughal or 'Indo-Persian' works was due partly to their comparative rarity, partly to the fact that a majority of works in both cases are portfolio pictures of moderate size, and finally to the fact that certain Rajput paintings show some traces of Mughal influence, while on the other hand many Mughal works are based directly on Rajput originals.

It may, nevertheless, be convenient to resume here the broad distinctions of Rajput from Mughal.

Mughal art is one of miniature painting, as Persian is an art of illumination. In the rare cases where Mughal art is executed on palace walls it has the character of miniature enlarged. Mughal art is at home in the portfolios of princely connoisseurs, but the Hindu paintings have stepped from the walls of shrines and palaces and public buildings, where their traces linger still. Mughal art is secular, intent upon the present moment, and profoundly interested in individuality. It is not an idealization of life, but a refined and accomplished representation of a very magnificent phase of it. It is dramatic rather than static; young, fond of experiment, and ready to assimilate. It is splendid and attractive, but it rarely touches the deep springs of life. Its greatest successes are achieved in portraiture, and in the representation of courtly pomp and pageantry. All its themes are worldly, and though sheer intensity of observation—passionate delineation—sometimes raises individual works . . . to the highest possible rank, yet the subject matter of Mughal art, as such, is of purely aristocratic interest: while that of the Rajput painter is universal. The distinction of Mughal from Rajput painting is indeed nowhere more apparent than in the fact that the former is aristocratic and professional, while the latter is at once hieratic and popular, and often essentially mystic in its suggestion of the infinite significance of the most homely events. Mughal courtiers would not have been interested in an art about herdsmen and milkmaids, nor Vaisnavas in pictures of elephant fights. . . .

The academic character of Mughal painting also appears in the fact that the painters' names are often known, and their pictures signed. There is, too, a very definitely and rapidly moving development, a rise and decline, of which the crisis occupies less than fifty years. It is thus possible to make of the study of Mughal art an affair of names and dates, after the approved European fashion. This will never be possible in Rajput art, which, like all ancient Indian art, is typically anonymous and conservative. Mughal art, however magnificent its brief achievement, was but an episode in the long history of Indian painting: Rajput painting, with the other Prakrit arts, belongs to the main stream. (Coomaraswamy 1916: 5-6)

Brilliant, penetrating, and misleading if not properly read and applied. Setting aside for a moment the question of how true this statement may be, and on what it was based, and what Coomaraswamy actually meant, his words have been taken (when they have been acknowledged at all) as a characterization of an essential foreignness, a non-Indian identity of the Mughal style. I might mention in passing that Coomaraswamy might thus be seen as implicitly responding to the colonial presence that sought to justify the British political control of India through parallels with the Mughal dynasty, from which the British claimed legal, as well as moral, descent. In the extremes of this opposition Mughal painting becomes an Indo-Persian style, by which name it was once known, a provincial Persian expression executed in India.

Stchoukine, on the other hand, relying on motif analysis at its best, rejects any suggestion of an alien identification for the Mughal style. As Chandra points out (1983: 90-3), he calls his great work *La Peinture Indienne à l'Époque des Grands Moghols*, not *La Peinture Moghole.* This is significant, for Stchoukine characterizes the birth of Mughal painting as part of a continuum that extends back to the ancient style, examples of which survive at Ajanta, and forward to the Rajput styles of the seventeenth to nineteenth centuries. He stresses the essential continuity, if not necessarily unity, of style.

It is important to remember that both scholars (especially Coomaraswamy) were operating with far less evidence than is available to us today; both present important, penetrating and still valid insights essential to the development of any understanding of Indian painting; and, I think, a careful reading of both moves them far closer to each other intellectually than is immediately apparent. Nevertheless, we need to keep a somewhat simplified view of their positions in mind as we move on to the question of how 'Mughal influence' has come to be understood in the field.

In what is broadly speaking the next generation of scholarship, Karl Khandalavala's pathbreaking study 'Leaves from Rajasthan' (1950) helped to free the study of Rajput painting from Coomaraswamian anonymity, and the directions of documentary study he indicated continue to bear fruit today. To a great degree, he sees artists as agents of artistic transmission. But his methods are not without their limitations. In the article he defines for the field at that time (and still for some) the conception of what constitutes 'Mughal influence' in Rajasthani painting, embracing motif analysis as the principal way of understanding style. His narrow application of this method, however, is derived not so much from the French school of Stchoukine as from the work of the German Hermann Goetz (1924 and later), who left Berlin for India in the 1930s. Though he uses various motif categories somewhat similar to those proposed by Stchoukine, he concentrates most heavily on elements of costume in the manner of Goetz. Thus, for Khandalavala, the appearance in a picture of what he defines as Mughal costume elements means Mughal influence on the style, as part of his general thesis at that time that the Mughal style influenced western Indian painting to produce Rajput art. In his exclusive reliance on motif, he ignores the essential and to my mind far more diagnostic questions of similarities or differences in palette, line, composition, and so on. If in later work he abandons the extremes of his position in the face of growing contrary evidence, he does not alter his essential approach (Khandalavala and M. Chandra, 1969; and Khandalavala and Doshi, 1987).

Another conception of influence is presented in a relatively recent article by Vishakha Desai (1990). Desai is sensitive to stylistic similarities and differences, relying more on formal relationships and less on pure motif analysis in her approach to pictures. Here, however, the discussion of Mughal stylistic influence is limited in another way. Taking as a given the assumption that art is exclusively the domain of royalty, the article asserts that the presence or absence of Mughal stylistic influence is directly diagnostic of a political relationship as defined by marital alliances, so that its relative lack, as in the painting of Mewar, indicates resistance to Mughal (and by extension Muslim) cultural patterns, dovetailing with the historical fact that Mewar was the last of the major Rajput states to submit to Mughal hegemony and enjoyed freedom from the requirement of providing princesses to marry Mughal princes. In this argument, the presence of Mughal influence, as in Bikaner, indicates an acceptance of Mughal culture based on the assumption that Bikaneri princesses married to Mughals transmitted their new culture to their home court, from which the reigning Rajput ruler was often absent.

While neat on the surface, such an interpretation does considerable damage to a broad range of art historical evidence that Desai's highly selective and empirically flawed argument distorts or does not acknowledge. At the outset it should be made clear that the main painters of the Mewar style in the first half of the seventeenth century were Muslim, a fact that weakens the implicit characterization of the style as Hindu in sectarian terms. In addition, more conservative even than the Mewar style is the so-called Malwa style in the seventeenth century. While it is true that the exact geographical range of this idiom remains unclear, it is fairly certain that the style was produced in Malwa as well as in contiguous regions. Malwa came under Mughal control as early as 1561, and it as well as the contiguous states did not enjoy special exemption from marital alliances. Furthermore, in addition to heavily Mughalized painting, a Malwa-derived (or related) style was produced in the seventeenth century in Amber, an area geographically, politically, and maritally close to the Mughal court (Glynn 1996, and Topsfield and Ehnbom 1987: 54-9, nos. 23-5).

One might also point to the very strong personal (though admittedly not marital) ties between the ruling family of Mewar and Shah Khurram, later Shah Jahan, expecting thus that Mewar painting of the second quarter of the seventeenth century might produce strongly Mughalized work. This is manifestly not the case, and when one does find growing Mughal influence in Mewar painting of about 1650 and later, the references are more commonly to the late Akbar period style than to the prevailing style of the Mughal court (for an example of about 1700, see Ehnbom 1985: title page and 114, no. 51). Desai, on slender evidence, would explain a lack of Mughal influence as a result of the lack of marital ties, but the relationship between artistic style and marital ties remains obscure. Following her argument for Mewar painting, the Rajput style of the state of Bundi should show little or no Mughal influence. But early Bundi (or Hadauti) painting of AD 1591 shows close affinities with the Mughal style, and its practitioners were Muslim artists trained in the Mughal court (Skelton 1981 and Bautze 1987). This enthusiastic acceptance of the Mughal painting style does not seem to have been mirrored directly in marital relations. No Bundi princesses married into the imperial family (*A'in* I: 510). So strictly was this observed that in the first year of his reign when Jahangir, himself the son of an Amber princess and already married to another, wished to marry a daughter of a Bundi princess and Jagat Singh, eldest son of Raja Man Singh of Amber, there was significant objection from the maternal grandfather, Rao Bhoja Hada, whose opposition was so strong that he incurred considerable imperial displeasure. The marriage did not take place until 1608, after his death (*Maathir* II: 603, n. 2; *A'in* I: 323 and 510; and *Tuzuk* I: 145).

I contend that the descriptions of Khandalavala and Desai, which I take as distinct but too generally symptomatic of scholarly approaches in general, obscure our ability to see clearly the relationship of Mughal and Rajput painting. If Khandalavala acknowledges the importance of the artist, he and his followers remain severely limited by too great a dependence on motif—the 'what' of painting rather than the 'how' (Chandra 1983: 93)—and Desai ignores entirely a model of workshop structure as a fundamental means of stylistic transmission (for a corrective to this view, see Goswamy 1968 and 1991). In the one view, the development of a style is all about the transmission of patterns and fashions in clothing, while in the other, it is entirely about patrons, politics, marriage, and diplomacy. When attention is paid to artists and their workshops, one convention of the scholarly study of Indian painting is that 'Mughal influence' on Rajput styles, however defined, was the result of unemployed painters turned loose by successive retrenchments in the Mughal workshop (see Khandalavala 1950 and after), retrenchments for which we have little evidence, and who then sought sub-imperial patronage among Rajputs and other nobles—a rather negative interpretation of the movement of artists and the commissioning of art. The engagement of such artists is often viewed in political terms, i.e. the ruler is aping the Mughal emperor in a manner indicating acceptance of Mughal rule and a desire to identify with Mughal power. In Desai's model, deracinated princesses who have married into the Mughal family are transmitting Mughal ideals to their homes.

I have not the space here to argue fully my contention, but it seems clear that miniature painting and manuscript illumination, unlike the highly public and often symbolically and politically charged art of architecture, are private arts directed at small audiences, unlikely arenas for highly politicized statements of a public nature. Both in pre-Islamic and Islamic India, painting was an essential element of aristocratic culture. Cultivated people were trained both as painters and as audiences for painting. Being patron of a workshop was just something the wealthy, both males and females, did if they could, and if we tend to think of the patrons as only aristocrats, there is considerable evidence that merchants too played a major role. Paintings could have many uses; they were often historical or didactic, sometimes entertaining and amusing, and very often devotional. The patronage of painting, then, should be seen less as a highly charged act weighted with political meaning than the ordinary action of a cultivated person of wealth.

If it is true that our understanding of painting workshops is limited by a dearth of evidence, much of what evidence there is has been systematically ignored. A careful analysis of illustrations surviving to us without clear inscriptional or documentary evidence can still reveal much about the nature and meaning of 'Mughal' elements in a Rajput picture. Let me take as an example a page from a *Rukmini-haran* series produced in the Hadauti region (probably in Kota) 1710. The surviving leaves are in public and private collections in India, Europe, and the United States (Bautze 1991: 230-1, no. 106). This one, illustrating Balarama's rebuke of Krsna for the humiliation of Rukmi, was formerly in the now-dispersed Koelz collection and has hitherto escaped scholarly attention. In its composition it shows clear references to Mughal painting, not, it must be noted, to the style of the late seventeenth and early eighteenth centuries, but rather to that of the Akbar period, and the leaf makes an instructive comparison with one from the Victoria and Albert Museum *Akbarnama* of the late 1580s. The vertical formats and compositions of the pictures are very similar, and the Hadauti picture, though it preserves conventions that can be traced to the pre-Akbar period such as the exclusive use of the profile in the depiction of human figures, and the river with lotuses at the bottom of the picture, reads like a simplified version of the Mughal. Note in both pictures (Plates 1 and 2) the high horizon lines, the broad divisions into three main registers with clusters of rocks with trees beside them at the top, and the strongly diagonal arrangements of the figures and other compositional elements. The faceted rock types of the Hadauti picture are clearly derived from Akbari sources, as is the marked shading of the figures. In addition, in both the main figures are isolated against plain, modelled grounds. Even the general refinement of the Akbari example is still preserved to some degree in the admittedly bolder Hadauti picture.

There are at least two explanations for these similarities, both based on a model of workshop production. First, as noted earlier, it can no longer be doubted that the earliest Hadauti painting was made by Muslim artists who had indeed trained in the Mughal workshop, a claim that can be amply supported visually, inscriptionally, and historically (in addition to sources cited above, see Bautze 1991: 107). Thus, such compositional types could represent survivals of conventions established at an early period. Indeed, such Akbari conventions certainly survived very directly and obviously in Hadauti painting at least until about 1640 (see Barrett and Gray 1963: 141), and if the intervening years are less clear in their evidence, perhaps we are hampered by accidents of survival. Another possible channel is through Mewar painting which had a particularly close relationship with the Hadauti style in the second half of the seventeenth century, a period during which Akbari elements exercised some impact on the painting of Mewar. Neither of these channels assumes recent contact with the Mughal court, and neither requires a highly politicized context in which to function. They indicate simply conventions existing as part of the repertoire of workshops that partake in a generalized spread of the Mughal style over a long period. Indeed, both suggestions may be true, a pre-existing tendency in

Plate 1: Leaf 84 from a manuscript of the *Akbarnama.* Opaque colour and gold on paper. The exhausted Akbar on a hunting expedition in AD 1571. Design and colouring by Mahes (Mahesa), portraits by Kesu. Mughal, *c.* late 1580s. The Victoria and Albert Museum, London (IS 2-1896 84/117). Photo by the author.

Plate 2: Leaf from a series illustrating the marriage of Krsna and Rukmini. Opaque colour and gold on paper. Balarama's rebuke to Krsna for the humiliation of Rukmi. Hadauti school (probably Kota), *c.* 1710. Private collection (ex-Koelz collection). Photo by John Listopad (ACSAA), reproduction courtesy the owner.

the Hadauti style being augmented and strengthened by awareness of developments in the Mewari idiom. (Indeed, it is not impossible that apparent Akbari elements in Mewar painting of the period were themselves derived indirectly from the Hadauti style.) Such exposure to the Mughal style may have been direct (as through artists trained in court) or indirect (probably through the spread of sub-imperial styles patronized outside the immediate court), but there is no need for ongoing contact with artists of the Mughal workshop for an awareness of much earlier Mughal conventions, though such contact certainly took place in certain historical situations (for example, in Bikaner in the mid-seventeenth century), and there is even less need to invest use of 'Mughal' elements with highly political meaning. Pramod Chandra (1976) has documented considerable debt to Indian sources in the formation of Mughal painting between 1560 and 1565, and I have demonstrated elsewhere (forthcoming) that many of the conventions of even late Akbari composition can be traced to pre-Akbar period indigenous Indian styles, supporting the continuum model of Stchoukine rather than an oppositional model. That the reverse is true in the development of Rajput painting is not surprising. The notion of Mughal painting as a culturally alien or even foreign idiom does not hold, and the highly politicized interpretations of stylistic development suggested, for example, by Desai seem unlikely.

If there is a lesson here it is that art historical evidence needs to be examined first in its own contexts, not as part of an externally applied grand scheme. Models of 'Mughal influence' too often assume highly unequal relationships wherein the dominant visual mode influences an essentially passive subsidiary mode of expression (by implication, the styles are conceived negatively as starting in a pure state and being overwhelmed and 'Mughalized', a culturally charged view), but such models too often limit the idea of what constitutes stylistic influence or take little or no notice of so mundane a concern as workshop structures as vehicles of stylistic transmission and development. Thus we obscure whatever part of the historical truth we try to reconstruct.

REFERENCES

Abu al-Fazl. *A'in-i Akbari by Abu-l-Fazl.* 3 vols. Vol. 1 trans. by H. Blochmann, Calcutta, 1871-3; Delhi, rpt. edn., 1965; 2nd edn., 1927; Lahore, rpt., 1975. Vols. 2-3 trans. by H.S. Jarrett, corrected and further annotated by Jadunath Sarkar, Calcutta, 1949 and 1948.

Barrett, Douglas and Basil Gray. *Painting of India* (Geneva, 1963).

Bautze, Joachim. *Drei 'Bundi'-Ragamalas. Ein Betrag zur Geschichte der rajputischen Wandmalerei* (Stuttgart, 1987).

———. *Lotosmond und Löwenritt* (Stuttgart, 1991).

Chandra, Pramod. *On the Study of Indian Art* (Cambridge, Mass., 1983).

———. *The Tuti-Nama Manuscript of the Cleveland Museum of Art and the Origins of Mughal Painting* (Graz, 1976).

Coomaraswamy, Ananda K. *Rajput Painting* (London, 1916; New York, rpt., 1975).

Desai, Vishakha N. 'Painting and politics in seventeenth-century north India: Mewar, Bikaner, and the Mughal Court', *Art Journal* 48 (Winter 1990): 370-8.

Ehnbom, Daniel J. *Indian Miniatures: The Ehrenfeld Collection* (New York, 1985).

———. *A Reconstruction and Analysis of the Dispersed Bhagavata Purana of the Caurapancasika Group* (forthcoming).

Glynn, Catherine. 'Evidence of Royal Painting for the Amber Court', *Artibus Asiae* 56, Nos. 1/2 (1996): 68-93.

Goetz, Hermann. 'Kostüm und Mode an den indischen Fürstenhofen des 16-19. Jahrhunderts,' *Jahrbuch der Asiatische Kunst* 1 (1924).

Goswamy, B.N. 'Pahari Painting: The Family as the Basis of Style', *Marg* 24, No. 4 (September 1968): 17-62.

Goswamy, B.N. and Eberhard Fischer, *Pahari Masters* (Zlrich, 1992).

Jahangir, Nur al-Din Muhammad, *The Tuzuk-i-Jahangiri*, 2 vols. Translated by A. Rogers and H. Beveridge (London, 1909-11; Delhi, rpt., 1965).

Khandalavala, Karl. 'Leaves from Rajasthan', *Marg* 24, No. 3 (1950-1): 2-24, 49-56.

Khandalavala, Karl and Moti Chandra, *New Documents of Indian Painting: A Reappraisal* (Bombay, 1969).

Khandalavala, Karl and Saryu Doshi, *A Collector's Dream* (Bombay, 1987).

The Maathir-ul-Umara: being biographies of the Muhammadan and Hindu officers of the Timurid sovereigns of India from 1500 to about 1780 A.D. By Shah Nawaz Khan and his son Abdul Hayy. Translated by H. Beveridge and revised, annotated, and completed by Baini Prashad. 2 vols. (Calcutta, 1911-41 and 1952).

Skelton, Robert. 'Shaykh Phul and the Origins of Bundi Painting', in *Chhavi* 2 (Banaras, 1981): 123-9.

Stchoukine, Ivan. *La Peinture Indienne à l'Époque des Grands Moghols* (Paris, 1929).

Topsfield, Andrew and Daniel Ehnbom. *Indian Miniature Painting* (London, 1987).

Piety, Religion and the Old Social Order in the Architecture of the Later Mughals and their Contemporaries

CATHERINE B. ASHER

THE EIGHTEENTH century has not been adequately studied, especially in the field of art history. Two interests developed when I was doing research on Mughal architecture which have direct bearing on this paper. One is my interest in the later Mughals and their successor states, in particular Islamic architecture of eighteenth- and nineteenth-century Delhi, but also of Murshidabad, Awadh and Rampur.[1] The second is an increasing awareness of the need to examine patterns of artistic patronage in non-sectarian terms. I started out by looking at the patronage of Raja Man Singh, a high-ranking Hindu noble under Akbar.[2] In the summer of 1994 I began examining Hindu architectural patronage in states dominated—or at least those who had once been dominated—by Muslims. Thus I started thinking about and literally looking at Hindu temples in Shahjahanabad, Awadh, Murshidabad and then for comparison some in Hindu states such as Jaipur and Burdwan. Because of my background, I know more about Muslim buildings and their patrons than about Hindu ones of the eighteenth and nineteenth centuries and their patrons. It is important to present a picture that includes more then the work of Muslim elites.

In 1657 Aurangzeb imprisoned his father, Shah Jahan, in the Agra fort allowing him only basic necessities and view of his famed Taj Mahal. That year and the event are traditionally viewed by art historians as the beginning of Mughal decline. [3] The next two hundred years until the uprising of 1857, is considered a period of crisis for indigenous authority in India, especially when established cultural values are challenged by an alien European presence. The architecture—be it Hindu or Muslim—of the late Mughals and their contemporaries is generally given short shrift by art historians. It is dismissed as decadent copies of earlier Mughal forms or as poor interpretations of European buildings.[4] Yet by examining this material we can address questions regarding visual symbols and cultural values.

Through the reign of Shah Jahan, the Mughals—imperial and non-imperial—were renowned for their patronage of architecture. After Aurangzeb's accession in 1658, it is generally assumed, concurrent with an ever-diminishing Mughal purse, that imperial patronage decreased.[5] Yet Aurangzeb himself repaired numerous old mosques and provided several magnificent ones. Examples include the so-called Moti Masjid, inside Delhi's Red Fort, and his 1673-4 Badshahi Masjid in Lahore.[6] His concentration on mosque construction, in contrast to secular structures provided more commonly earlier, signalled a tendency toward religious construction that began across north India among Muslims and Hindus alike. Commencing with Aurangzeb's reign the use of certain motifs in Islamic religious buildings formerly associated *only* with imperial presence suggests that features once associated with royalty were now connected with piety and Islam.[7] During Shah Jahan's reign, for example, the curved baldachine roof was only used on structures intended for the emperor's personal use, but by 1660 are found on the courtyard of the Mathura Jami[c] Masjid.[8] Its is not until Aurangzeb's reign that mosques built in conjunction with palaces are decorated with the sort of ornateness earlier associated only with imperial palaces.[9] To what extent did this new meaning given to older forms influence Muslim building in crisis-ridden north and east India of the eighteenth and nineteenth centuries? And what impact did such symbolism have on contemporary Hindu religious architecture, some of which was formally protected by the Mughals? Before answering these questions, let us first examine the Muslim-sponsored architecture in northern India, especially Delhi.

Between about 1680, when Aurangzeb left for the Deccan,

and 1858, the end of the Mughal dynasty itself, the patronage of Muslim and Hindu elites began to replace that of the emperor, especially in Delhi, still the symbolic centre of Mughal India.[10] For example, the most powerful officer in Muhammad Shah's court, Raushan al-Daula Zafar Khan, spent vast sums on the ᶜUrs ceremony at the *dargah* of the Chishti saint Bakhtiyar Kaki in Mehrauli, south Delhi. By providing elaborate lighting devices along the 15 km road that led to the *dargah* from the imperial palace in Delhi, he created a spectacular visual link between the capital and this shrine.[11] The support of such celebrations, popular among Muslims and Hindus alike, underscores the public nature of much patronage in the eighteenth century.

This same courtier, Raushan al-Daula, also provided in 1721-2 the Sunahri Masjid (Plate 1), one of many constructed by nobles and the emerging wealthy Muslim class, who by now largely replaced the emperor as patron.[12] Located in the heart of the walled city of Shahjahanabad, the mosque is in the main bazaar, the street that today we call Chandni Chowk situated midway between the Mughal palace (the Red Fort) and the city's Lahori Gate, no longer extant. This single-aisled three-bayed mosque, originally flanked by two slender minarets, stands on a high plinth. While the mosque seems lost in today's Chowk, even turn-of-the-century photographs make clear that it dominated the street.[13] A close look at its facade and interior indicates the greatest care was taken with its construction. The mosque is embellished with moulded stucco arabesques and floral motifs similar to those on Aurangzeb's palace mosques, for example the Moti and Badshahi Masjids.[14] Thus features once reserved for mosques associated with Mughal palaces were now used throughout the capital. This appropriation reflects the increasing power assumed by the nobility—often overshadowing that of the ruler himself. This power extended even to the moneyed elite, a significant portion of which was Hindu.

The elite include, of course, Muslims as well, for example, Tahawwar Khan, a zamindar who embellished Delhi with a mosque in 1727-8 (Plate 2).[15] Others were Abu Said, a *muhtasid* who provided a mosque in 1723-4, and Kalil Allah who built one in 1698-9.[16] Men we know only by their names, for example Haji

Muhammad Sultan, son of a local religious official, were often responsible for monuments in the hinterlands.[17] Haji Muhammad built an unusually striking Jami[c] Masjid in Merta, Nagaur District, Rajasthan. It is rare to find a regional mosque of this scale and with fine craftsmanship. Moreover, the stone appears to have been transported from a considerable distance, probably from the Dholpur quarries.[18] The reasons for such large fine mosque in Merta are not clear, but I suspect that it was to counter a temple in the vicinity where the young Mira Bai first revealed her devotion to Krishna.[19]

Women belonging to the imperial house had, since Shah Jahan's reign, provided Shahjahanabad and its surroundings with some its finest mosques, markets, and gardens. During Aurangzeb's reign one of his daughters, Zinat al-Nisa, provided a mosque and her own tomb; another, Raushan Ara, embellished a suburb with her tomb set in splendid garden.[20] By the second quarter of the eighteenth century, and in the early nineteenth, not only the queen but lesser women also provided buildings in Delhi. Qudsiya Begum, concubine turned queen under Muhammad Shah, endowed a large estate that included a mansion, a mosque and elaborate grounds, and several public mosques; she also was responsible for embellishing much of the Shia *dargah* of Shahi Mardan near Jor Bagh.[21] So too Fakr-al Jahan, the widow of Aurangzeb's artillery commander, in 1728 funded a mosque, known as the Fakhr-i Masjid, just inside the walled city's Kashmiri Gate.[22] Before the eighteenth century the construction of a mosque in such a prime location by a relatively insignificant woman would have been highly unusual. Even less likely would have been the prominence of a mosque commissioned in 1822 by Lal Kunwar (Plate 3), an Englishman's concubine, or the charitable complex donated by Saddho who calls herself a humble milkmaid, a designation that merits further investigation.[23]

Among the public building provided by newly affluent Muslims, that is those assuming a role once performed by the emperor and his immediate family, mosques are the type most commonly built. In our list there are no tombs at all, not even the well-known 1754 mausoleum of Safdar Jang in Delhi, a structure often called the last Mughal tomb.[24] As will become apparent, it is an anomaly, not the rule. By the beginning of the eighteenth century in most of north India, Shia Awadh possibly excepted, the taste for monumental mausolea ceased and orthodox Islam gained favour. Now modest grave markers, more in keeping with the Koranic mandate, replaced large structural tombs such as the Taj Mahal or even more modest ones such as Shaikh Chilli's tomb at Thaneswar.[25] Across north India these simple cenotaphs frequently were surrounded by screens. Often these screens were made of marble, for example the tomb of ᶜAbd Allah's wife (1702-3) in Ajmer, or the tomb of Ghazi al-Din Khan Bahadur at his Delhi *madrasa*, built about 1709.[26] Thus these tombs utilized materials associated earlier with the tombs of saints and kings. These screened tombs of the nobility or affluent elite were built in gardens, private estates, and family burial grounds, but rarely within the confines of a saint's shrine or *dargah.* Curiously, this was the time when the Hindu elite began to commemorate the dead with memorial cenotaphs on a large scale.

The new Muslim patrons show consistent interest in architecture that can be used by a public. This trend favoured by Aurangzeb escalated in the centuries to come. Mosques were almost invariably an intimate part of the urban fabric. Visible from the main streets, they tended to be situated over shops (Plate 3), and were clearly intended to serve the inhabitants of a *mohalla* or locality; every large city had dozens of these late Mughal period mosques.

Underscoring the interest in public architecture instead of private monuments such as the Taj Mahal, or pleasure pavilions in which earlier monarchs had invested, is the later Mughal rulers' almost exclusive support of *dargahs.* Among the most significant was the *dargah* of the fourteenth-century Chishti saint, Bakhtiyar Kaki, just south of Delhi.[27] Before the eighteenth century there had been virtually no Mughal patronage at this shrine. Then about 1710 Shah ᶜAlam Bahadur Shah commissioned a mosque and his own open-air screened grave. At other *dargahs* in Delhi similar patterns developed as rulers commissioned marble-screened tombs for themselves, for example the grave of Shah ᶜAlam (died 1712) at the *dargah* of Bakhtiyar

Kaki, and that of Muhammad Shah (died 1748) at the shrine of Nizam al-Din Auliya.[28] These imperial screened graves were similar in form and appearance to those erected throughout north India by the wealthy, but those screened ones were virtually never in *dargahs*.[29] By contrast, the later Mughal rulers, in lieu of private monumental mausolea erected for self or family, and in keeping with the new trend for publicly accessible architecture, placed their own tombs constructed of the finest material in such *dargahs*, as if making a public statement about their own piety.

In addition the Mughal rulers often added a series of gates. The most notable example is at the *dargah* of Bakhtiyar Kaki, where in 1717-18 Farrukh Siyar added two white marble gates inscribed in black stone[30] thus creating a perceptible resemblance between these Delhi shrines and the premier *dargah* of Muᶜin al-Din in Ajmer, where during Shah Jahan's reign most of the major structures had been built by the royal family.[31] Unfavourable political conditions around Ajmer made access to Muᶜin al-Din's *dargah* difficult, so the later Mughals revitalized Delhi's *dargahs* with white marble buildings that evoked a glorious Mughal past.

The memory of that past remained a vital visual symbol. Perhaps underscoring this is the last significant Mughal building erected within Delhi's walled city, the mosque of Hamid ᶜAli Khan.[32] He was the first minister of the last Mughal emperor, Bahadur Shah II, who ruled from 1837 to 1858. Hamid ᶜAli Khan built the mosque in 1841-2 and commissioned Ghalib, the most famous poet of the time, to write its inscription.

The central bay of the mosque is marked with an arch whose central lobe forms a curved cornice, recalling Shah Jahan's throne in the nearby Red Fort.[33] So too its flanking sidewings are surmounted with parapet of miniature domes. All these are features derived from earlier Mughal entrance gates including those on the entrance to the Taj Mahal, but they are not exclusive to it. Features of the interior—cusped arches supported on baluster-type columns—derive from those first used in Shah Jahān's palace architecture.

This evocation of the past was perhaps intentional. In 1803 Delhi was incorporated into the domain of the East India Company; increasingly Western-style architecture became part of the cityscape. Yet Hamid ᶜAli chose not to include Westernized features on his mosque; instead he looked back to motifs manifest most clearly during Shah Jahan's reign. In this same manner, Bahadur Shah only a decade later commissioned Ghalib, the very poet who wrote the verses embellishing Hamid ᶜAli's mosque, to write a history of the entire Mughal house commencing with Timur.[34] Ghalib laments the passing of the past, a major theme in his verse and letters, evoking Shah Jahan's reign as a golden age.

In support of the notion that elements from an older Mughal style come to stand for piety, Islam, and the old social order, we might examine very briefly the architecture of two Mughal successor states—Murshidabad and Awadh. In each state European styles were often preferred for secular buildings. Examples include the palace at Murshidabad, built in 1829 for administrative purposes and to entertain the British, or the Bibipur ki Kothi in Lucknow built in the late eighteenth century.[35] Each contrast, very little religious architecture bears any European imprint.[36]

In both Lucknow and Murshidabad religious structures were built in prolific numbers. This can be interpreted as a desire to rival Mughal cultural centres. In Murshidabad the situation is especially poignant. For as early as 1757, when it had become a Company puppet state, exercising religious authority was the only domain from which the British were excluded.[37] In architecture, while both courts now relied heavily on older Mughal building forms, in fact, with their devotion to the Shia sect, new types came into existence. While the history of the Imambara, Medina and Karbala in north India is still obscure, the building types seem to develop concurrently in Awadh and Murshidabad.[38] In essence, both houses, but especially Awadh which had greater wealth, indulged in religious buildings on older Mughal models; yet, even as the cultural heirs of the Mughal house, they promoted the Shia heritage that distinguished them from their Delhi counterparts. If the style of these buildings suggests that they were deeply rooted in distinguished and legitimate cultural values, the types constructed indicate a new religious authority.

The picture I have presented so far portrays Islamic buildings provided by Muslim patrons in eighteenth- and nineteenth-century north India, the kind of picture my Islamic art historian colleagues are interested in at the Middle East Studies Association or even the meetings of the College Art Association, and it is one I am accustomed to painting. But for South Asianists it is not a complete picture. Where do Hindus and their buildings fit in? After all, we know that the Hindu population—some of it very wealthy—of Delhi, Lucknow and other so-called Muslim cities was indeed sizeable.[39]

Indeed, during this very period, in parts of Shahjahanabad Hindus built about a hundred temples.[40] Unlike Delhi's mosques and tombs which often bear dated inscriptions, these temples rarely do. I have visited many of them. Although a chronology based on style is yet to be established, I think most were built in the early or middle nineteenth century, but is seems highly likely that some were founded earlier and then rebuilt. Some portions of these temples probably even date to the eighteenth century itself. As yet no one has considered these temples; and until a careful study is made it will be difficult to date precisely this conservative building type.

At this point it might be useful to consider these temples in the light of their better-known contemporary Islamic counterparts, although I do not want to suggest that there were distinctive religious styles or that one was derivative of the other. The eighteenth- and nineteenth-century mosques built throughout the walled city are easily visible from a distance. The largest take up a considerable space, while the smaller ones are located on the second storey above a main street intended for both vehicular and pedestrian traffic (Plate 3). In contrast, temples are not as immediately visible and, for the most part, stand in small courtyards just off the narrow pedestrian lanes of the city (Plate 4). None of these temples is surmounted by a high *shikhara* which we so often associate with temple construction;[41] those with domes, almost always Sivalayas, are low and small (Plates 5-6).[42] The dome in some is barely visible since the courtyard is narrow. In fact, these temples are only apparent during the timings for *darshan*, that is when the doors to the courtyards are open, a situation today that probably reflects original use. Even in areas such as Katra Nil, predominantly Hindu,[43] there are no large temples. Rather, as many as four or five small ones might be found on a single short lane as is the case in Katra Nil.[44]

To understand the surprisingly low visibility of Shahjahanabad's temples I think it is instructive to look at temple construction in Jaipur, a city planned and ruled by a Hindu monarch. Founded by Sawai Jai Singh in 1727, the city today boasts more temples than any other but Varanasi.[45] Most of these date to the eighteenth and nineteenth centuries, that is, exactly contemporary with those in Delhi's city.[46]

Even though Jaipur was built by a Hindu ruler and (one might even argue) as a Hindu city,[47] temples are no more visible here than in contemporary Shahjahanabad. Only one, the Kalkiji temple, built by Sawai Jai Singh in 1740, bears a *shikhara* (Plate 7).[48] While the entire temple is easily visible from its platform on the second storey above shops, as shown in Plate 7, from the main street in the major Sireh Deorhi Bazaar the temple is not readily visible, especially in the context of the busy street. The other two temples with dominant *shikharas* visible from a distance were not built until the very late nineteenth century.[49] The rest are, like those in Delhi, within courtyards. Examples include the Ramachandraji temple (1854), located above shops in Sireh Deorhi Bazaar, and Sri Brijraj Behariji's temple in Tripolia Bazaar (Plate 8). Today signs in Hindi indicate the presence of some; others have none. For example, there is no indication that an almost unnoticeable entrance, off the main Jalab Chowk, leads the Sri Brijnandji temple (Plate 9) of Maharaja Sawai Pratap Singh in 1792.[50] We do not know how they were marked at the time of construction, but chances are there were few written indications to tell of their existence. Thus while larger than those in Shahjahanabad, they are no more nor less visible from the exterior. We can therefore conclude after examining temples in Jaipur that the Delhi temples are obscure to those who don't know their location not because their builders and patrons sought to hide them from Muslim rulers and Muslim neighbours, but because they follow the trend of the time.

It may be, my research indicates, that the situation in Jaipur and Shahjahanabad is not typical. Certainly in Bengal, where the most innovative and widespread tradition of temple building had developed, temples continue to be a highly visible part of the landscape. For example those in Puthia or Kantanagar are easily visible and most bear the customary *shikhara.*[51] Even the 108 Siva *linga* temples in the Nawab Hat section of Burdwan town, although entered through formal gates and intended to be viewed from an interior courtyard, are clearly visible from a distance because of their superstructures (Plate 10).[52] So too in places such as Ayodhya, Lucknow and Varanasi, temples are readily seen.[53] One issue here though is that with some exceptions, for example Chait Singh's Sumeru temple in Ramnagar (Varanasi) (Plate 11), we cannot differentiate between temples of the eighteenth and those of the succeeding centuries.[54] Views such as the general riverine ones of the Varanasi and Ayodhya ghats probably reflect nineteenth-century temple construction and are not characteristic of the eighteenth century.

This suggestion is made in part on the basis of two buildings. One is a Jagannath temple (Plate 12) reputedly provided by Nawab Asaf al-Daulah in a village known as Serai Shekh, about 15 km from Lucknow.[55] The temple is enclosed in a high-walled courtyard and entered through a gate on the east. A small dome, virtually indistinguishable from those used on mosques and tombs, serves as the superstructure and marks its presence from a distance. In short, this eighteenth-century structure is clearly a religious building, but nothing from a distance further defines its affiliation. The second structure is the famous Kalkaji temple in south Delhi.[56] Today the twelve-sided temple is surmounted by a tall tapering *shikhara*, but this was not provided until 1816 under the auspices of Mirza Raja Kedar Nath, *peshkhar* of Akbar II. Originally the temple was flat-roofed. So too the site of the Yoga Maya temple near the Qutb Minar is of great antiquity, but the extant building dates to the previous century.[57]

Although my work on temples in Shahjahanabad is very much at a nascent stage, the types from *mohalla* to *mohalla* appear to vary a good deal more than do the mosques built in these areas. The illustrations here show, for example, two different settings for the lustrated *linga* (Plates 13-14). In contrast, the mosques, regardless of *mohalla*, almost invariably follow a similar pattern:

single-aisled multi-bayed structures surmounted with domes (Plate 1). The temples show a greater variety of types. For example in Katra Nil, nearly all the temples are small domed Sivalayas situated within open courtyards (Plates 5-6), while in nearby Balli Maran, Sivalayas are incorporated into walls almost as if they were shops (Plate 15).[58] It is not clear what conclusions can be drawn from this, but the variety of temple types has nothing to do with sect. In that period almost all temples in Delhi are dedicated to Siva.[59] Most of these are domed. The few dedicated to Vishnu, usually in the form of Radha-Krishna temples, are known as *haveli* types.[60] That is, they are flat-roofed temples that are modelled on Jai Singh's 1734 Govind Deva temple in Jaipur (that, in turn, I believe is derived from a Mughal-style Diwan-i ᶜAm or Public Audience Hall). Temples of this sort, for example the temples of Charan Das and Ladliji (Plate 16), are usually located within high enclosure walls and have an open central courtyard recalling a traditional house.

The uniformity of mosques in Shahjahanabad may reflect a conservative adherence to a pattern of imperial patronage established earlier in the Mughal period. There is no such parallel for the Hindu material; thus individual patrons or buildings may have served as local models. By the eighteenth and nineteenth centuries all of these structures—temples and mosques—were sponsored by individuals, not by the state. The more exclusive nature of the Delhi temple—both in location and size—may reflect patterns of use that in turn reflect the sociological make-up of the *mohalla*.

Although a number of temple types in Delhi and elsewhere were built throughout eighteenth- and nineteenth-century north India, the two most common types are the domed circular or polygonal ones and what is known as *haveli* type. The latter probably derives from an imperial audience hall with the throne known as a *jharoka-i-darshan*. The best known example is Shah Jahan's throne inside his Public Audience Hall (Diwan-i ᶜAm) in the Delhi Red Fort.[61] The *darshan* bestowing deity is installed similarly, for example the image of Govind Deva installed in the Jaipur temple in 1734 (Plate 17), probably the first temple of this sort.[62] The main image in the Charan Das temple, originally founded in the eighteenth century with later additions, is installed similarly (Plate 18). The *haveli* temple type may well be closely associated with Jai Singh's concept of regional authority as validated by the divine.[63]

The small domed Sivalaya seems to have had a longer, albeit more obscure, history. For example a small domed temple, enshrining a lustrated Siva *linga*, is depicted in the 1591 Chunar Ragamala, probably a manuscript commissioned by the Bundi raja.[64] Since our knowledge of seventeenth-century temples is restricted only to a very few large-scale ones, the development of the domed Sivalaya is unclear.[65] However, to my mind the visual relation between two types of structures—the Muslim tomb and the Hindu memorial *chattri*—is most apparent.[66] I am not trying to suggest that temples are transformed memorials—Hindu or Muslim—but rather the domed *chattri*-like structure was simply associated with the visual vocabulary of religion.

I suggest that forms originally associated with Mughal authority—that is, the Diwn-i ᶜAm—and religious commemoration become appropriate forms for temples. The surface decoration of temples too is similar to contemporary Muslim architecture: for example, there is no difference between the arches on the Charan Das temple (Plate 19) and those on the mosque of Tahawwar Khan (Plate 2).[67] So too are their baluster columns close in appearance, resembling the ones from a raja's palace in Dig (Rajasthan).[68]

Earlier I had suggested in the context of Muslim mosque architecture that the use of arches, domes, curved cornices, and so on was associated with Islam, piety, and the old social order.[69] But if this is what they mean for a Muslim, what do they mean in the Hindu context (be it palace or temple)? I suggest that it is not really an issue of Hindu *versus* Muslim, but rather an issue of Indian *versus* non-Indian. That is, we may see the use of Europeanized forms on administrative structures, Hindu or Muslim, as we do increasingly into the nineteenth century, but these forms, with remarkably few exceptions, are avoided across sectarian lines in religious architecture. This only widens a suggestion I made in print earlier—one I made when looking at only part of the South Asian context. Then I said that the architectural features and forms discussed there stand for Islam, piety and an old social order. I now apprehend that the forms stand for *religion*, piety and the old social order.

NOTES

1. See Catherine B. Asher, *Architecture of Mughal India* (Cambridge: Cambridge University Press, 1992), Chapter 7; 'The Architecture of Murshidabad: Regional Revival and Islamic Continuity', in A.L. Dallapiccola and S. Zingel-Ave Lallemant, eds., *Islam and Indian Regions*, 2 vols. (Stuttgart: Franz Steiner Verlag, 1993), pp. 61-74 plus plates; 'The Later Mughals and Mughal Successor States Architecture in Oudh, Murshidabad, and Rampur', in Christopher London, ed., *Architecture in Victorian and Edwardian India* (Bombay, 1994), pp. 85-98.
2. Catherine B. Asher, 'Mughal Sub-Imperial Patronage: The Architecture of Raja Man Singh', in Barbara Stoler Miller, ed., *The Powers of Art: Patronage in Indian Culture* (Delhi, 1992), pp. 183-201; 'Kacchavaha Pride and Prestige: The Temple Patronage of Raja Man Singh', in Margaret Case, ed., *Govindadeva: A Dialogue in Stone* (Delhi, in press); and 'Authority, Victory and Commemoration: The Temples of Raja Man Singh', *Journal of Vaisnava Studies*, vol. 3, 3 (Summer 1995), 25-36.
3. See, for example Percy Brown, *Indian Architecture* (*Islamic Period*), 5th edn. (Bombay, 1968), p. 111, although historians such as John F. Richards, *The Mughal Empire* (Cambridge, 1993), pp. 253-81 tend to place the Mughal decline after Aurangzeb's reign.
4. Brown, pp. 111-16. For a more accurate view, see Ebba Koch, *Mughal Architecture: An Outline of Its History and Development* (1526-1858) (Munich, 1991), p. 125.
5. Satish Chandra, 'Cultural and Political Role of Delhi, 1675-1725', in R.E. Frykenberg, ed., *Delhi Through the Ages* (Delhi, 1986), pp. 207-8.
6. For plates, see Asher, *Architecture of Mughal India*, pp. 256-9.
7. Asher, *Architecture of Mughal India*, 258-9.
8. Ebba Koch, 'The Baluster Column—European Motif in Mughal Architecture and its Meaning', *Journal of the Warburg and Courtauld Institutes*, 45 (1982), p. 259. For a plate of the Mathura example, see Asher, *Architecture of Mughal India*, p. 277.
9. Examples include the Badshahi and Moti Masjids of Aurangzeb's reign. See note 6.
10. Chandra, pp. 214-15.
11. Zahir Uddin Malik, *The Reign of Muhammad Shah* (New York, 1977), p. 362.
12. There are three mosques in Shahjahanabad known as the Sunahri Masjid, each constructed by Raushan al-Daula. For an account of them,

see *List of Muhammadan and Hindu Monuments*: *Delhi Province*, 4 vols. (Calcutta, 1916-22), I: 29-30, 32-4, 121-2 (hereinafter this work will be cited as *List*). The Sunahri Masjid discussed here is the earliest of the three.

13. For a turn-of-the-century photograph, see H.C. Fanshawe, *Delhi: Past and Present* (London, 1902), illustration facing page 50. For a recent view of the facade, see Asher, *Architecture of Mughal India*, p. 297.
14. See note 6.
15. *List*, I: 98-9, and Asher, *Architecture of Mughal India*, pp. 299-300.
16. *List*, I: 78-9, 171-2 and Asher, *Architecture of Mughal India*, p. 299.
17. Z.A. Desai, *Published Inscriptions of Rajasthan* (Jaipur, 1971), pp. 108-9, and Asher, *Architecture of Mughal India*, pp. 269-70.
18. The sixteenth-century mosque in the Merta fort is made of a pale stone, probably quarried nearby, while the facade of the Merta Jami[c] Masjid is similar to that of the Fatehpur Sikri monuments.
19. K.K. Sehgal, *Nagaur*, vol. 16 of *Rajasthan District Gazetteers* (Jaipur, 1975), pp. 371, 394, and H. Bisham Pal, *The Temples of Rajasthan* (Jaipur and Alwar, 1969), Plates 84-5.
20. Koch, *Mughal Architecture*, pp. 127-8, and Asher, *Architecture of Mughal India*, pp. 203-5.
21. For her patronage, see Hermann Goetz, 'Qudsia Bagh at Delhi: Key to Late Mughal Culture', *Islamic Culture*, xxiv, I (1952), 132-52; *List*, I: 29-30, 195-210, 295-6; Mildred Archer, *Early Views of India: The Picturesque Journeys of Thomas and William Daniell, 1786-94* (London, 1980), Fig. 37; Asher, *Architecture of Mughal India*, pp. 302-5.
22. *List*, I: 183-4; Asher, *Architecture of Mughal India*, 298.
23. *List*, I: 83, 114-15, 308-9.
24. Literature on tomb includes *List*, II: 190-4; Brown, pp. 112-13; Asher, *Architecture of Mughal India*, pp. 305-6.
25. Asher, *Architecture of Mughal India*, pp. 228-9.
26. S.A.A. Tirmizi, *Ajmer Through Inscriptions, 1532-1852* (Delhi, 1968), pp. 57-8; *List*, II: 1-3; Asher, *Architecture of Mughal India*, pp. 268-9, 274-5.
27. Matsuo Ara, *Dargahs in Medieval India* (Tokyo), pp. 87-176 for patronage at this *dargah*. Asher, *Architecture of Mughal India*, pp. 293-5.
28. Zafar Hasan, *A Guide of Nizamu-d Din*, Memoirs of the Archaeological Survey, No. 10 (Calcutta, 1922), p. 18, Plate VII a. Ara, pp. 137-40.
29. Ara, pp. 109-10 notes that Mut[c]ammad Khan, a eunuch at Aurangzeb's court, is buried within a screened enclosure at Bakhtiyar Kaki's *dargah*. But screened enclosures during this period appear to be reserved mainly for religious figures or rulers of various ranks.
30. Ara, pp. 126-8, and Asher, *Architecture of Mughal India*, pp. 293-5.
31. P.M. Currie, *The Shrine and Culture of Mu[c]in al-Din Chishti of Ajmer* (Delhi, 1989), pp. 107-10.

32. *List*, I: 185-6; Asher, *Architecture of Mughal India*, pp. 309-11.
33. Asher, *Architecture of Mughal India*, pp. 194-6.
34. Mirza Asadullah Khan Ghalib, *Ghalib, 1797-1869*, ed. and tr. Ralph Russell and Khurshidul Islam (London, 1969), p. 73.
35. Sten Nilsson, *European Architecture in India, 1750-1850* (London, 1968), pp. 110-11; Darogha Ubbas Ali, *The Lucknow Album* (Calcutta, 1874), Plate 3. For a more recent discussion, but without plates, see Rosie Llewelyn-Jones, *A Fatal Friendship, the Nawabs, the British and the City of Lucknow* (Delhi, 1985), pp. 134, 148.
36. One exception is the Murshidabad Palace Imambara. For an explanation of its appearance, see Asher, 'The Architecture of Murshidabad', p. 71.
37. Asher, 'The Architecture of Murshidabad', pp. 69, 71-2.
38. Asher, 'The Later Mughals', p. 94.
39. For example, Jamal Malik, 'Islamic Institutions and Infrastructure in Shahjahanabad', in Eckart Ehlers and Thomas Krafft, eds., *Shahjahanabad/Old Delhi: Tradition and Colonial Change* (Stuttgart, 1993), p. 45 assesses the Hindu and the non-Muslim areas of the city.
40. See the index of *List*, I, under entries for Sivalayas and Temples.
41. In the entire walled city, I saw only one temple with a *sikhara* that appears to date prior to the twentieth century; it was in the area of Sitaram Bazaar. Today it is enclosed by walls, and cannot be examined.
42. Notable examples include numbers 351, 354 and 360 of *List*, I: 161-3, 165. On the map the locations of 351 and 360 are reversed.
43. Thomas Krafft, 'Contemporary Old Delhi: Transformation of an Historical Place', in Eckart Ehlers and Thomas Krafft, eds. *Shahjahanabad/Old Delhi: Tradition and Colonial Change* (Stuttgart, 1993), p. 81.
44. See *List*, I: 160-6 and the map included at the back.
45. Ashim Kumar Roy, *History of Jaipur City* (Delhi, 1978), p. 29.
46. For a list of structures including temples provided by the royal family, see Roy, pp. 227-32.
47. Joan L. Erdman, *Patrons and Performers in Rajasthan* (Delhi, 1985), p. 28.
48. While this appears true for the temples in the city itself, those on the surrounding hills do bear *shikharas* including the Ganeshgarh temple with which the Govind Deva temple and City Palace are aligned. The significance of this is not clear, although the date of the Ganeshgarh and other hill temples may be a factor. For distant views of the Ganeshgarh temple and others see Aman Nath, *Jaipur, The Last Destination* (Bombay, 1993), pp. 4-5, 72, 73, 147, 198. There is no published photograph of the Kalkiji temple proper, but Nath, p. 162 illustrates its small fore-shrine, and G.H.R Tillotson, *The Rajput Palaces: The Development of an Architectural Style 1450-1750* (New Haven and London, 1987), p. 168 show a view of the bazaar; the *shikhara* visible is that of the Kalkiji temple.

49. These include Ramchandraji's temple in Chandrapole Bazaar (1894) and the Lakshmi Narayana temple in Bari Chopra.
50. These temples are listed by Roy, pp. 229-31, but I know of no published illustrations of them. The exception is a detail of the 1854 Ramchandraji temple's exterior in Nath, p. 68.
51. George Michell, ed., *Brick Temples of Bengal* (Princeton, 1983), Plates 165, 169, 185, 605-6.
52. J.C.K. Peterson, *Gazetteer of the Burdwan District* (Calcutta, 1910), pp. 190-1. They were provided by Maharani Adhirawri Bishti Kumari.
53. For example, see Pierre-daniel Coute and Jean-Michel Leger, *Benares: Un voyage D'Architecture* (Paris, 1989), p. 17.
54. Coute and Leger, p. 51.
55. Yogesh Praveen, *Lucknow Monuments* (Lucknow, 1989), pp. 17-19 gives a description, but no illustration. Interestingly it is not included by B. Tandan, 'The Architecture of the Nawabs of Avadh between 1722 and 1586 AD: A descriptive Inventory and An Analysis of Types' (Cambridge: Ph.D. dissertation, University of Cambridge, 1978).
56. *List*, IV: 9-11; Sayyid Ahmad Khan, *Asar al-Sanadid* (Delhi, rpt. 1965), pp. 337-40.
57. *List*, III: 86; Ahmad Khan, pp. 344-7; M.M. Kaye, ed., *The Golden Calm, An English Lady's Life in Moghul Delhi* (New York, 1980), p. 188.
58. See *List*, I: 103-12, 160-6 for temples in these two *mohallas.*
59. See *List*, I, for the temples which are almost all dedicated to Siva.
60. The two major ones are the temple of Charan Das (*List*, I: 109-10) in Hauz Qazi (although the *List* includes it under Balli Maran), and Ladliji's temple in Katra Nil (*List*, I: 163-4).
61. Asher, *Architecture of Mughal India*, pp. 194-6.
62. For a distant view of temple and its interior image, see Nath, pp. 146-7. Erdman, p. 37, reiterates a story that the temple was first constructed as Jai Singh's sleeping quarters, but after divine revelation in a dream he gave the structure over to Krishna as Govind Deva. It is not possible to trace the antiquity of this belief.
63. See Erdman, pp. 27-44 for the interaction of religion and authority in the city's construction.
64. The manuscript is discussed in Milo Cleveland Beach, *Mughal and Rajput Painting* (Cambridge, 1992), pp. 41, 44-7. However, this particular page is illustrated in Douglas Barrett and Basil Gray, *Painting of India* (Lausanne, 1963), p. 143, although the date is incorrectly given. A similar and probably earlier Sivalaya is depicted in an undated *Bhairava Raga* by Beach, p. 47.
65. In Vrindaban are several large temples reputedly erected during the seventeenth century, for example, the Jugal Kishore in Asher, *Architecture of Mughal India*, pp. 164, 166. The 1652 Jagannath temple in Udaipur is

a well-known western Indian example, mentioned but not illustrated in George Michell, *Buddhist , Hindu, Jain* , vol. I of *The Penguin Guide to the Monuments of India,* p. 311.

66. Examples of tombs are numerous. See Tatsura Yamamoto, Matsuo Ara and Tokifusa Tsukinowa, *Delhi: Architectural Remains of the Delhi Sultanate,* 3 vols. (Tokyo, 1967-70), vol. 3, Plates 73-121. Among the earliest Hindu memorial *chattris* are probably those of the Kachhawaha rulers of Amber. See Nath, pp. 52-3 for a general view.
67. Asher, *Architecture of Mughal India,* pp. 299-300, for Tahawwar Khan's mosque.
68. Tillotson, p. 190.
69. Asher, 'The Architecture of Murshidabad', p. 72.

Plate 1: Sunahri Masjid, Delhi (Shahjahanabad), Chandani Chowk, 1721-2. East facade.

Plate 2: Mosque of Tahawwar Khan, Delhi (Shahjahanabad), Lal Kuan 1727-8. East facade, central bay.

Plate 3: Lal Kunwar's Masjid also known as the Masjid of Mubarak Begum, Delhi (Shahjahanabad), Lal Kuan, 1822. View from street showing entrance and mosque on second storey above shops.

Plate 4: Main gully of Mohalla Katra Nil. The entrance to a Sivalaya (*List* I: No. 351) is below the overhanging window on the right. Delhi (Shahjahanabad), Katra Nil.

Plate 5: Sivalaya known today as Bara Sivalaya or Sivalaya Kunniji Maharaja (*List* I: No. 354), Delhi (Shahjahanabad), Katra Nil. View from the courtyards's roof.

Plate 6: Sivalaya (*List* I: No. 351), Delhi (Shahjahanabad), Katra Nil. Interior courtyard.

Plate 7: Kalkiji Temple, Jaipur, Sireh Deorhi Bazaar, 1740. View of temple from interior courtyard above shops.

Plate 8: Sri Brijraj Behariji's Temple, Jaipur, Tripolia Bazaar, 1813. View from east of interior courtyard.

Plate 9: Entrance from street to Sri Brijnandji's Temple, Jaipur, Jalab Chowk, 1792. The entrance is the arch partially obscured by tree on the right.

Plate 10: Exterior of 108 Siva *Linga* Temples, Burdwan, Nawab Hat, 1788.

Plate 11: Sumeru Temple, Ramnagar (Varanasi), *c.* 1770-1.

Plate 12: Jagannath Temple, Serai Shekh, Lucknow District, eighteenth century. Exterior walls and temple's dome.

Plate 13: Lustrated *Linga* Sivalaya (*List* I: No. 351), Delhi (Shahjahanabad), Katra Nil.

Plate 14: Lustrated *Linga*, Sivalaya Ghantesvara Mahadeva (*List* I: No. 358), Delhi (Shahjahanabad), Katra Nil.

Plate 15: Sivalaya (*List* I: No. 238), Delhi (Shahjahanabad), Balli Maran. The door on the right leads to the Sivalaya.

Plate 16: Temple of Ladliji, Delhi (Shahjahanabad), Katra Nil. Interior courtyard, view from east.

Plate 17: Govind Deva with Radha, Govind Deva Temple, Jaipur, City Palace. Installed 1727.

Plate 18: Interior Shrine, Temple of Charan Das, Delhi (Shahjahanabad), Hauz Qazi. Eighteenth Century with later additions.

Plate 19: Interior, Temple of Charan Das, Delhi (Shahjahanabad), Hauz Qazi. Eighteenth Century with later additions.

PART III

Language, Knowledge and Identity

Making 'Manly' Poetry: The Construction of Urdu's 'Golden Age'[1]

CARLA PETIEVICH

I ATTEMPT IN this essay to reconsider, in the light of recent and standard literary histories, some of the ways in which we have been taught to think about the 'development' of Urdu literature, specifically the centrality of Mughal Delhi as the primary site of this development, and the conventional wisdom that orients the Urdu *ghazal* with Persian rather than Indian antecedents. I argue that this orientation towards Persian reflects, in part, a mandate engendered by British colonialist discourses which constructed Indian culture as effeminate, or 'lacking in vigour'. It appears to have been in connection with these colonialist discourses that the Indo-Muslim cultural elite has taken care, over the past century, to ally itself with the perceived vigour of Urdu's Islamic (Perso-Arabic) roots and to distance Indo-Muslim literature from its 'Indian' (Hindu) roots.

This process can be seen at work in the apparent excision of a remarkable phenomenon in the Dakani *ghazal*, that of its sometimes female narrator. It can also be seen in the association of Lucknow (Delhi's rival city) with decadence and effeminacy. The Persian connection in Indo-Muslim culture is by no means spurious, as we know. But the denial of the 'Indian' in that same culture is; so also is it spurious to connect only Mughal Delhi with the Persian in 'Indo-Persian' culture, and not include such alternate sites of Indo-Muslim cultural productions as Lucknow, Bijapur, Golkunda, and Aurangabad.

Let us begin by considering Urdu poetry as we currently 'know' it. Take, for example, Ahmed Ali's *The Golden Tradition*,[2] an anthology popular in North American classrooms for the past twenty years, by a writer held in the highest esteem, and himself part of the modern canon. His translations of Urdu *ghazal* into English have yet to be superseded, and the contents of this particular anthology include all the familiar names from the eighteenth and nineteenth centuries: Vali, Siraj, Sauda, Dard, Mir, Nazir Akbarabadi, Mir Hasan, Insha, Zafar, Atish, Zauk, Momin, Anis and Dagh. *The Golden Tradition's* dedication reads, 'To Delhi, the city of memories—of poetry, my ancestors and vanished glory'.

Why other poets are not included in such 'representative' anthologies, why they are not part of the 'Golden Tradition', is the question this essay attempts to answer. The answer is tied up with telling Urdu's mythic past, a past centred on the eighteenth century and its constructed 'Golden Age'. Pivoting on the history of Iran and India in the seventeenth and eighteenth centuries, this construction reflects modern culturo-political mandates. The story of Urdu is employed variously to serve various versions of 'Muslim identity' that have developed under the strains of regional rivalry and colonial discourses of the British Raj.

In this essay I challenge the version implied by standard anthologies and literary histories, and myth of an eighteenth-century 'Golden Age' and the fundamental assumption that the Urdu *ghazal*—the most popular genre of classical poetry—is an expression of Dehlavi,[3] or Hindustani, genius. I argue instead for a far more comprehensive past, one that includes, on the one hand, Dakani poetry from the Muslim courts of Bijapur and Golkunda during the century and a half before Urdu poetry came to Mughal Delhi; and on the other hand, the centre of culture (*markaz*) represented by Lucknow from 1775 to 1856.[4]

Rekhta: The 'Original' Urdu Poetry

Khugar nahin kuchh yun hi ham rekhta-goi ke
Ma'shuq jo apna tha bashinda-i Dakan tha

I did't just happen to take up the practice of
writing Urdu verse:
I once had a lover who hailed from the Deccan.

Mir Taqi Mir

The average student of Urdu literature would recognize all names listed in *The Golden Tradition's* table of contents. S/he would be expected to repeat the following legend of Urdu poetry's creation and development,[5] the 'received' version that goes something like this: Very near the turn of the eighteenth century a poet from the Deccan named Vali (1668-1727) visited Mughal Delhi, where he was exhorted by a local *ustad*, Sa'adullah Gulshan, to abandon the Dakani idiom in which he wrote and compiled a *rekhta divan* (to compose a collection of *ghazals* in the vernacular) 'after the manner of the Persian poets'. Vali returned some years later with his new *divan* and it met with wild and enthusiastic response from the Delhi literati, who began to emulate the new style. Thus into Indo-Muslim poetry was born a corpus of verse referred to as *rekhta*, the name by which Urdu poetry was first known. It meant 'scattered' in Persian, and reflected the vernacular's mixture of Persian and Hindi.[6] Persian remained the primary literary language of Mughal India, but *rekhta* was taken up with such enthusiasm by Dehlavi poets as to create a sensation.

The approximate time of this sensation was 1720 and those early years (so our student would tell us) were the best Urdu literature has known. *Rekhta* required some overhaul because the Dakani idiom in which Vali wrote was a 'very poor dialect [which] had not attained the status of a language on account of having a limited vocabulary and [being] crude and unrefined, incapable of expressing subtleties and varieties of thoughts though it had beauties of its own'.[7] Under the tutelage of a gener-ation of distinguished Dehlavi *ustads* (Vali's contemporaries), most notably the great Khan-i Arzu and Shah Hatim, the new poetic style ushered in a glorious period of Indo-Muslim culture. The following is a condensed summary of critics' take on how the coarse and crude Dakani idiom became elegant, refined *rekhta*:

Arzu and Hatim were the 'early fathers of Urdu in the North', the 'pioneers of Urdu poetry', [These] 'early fathers of *rekhta*, who nursed and reared the newly found babe'[8] were 'perfect Persian scholars and poets'.[9] 'Khan-i Arzu directed Urdu writing into orderly ways.'[10] Urdu continued to flourish under Arzu's and

Hatim's pupils, among whom were the famous 'Four Pillars' (Mazhar Jan-i Janan [1702-81], Mirza Rafi Sauda [1713?-81], Mir Taqi Mir (1722-1810), and Mir Hasan (1736-86). These masters were succeeded by yet another generation of Delhi genuises, Ghalib (1797-1869), Momin (1800-51), Zauk (1789-1854), and Bahadur Shah Zafar (1775-1862), the last Mughal poet-king.

Let us for a moment stop to examine this familiar narrative and point out some of its problems. In the first place it is remarkably selective, excising the enormous corpus of literature produced in Lucknow from 1775 to 1856 as well. It gives little, and apologetic, place to the influence of earlier vernacular literature on *rekhta*, making it easy to form the impression that 'vernacular' Indo-Muslim poetry was non-existent before Vali. Vali Dakani (as he is also known) is credited with having introduced Delhi to the delights of *rekhta*; and Aurangabad is credited with being the place from which he journeyed there in 1700 or 1707 and 1722;[11] but the histories say almost nothing about the cultural milieu which produced him and in which he matured as a poet.[12]

In the pioneering work of literary history in Urdu,[13] for example, Muhammad Husain Azad begins the epoch of Urdu with Vali, but refers to him as 'the pupil of nobody', thus denying him the requisite pedigree for literary credibility in a culture which identifies and values a person as much by his family and social circle as by his own deeds.[14] With Vali, then, appearing in Delhi largely uneducated and producing his most famous work in accordance with the advice of a Dehlavi master, the link between the Deccan and *rekhta* becomes seriously accentuated. Another critic, Muhammad Sadiq, drives the wedge further between 'classical' Urdu and its Dakani origins by characterizing Dakani poetry as 'more than ever the province of the specialist, [being] so excessively archaic that a layman can neither understand nor appreciate it. For the student of Urdu literature it can at best be an acquired taste and no more.'[15]

The impression of Dakani's non-existence, or the sense of its crudeness as a literary language, would probably have come as a surprise to the poets of Bijapur and Golkunda. Vali may well represent the beginning of 'vernacular' poetic composition in

Delhi, but he represents perhaps its final culmination in the Deccan. The names of Vajhi, Nusrati, Ghavasi, Ali Adil Shah Sani, Abdullah Qutb Shah and a host of others almost never figure in Urdu literary histories, though all of them wrote poetry—many would argue— 'after the manner of the Persians'. Why, then, have their names and poetry been kept unknown or unfamiliar to us?

As mentioned at the outset, the standard version of Urdu's past focuses on Mughal Delhi. Yet its neglected Dakani and Lakhnavi chapters offer valuable insight into the evolution of Indo-Muslim cultural identity.[16] They also shed light on how literary criticism can serve a particular community's master narrative of its past and present. Delhi and Lucknow had engaged in fierce cultural rivalry almost from the establishment of the Lucknow court in 1775, with both cities competing for the prestige of being known as 'Urdu *markaz*'. In the post-1857 period this regional rivalry as deployed to defend Mughal culture in the face of an onslaught in colonial discourse.[17] At the centre of that attack were the issues of cultural masculinity and femininity.

As it happens these Dakani poets wrote not only 'after the manner of the Persians' (employing the genres and tropes of the Perso-Arabic literary tradition), but also 'after the manner of the Indians', using a feminine narrator for the love of poetry of separation.[18] Witness the following *ghazal* verses from the *Kulliyat-i Muhammad Quli Qutb Shah* of Golkunda (1566-1611):

Suno meri sati piya hauron rata
ki sej par sain parsang gamata

Listen, girlfriend, my lover makes love elsewhere
My lord disports himself on another['s] bed.

Hua be-sabab sa'in hamna sun karvat
Pakar duti ka man, haman man santata

There's no good reason my lord has turned away from me:
Capturing another woman's heart, he tortures mine.

Piya yun sun mil ke jhal khave dutin
Main hun teri mati, tun hai mera mata

I am drunk with you and you with me.
Beloved, come to me and make *her* burn with jealousy!

Hikayat parim ka nako munj the puchho
Piya hat di hun main sab man ka bhata

Don't talk to me about the story of Love,
I've given my beloved all his heart's desire.

Nabi sadke Qutba ki mati kati hai
Qutb Shah sundar-guni maddamata

By the grace of the Prophet, Qutb's drunken one declares:
Qutb Shah features many fine qualities and is
a drunkard of love.

Conservatives may view this *ghazal* as frivolous and crude, lacking the deep emotional essence of *ghazal* as the poetry of Love (*'ishq*). Others might argue that its directness and concreteness of imagery recommend it over the more abstract expression often displayed in the Urdu *ghazal*. To both sets of critics one could present the following *ghazals*, whose wistful lamentation is neither crude nor concrete, nor alien in any way to the convectional melancholy of *'ishq*:

Piya baj pyala piya jaye na
Piya baj yak til jiya jaye na

Without the Beloved the cup will not be drunk
Without the Beloved not a moment will be lived.

Kahi the piya bin saburi karun
Kahiya jaye amma kiya jaye na

They say, 'Be patient in the Beloved's absence.'
It may be said, but how is it accomplished?

Nahin 'ishq jis vo bara kur hai
Kadhin us se mil biisiya jaye na

He who does not love—greater fool he!
Neither meet with such a one, nor sit down with him!

Qutb Shah na de muj divane kun pand
Divane kun kaj pand diya jaye na

Qutb Shah, do not advise me in my madness:
The mad simply cannot be given advice.

Saki batan shakar karti vale mithai asi na
Divani nishkar men koi kad hain nabat basi na

My girlfriend speaks in sugared terms,
but sweetness doesn't come.
Mad one, you can't get the concentration
of rock candy in sugarcane.

Khabar hui shah hue savara yakayak aye muj thara
Na puchhe tik phire bhara to ab birha saha si na

I heard that the king came riding up to my door
on horseback.
Not even asking after me, he turned and
rode away again—
Now how will separation's grief be borne?

Kahun apan birah jis kan agin sho'le pare is tan
So mushkil datiya muj man haman dukh koi suna si na

Were I to speak to anyone of separation's burning tumult
Its flames would scorch *their* body so I keep it
locked in my heart.

Ma'ani, tha'un tun jane ghavas ho kar ratan pane
So khali sipiyan liyane dujiyan sam tuj kun asi

Ma'ni, you know your place:
Be a pearl-diver and come up with gems!
It's not for you to bring forth
The empty shells of others.

The diction is indeed archaic when compared with modern Khari Boli Urdu, and does require extra effort, at times, to be comprehended by those uninitiated into old Dakani. But we must maintain a distinction between linguistic archaism and the sort of aesthetic archaism that renders Dakani inaccessible to modern Urdu readers, if we are to believe Muhammad Sadiq.

If a dramatic aesthetic difference exists between these poems and those from the northern 'classical' corpus, it lies in the gender of the narrator, suggested here by the use of the term *piya* (this is agreed even when the verb conjugations and pronouns do not explicitly point to a feminine-gendered narrator).[19] The aesthetic of love in separation (called, in Persian, *firaq-i yar*) is very much that reflected in late *ghazals*, except that the narrator-lover, the *'ashiq*, is there constructed unambiguously as male. These images of suffering and pining are also familiar to the reader of Indic ('Hindi')[20] love poetry—especially not exclusively, Radha-Krishna *bhakti* poetry, where the theme of separation is called '*viraha*'. *Viraha* often causes the lover to refuse food and drink, in addition to the feverish writhing in the body suggested above in the verse where the narrator kept her suffering to herself 'lest it burn others'. Almost anyone who has been exposed to *bhakti* (devotional) poetry or *geet* in Indian languages will recognize the *virahini's* voice—that of a woman pining for her absent beloved—and find the verses emotionally familiar. Additional common features of Dakani *ghazals* in the feminine voice which we also see here are mention of the *virahini's* female companions (*sahelian/sakhiyan*), the fire of separation (*biraha ki aag*) and mad jealousy toward other women. These terms or phrases would constitute a rare exception in 'classical' Urdu *ghazal*.

Rekhta v. *Rekhti*

As I have discussed elsewhere,[21] another way of understanding this opposition is to associate Delhi with *rekhta* and both Lucknow and the Deccan with *rekhti*. The latter is the feminine form of the word. The Dakani scholar Hafeez Qateel wrote of *rekhti* that it is 'a *badnam* (disreputable) genre of Urdu poetry which is thought to serve especially for the expression of women's particular emotions and generic concerns in women's idiom' (*auraton ki boli*).[22] The term '*rekhti*' is generally agreed to have been coined toward the end of the eighteenth century by the Lakhnavi poet Rangin (who was also reputedly a pupil of Hatim), one of the guardians of the Golden Age.[23] Rangin himself claims credit for the coinage and it would seem to be corroborated by Insha in the following (*rekhti*) *she'r*:

Rekhti kahin aji Rangin ki yih aijad hai
Munh churata hai mu'a Insha ji(a)ya kis vaste?

Rekhti writing is Rangin's creation
Why attempt imitation, Insha, you wretch?[24]

This corpus of poetry is characterized as light and racy, often salacious and obscene, and expressed in 'women's idiom' usually by male poets (sometimes in male drag).[25] Mirza Muhammad Askari writes that the 'artificial dialect spoken in *rekhti*' is 'completely different than the language of *sharif* women' as he has never heard such language uttered from the mouth of any woman of respectable family.[26] The disrepute of the genre, its characteristic effeminacy, and its 'origin' in Lucknow with a poet reputed to be a great companion of courtesans, have contributed to the easy equation of *rekhti* with decadence, effeminacy, artifice and general decay ascribed by conventional wisdom to late-Mughal India and crystallized in Lucknow.

But Dakani *ghazals* in the feminine voice cannot be so easily dismissed as salacious or frivolous. To underline this claim, let me offer another example of Dakani *ghazal*, written by the great Mullah Vajhi (d. 1655?). It is found embedded in his longer poem, the *manasvi Qutb Mushtari* (composed in 1609), featuring Qutb Shah and Mushtari, his paramour:

Taqat nahin duri ki ab tun beg a mil re piya
Tuj bin munje jiv na bahut hota hai mushkil re piya

I haven't the strength for the long stretch—
    Come quickly, now Beloved!
Without you living is extremely troubled, Beloved.

Khana biraha kiti hun main pani anjhu piti hun main
Tujti bichhar jiti hun main kya sakht hai dil re piya

Separation is what I swallow
    The water I drink is tears,
Cut off from you, the life I live is
    Hard as your heart, Beloved.[27]

Har dam tun yad ata minje ab aishi nain bhata munje
Biraha yu santata munje tuj baj til til re piya

Within me your memory swells with each breath,
    I can't even enjoy pleasure now,
Oppressed at each moment with parting—
    this is what it's like without you.

Munj tan tapish jane tuhin munj thar jiv lane tuhin
Munj dil mandhir miyane tuhin kita hai manzil re piya

My body's become Austerity itself
 You alone can replenish living
Beloved, my heart is an empty temple, You alone
 can [ful]fill it.

Tun jiv mera men so dil tuj sat rahna kyun na mil
Din rat men main ek til nain tuj ti ghafil re piya

Since you are my life, and I but a heart
 Why don't we join together and live?
As it is, Beloved, night and day
 theirs is not a moment I'm not mindful of you.

The theme here is of love in separation (*firaq-i yar*), the central topic of classical Urdu *ghazal*, featuring graphic portrayal of pining: the assertion that separation is a living death; the narrator's (*'ashiq's*) indifference to her own body, to food and drink; her personification of herself as a heart, etc. Aesthetically, then, the *ghazal* should be viewed as *rekhta*. The one feature rendering it *rekhti* in the eyes of the critics is its unambiguously feminine narrative voice, which is evidenced grammatically. Such absence of ambiguity signed for Dakani poetry its death warrant at the hands of later Urdu literati, because it personified feminized, Indian space.

It is significant that Vajhi used the *ghazal* above to highlight a moment of acute poignancy in the *Qutb Mushtari*, when the lovers Qutb Shah and Mushtari were separated from one another. It indicates that the Dakani poets consciously blended Perso-Arabic and Indic literary ideas and genres. *Qutb Mushtari* is a *masnavi*, a narrative genre from Persian. Vajhi chose to express separation first in the *ghazal* genre and second in the voice of the *virhini*[28] rather than in the lexicon of the Perso-Arabic tradition's *firaq-i yar*. Since we know that Vajhi also wrote in Persian, we can assume that choice of *viraha* terminology was conscious, and not an indication of his limited repertoire. On the contrary, it seems to indicate a deliberate choice to follow the 'Hindi' convention of male poets addressing the beloved in the feminine. The Dakani masters' choice of the *virahini* voice to express love in separation, and the choice of the *ghazal* genre for expressing *'ishq*, would seem to suggest a creative environment in which Hindu/Muslim (or Indic/Perso-Arabic) distinctions were not strictly observed; rather, such borrowings were free. It seems clear also that writers of early *ghazal*—whether we call their language Ḍakani or Hindi, *rekhta* or Urdu—were both cognizant of, and receptive to, the idea of a female narrator, even in poetry where the Beloved was sometimes understood to be the divine.[29]

Compare now the following verses from 'classical' Hindustani *ghazals*, all of which eschew the feminine:

Dagh sine hote hain gul khate hain 'ashiq tire
Garm bazar in dinon men marham-i kafur ka

Branding rosy scars across their breasts, your
lovers attest fidelity
There's a hot trade these days in camphor dressings. Atish

Whereas the Dakani *ghazals* are often narrated in explicitly feminine grammatical terms, here the *'ashiq(s)* speak(s) in the masculine plural. When lovers brand rosy scars across their breasts in the verse above (*gul khate hain*), they do so in the masculine plural. In the following verse the audience pictures a single feminine beloved (referred to as '*but*', idol) although the subject is grammatically ambiguous:

Mere marne ki du'a mange voh but parh kar namaz
Kis taraf ja kar karun main sajda-i shukrana aj

If while praying [she] pleads for the blessing of my death,/
Where should I direct my grateful prostration
[toward Mecca or to her]? Atish

This elimination of the feminine voice/grammatical gender in the 'classical' *ghazal*, is explained by Urdu scholars as a convention in keeping with Persian (where, as in English, and unlike Urdu, verb conjugations and pronouns do not contain gender markers). It is a convention that often requires a certain dexterity from the poet and from the audience as well.[30] Overt gender references can be avoided in a number of ways. For example, in the verse just cited the idol who prays for the 'blessing' (*du'a*) of the *'ashiq's* death is the beloved (*mahbub*). Ironically, the *mahbub* is always grammatically masculine in the classical *ghazal*, even though its audience tends to picture a female beloved. By contrast, the *'ashiq* (the 'I') of the verse is male both grammatically and according to convention. Often a poet's choice of verb form will leave ambiguous the gender of both the *'ashiq* and the *mahbub*, as when the subjunctive mood is employed. For example, the idol [who] having prayed, might beg the boon of my death . . .' is not explicitly gendered in this verse. Nor is the gender of the narrator, who queries, 'In which direction should I bow in gratitude?' because the subjunctive mood, unlike other Urdu verb forms, does not contain gender markers. The 'she' who appears in English translation has been injected for intelligibility by the translator.

In most cases, however, verb forms do contain gender markers, as in the case of this last verse below, and in these cases the masculine is employed regardless of the gender of either the character who is speaking or the one being addressed:

Kahte hain tum ko hosh nahin iztirab men
Gare gile tamam hue ik javab men

You say: 'You seem so distraught—are you quite in
your right mind?'
All my complaints were thereby disposed of in a single reply.

Momin Khan Momin

Here the scene evoked is that of the agitated, tongue-tied lover in the presence of the beloved. (He) can neither declare (him) self nor complain of the cavalier treatment he receives at (her) hands. The person who says, 'You seem so distraught . . .' is grammatically masculine plural, yet the audience/reader conventionally pictures a 'she'. Grammatically, the translation of *kahte hain* could read as 'he says' or 'they say' as well as the 'you say' that I have chosen here; and in the gender-bending semantics of the post-Dakani Urdu *ghazal*, even 'she says' would be a semantic possibility.[31] Yet this verse would never be translated 'she says', because a pact exists among readers of the Urdu *ghazal* to maintain grammatical masculinity no matter what the gender of the speaker. The explicitly feminine is thereby eliminated.

I am arguing, then, that there is a clear relationship between the aesthetic of *'ishq* in these early Dakani *ghazals* and the more familiar Hindustani *ghazals* of the eighteenth and nineteenth centuries; that, furthermore, the northern authors who have diminished Dakani's importance to the development of Urdu poetry, or who have excised it from literary histories, did so less because they could not understand this poetry than because its female narrator posed problems to a unitary myth of origin tracing Urdu back directly through Delhi to Isfahan and Arabia. In other words, (masculine) gender is central to the Indo-Muslim cultural identity constructed in modern Urdu literary histories, While my formulation of the Urdu *ghazal's* indebtedness to a feminine aesthetic proceeds primarily from Dakani's feminine narrator/*'ashiq/virahini*, it is worth noting as well that the earliest extant examples of Urdu literature are Sufi appropriations of (indigenous) women's work songs, e.g. the *chakki-nama* and the *charkha-nama*[32] where we find, as much as in the Dakani *ghazal*, a distinct idiom identified as 'women's language' (*auraton ki boli*).[33] So the feminine is widespread in Dakani literature, can be found in numerous genres, and would seem to have been there from the earliest times.

Gender v. *Genre*

Another point worth reiterating is that the *masnavi* genre features a female character of very strong voice, in both Dakani and in later Urdu poetry.[34] *Masnavi* represent about 70 per cent of extant Dakani literature, but that ratio dwindled dramatically during the eighteenth century's 'Golden Age' in the north. Even the great eighteenth-century poet Mirza Rafi Sauda, characterized as primarily as a *qasida-go* (satirist), leaves us more than twice as much *ghazal* verse in Urdu as *qasida* verse.[35] By the nineteenth century *rekhta* features relatively few *masnavis* or *qasida* or any other narrative poetry (with the possible exception, in Shi'a Lucknow, of the *marsiya*).[36] Thus, while the feminine *gender* has been eliminated from the 'classical' *ghazal*, the *masnavi genre*—

with its strong female voice—is practically displaced by *ghazal* composition in northern *rekhta-goi.* The de-feminized (neutered?) *ghazal* prevails, and all poetry featuring a feminine narrator becomes designated *rekhti.* Thereby distinguished from *rekhta,* it is effectively eliminated from the canon.[37]

The 'golden phase' of Urdu took place during the time of tremendous social and political upheaval for the Mughals. Yet throughout the second half of the eighteenth century—according to our story—Delhi remained the scene of intense and brilliant literary activity. And even during the nineteenth century's 'age of decadence . . . when Delhi had been destroyed and the centre of Urdu had, for the time, been transferred to Lucknow . . .' from within the walls of the Red Fort the beleaguered Mughal emperor-poet, Bahadur Shah Zafar, patronized a revival wherein 'Momin, Zauq, and Ghalib revived the healthy trends which had been characteristic of Delhi poetry during the eighteenth century'.[38]

How did the Indian space, lacking in ambiguity, become feminized? It happened courtesy of the colonial discourse that characterized Indian rulers as lazy, effeminate sensualists who preferred to dally with their multitudes of wives and concubines, composing and listening to poetry rather than pursue the models of kingship favoured by the British. (The model most favoured tended to be the Indian king who diligently collected revenues and turned them over to the British.[39]) Here are some of the portraits drawn by critics of Dakani and Lakhnavi poet-kings.

Muhammad Quli Qutb Shah (r. 1580-1611), whose poetry appears above, has begun to be incorporated into standard literary histories as of the mid-twentieth century. Although he seems to be the earliest Urdu *sahib-i divan* (poet with a full collection of *ghazals* to his credit), and this extends the history of the Urdu *ghazal* by more than a century, his treatment at the hands of critics has not always been the gentlest. Muhammad Sadiq has this to say:

> In some respects he is a landmark in the history of Urdu poetry; for he is the first to introduce a secular note in a poetry which had been so far mainly religious. He writes of love, nature, and the social life of the day . . . his sensuousness is no less observable in his love of nature and female beauty.

Of all that pertains to the mind there is no trace in him. And no wonder. Living in regal splendour, what occasion could he have for thought?[40]

Wajid Ali Shah, the last king of Awadh, known also by his *nom de plume,* Akhtar, is characterized by Ram Babu Saksena as sensual, prodigal, and extravagant; and, though a generous patron of Urdu poets, a voluptuary influenced by unworthy social inferiors who led him to ruin:[41]

Money was spent like water and . . . [he] pursued his insensate course until he was deposed and transported to Calcutta. . . . In fact the passion for poetry and music was responsible to a certain extent for the decay and ruin of his kingdom. . . . Urdu poetry in his Court busied itself in describing the toilets of women and the physical beauty of courtesans. The coarse and sensual poetry was a direct incentive to his debaucheries, and when sung by beautiful girls in alluring toilets amidst his lascivious courtiers it had a most deleterious effect on the easy morals of the King. . . . Akhtar, though a fertile writer, was not highly gifted. His verses have no lofty sentiments and they do not vibrate with genuine emotion. The cult of the Lucknow School possessed him and he wrote *a la mode*. . . .[42]

Sadiq, too, says:

Vajid Ali Shah (r. 1847-56) revived to the full the gay traditions . . . fond of fine arts and music, he spent his time in the company of courtesans & musicians, and awarded offices to upstarts and musicians. His life was an orgy of sensuality . . . and his poetry is a frank account of his sexual excesses and vulgar intrigues. . . . All this riot and madness suddenly came to an end when Lord Wellesley, the Governor General, decided to annex Oudh in 1856.[43]

Putting aside a number of highly debatable 'truths' in the above passage, it is important to note that Sadiq gives us no sample at all of any of Wajid Ali Shah's verse. We are obliged to accept both his historical reportage and his literary judgements.[44] It would be difficult to find an assessment more consonant with colonial discourse, or more redolent of a conflation between 'Indianness' and decadent sensuality, even effeminacy, on the one hand; and a masculine vigour, on the other, with Englishness. This account does nothing to acknowledge those aspects of Lucknow's legend which paint the king in more favourable colours, e.g. reports that his songs were sung in all the alleys and lanes, by the nobility as well as the working class; or that from Wajid Ali Shah's time onward the local idiom—indeed the city's entire ethos, called *Lakhnaviyat*—was so delicate and refined as to win an all-India (and later, all Pakistan) reputation as exemplary of the heights Indo-Muslim culture had attained.

The sensuousness, love of nature and female beauty, and mindlessness evoked in the characterizations of Muhammad Quli Qutb Shah and Wajid Ali Shah are all part of a harsh rhetoric employed especially after 1857 and directed at kingdoms which had been targeted for annexation by the British. The sensuality is often coupled, in such discourse, with an effeminacy and hedonism implicitly characteristic of 'the Orient' (of which Hindu India came to be seen as an even more dramatic example than Muslim India). Considering that Quli Qutb Shah celebrated the Indian environment in words, themes, and genres; that Bhagnagar, the original name for the city he built near Golkunda (present day Hyderabad) was reputed to commemorate his love for Bhagmati, a Hindu woman; and that, as a poet, his imagery is often more direct and concrete than the abstract and lamenting quality modern critics have tied to claim for Urdu *ghazal*; it is easy to see how Muhammad Quli might have become their target.[45]

Considering that Lucknow gained mythic proportion in the lore of the British Raj because of the legend charging Wajid Ali Shah with allowing the British to annexe his kingdom without armed resistance, without 'standing up and fighting like a man'; because of the bloody and protracted armed struggle, by contrast, between Indian soldiers and British officials as well as civilians in the Lucknow Residency during the siege of 1857-8; it is also easy to see how Lucknow's last king excited such condemnatory judgement later on. This is especially the case if we recall that Urdu literary histories have tended overwhelmingly to be written by northerners, indeed by Mughal- and Delhi-identified scholars. In the late nineteenth century, Muhammad Husain Azad and Altaf Husain Hali[46] still smarted from the dual humiliation of Delhi's displacement by Lucknow as Urdu *markaz* followed by defeat in 1857 at British hands. In the twentieth century, critics like Muhammad Sadiq and Ram Babu Saksena had been educated by the British and fed on a fairly steady diet of colonial discourse about the recent past.

Regional rivalry (between Mughal Delhi and other centres) seems to have joined hands with colonial discourse to erase 'provincial' courts in favour of a Delhi-centred mythic past for Urdu and, by extension, Indo-Muslim culture in general. And as these discourses erased the 'Indian' from an Indo-Muslim culture personified by Delhi, they substituted the notion that Mughal Delhi had developed solely along lines loyal to 'traditional' Persian culture. How could this mythical picture stand in the face of contesting pictures of Lucknow and Golkunda?

The following remark sheds light on the appeal of the sort of Mughal past evoked first and foremost by Maulana Azad in *Ab-i Hayat.* It is offered by Azad's biographer, Muhammad Sadiq: '[*Ab-i Hayat*] . . . is a living page torn out of the past, which was, perhaps, never present, but which, as presented to us, throbs with life, and is, therefore, real.'[47]

Here Sadiq acknowledges the greater power of myth over empirical knowledge. Sadiq, writing some eighty years after—but clearly inspired by—Azad continues to emphasize the 'traditional' character (for which read 'Persian') of Dehlavi culture over the 'Hindi'. By tying the Mughals to Persian, Indo-Muslim culture could lay claim to several additional centuries of high civilization than a strictly Indian Urdu cultural history might have justified. So, despite the conventional wisdom that identifies Mughal genius as the successful integration of Persian with Indic cultural modes (architecture being the most oft-cited case in point, but *rekhta* no less appropriate an example), in the last century there has been a sustained effort on the part of some to diminish, even deny, the Indian (Dakani and Lakhnavi) part of Indo-Muslim culture.

I am arguing that this de-Indianization was partially effected by the de-feminization of the Urdu literary aesthetic. The *masnavi* is undeniably a Persian genre, the *virahini* undeniably an Indian convention. Critical assertions that the Lakhnavi *ghazal* concentrated on descriptions of feminine toiletries and accoutrements[48] and descriptions of the beloved's physical features serve also to suggest that Lakhnavi poets had 'gone native' and taken up decadent literary genres from Indic poetry. A genre often cited in this context is the *sarapa* a 'head-to-toe' description of the beloved's physical features.

To conflate the feminine with decadence and Indianness works, in a complicated way, to also assert a contrasting, Perso-Islamic essence for the mythical Mughal Delhi which is being promoted in the literary histories. The *sarapa* echoes, perhaps, Sanskrit poetic motifs such as *keshadipadavarnana*[49] in which a beautiful woman (or a deity) is described in elaborate iconographic detail, fashioning a sort of verbal sculpture. The *virahini* in Dakani recalls *bhakti* poetry. The Urdu *ghazal*, though secular (even if ideologically constructed as essentially spiritual and therefore 'legitimate' in the face of potential clerical disapproval), is the central icon of Indo-Muslim culture. It cannot afford such associations.

Identification with Islam is what had separated the Muslim ruling elite in India from those whom they ruled; what justified conquest of non-Muslim lands was a religious mandate. Both the female narrator of Dakani poetry, and the effeminacy of Lakhnavi poetry (personified in such genres as the *sarapa*) smacked entirely too much of Ḥindu idolatry; of that which ought to have remained eternally separate from Islam in India. This kind of 'Indianness' threatened to suggest too strong a connection between Indo-Muslim literature and the Perso-Arabic legacy so central to its exponents' and audience's self-identification. It needed to be nullified and textually, at least, it was.

Indian elements in Mughal poetry—when Muslim rule was still intact—were not nearly the threat they became after 1857, when the Mughal empire was utterly and finally defeated by the British. A newly displaced, non-ruling, non-Hindu minority was now obliged to negotiate a new relationship in a different hierarchy. These negotiations were double-edged—with the new British rulers on one side, and with the Hindu majority over which this minority had ruled for many centuries on the other. Evocation of Mughal glory as the quintessential Muslim chapter in Indian history, a chapter with whose glory even non-Muslims identified to a certain extent, perhaps promised this displaced group a niche in British India.[50]

As stated before, there is quite a bit at stake in this imaginary construction of Urdu literature as the pre-eminent product of Mughal courtly culture; and therefore as the featured cultural product of an eighteenth-century 'Golden Age' Delhi. Had not this very Mughal culture dazzled the minds of early English traders so that they held in awe the notion of the 'Great Mughals'? And had the 'Great Mughals' not gained, and held, their tremendous empire through military prowess? What room was there, then, to accuse Mughal India of effeminacy and decadence as colonial discourse was prone to do? No, those things needed to be sought elsewhere, e.g. in Lucknow or Golkunda.

This constructed mythic past, then, effectively countered colonial discourse at the same time it served to separate a 'Persianate' recently-powerful Muslim elite from the dominant culture of indigenous Hindus whom they no longer ruled. Not only did such a diminished picture of cultural syncretism in Indo-Muslim history serve the contestation for a place in British India, it could also serve an evolving national myth of Pakistan. After all, once again, it was Islam, which distinguished Pakistan from India in post-Independence South Asia.

Conclusion

Perhaps a different portrait of the eighteenth-century literary imaginary would emerge through study of its extant poetry in addition to analysis of the critical literature. Because we lack extant contemporary cultural histories it could be said that the eighteenth century remains the period of Urdu culture about which we know the least, though we have said so much. The very absence of empirical data for this time enables discourses that continue to privilege it over the dramatically more productive seventeenth and nineteenth centuries. This absence of empirical data leaves little concrete impediment to discursive preservation of a comfortable myth of an eighteenth century as a golden phase of purity and simplicity; to seeing in the cultural hybridity and 'Indianness' of more critically-documented eras the decline and fall required by neo-Islamic national (and transnational) narratives. For such narratives as those a 'Persian' rather than 'Hindi' mythic past makes perfect sense. Neither need we accept those discourses, nor need we credit other, neo-Hindu, discourses that might seek to diminish the Muslim elements in Indian culture. To understand early modern, indeed contemporary, South Asia, we need to retain all elements constituting this blend. Not to do so is either short-sighted, or intellectually dishonest, or both.

NOTES

1. An earlier version of this essay was presented at the University of Virginia's workshop on Rethinking Early Modern India where it received an insightful response from David Gilmartin. Sincere thanks also to Stewart Gordon for incisive editorial comments, and to George Bretherton for helpful comments on the penultimate draft.
2. Columbia University Press, 1973.
3. Dehlavi literally means 'of Delhi' just as Lakhnavi means 'of Lucknow'; Dakani means 'of the Deccan'; and Hindustani means 'of Hindustan' (which refers to the heartland of Muslim north India).
4. The case for Dakani is highlighted here, as I have discussed Lucknow at length elsewhere (Petievich 1992).
5. I use the term 'legend' for two reasons: (1) it underlines the imaginative nature of writing history; and (2) it reflects the wording employed by historians of Urdu literature, who have published any number of histories entitled, e.g. '*Dastan-i tarikh-i Urdu*' or '*Dastan-i Adab-i Avadh/ Haidarabad/Dakhan*', etc.
6. It is not clear when 'Urdu' came to replace the term '*rekhta*' but it would seem to have been well into the nineteenth century.
7. Saksena, p. 6. Samples of Dakani poetry featured later in this paper will challenge this assessment.
8. Saksena, p. 45.
9. Ram Babu Saksena, *A History of Urdu Literature* (Allahabad, 1927, 1940), p. 13.
10. Annemarie Schimmel, *Classical Urdu Literature from the Beginning to Iqbal*, Wiesbaden: Otto Harrassowitz, 1975, p. 164. Khan-i Arzu (1689-1756). Shah Hatim (1699-1781).
11. In keeping with the argument developed later about regional loyalties of literary critics, let us not overlook the importance of Aurangabad as a Mughal court centre during the several decades-long campaign to conquer Golkunda. In other words, if Urdu poetry is to be a Mughal

achievement, and some recognition must be given to its southern origins, it is reasonably safe to identify a southern Mughal *markaz* as that original locus, rather than *markiz* (cultural centres) such as Bijapur and Golkunda, which were independent Muslim courts, and which resisted fiercely the Mughal annexation which finally occurred in 1686 and 1687, respectively.

12. Muhammad Sadiq, in *A History of Urdu Literature* (2nd edn., Delhi, 1984: 50), mentions that Urdu (known as Dakani or Hindi) had had a flourishing literary career for a century and a half [between] 1590-1730 he nevertheless presents the presence of 'Urdu' in the Deccan as a 'transplantation' from the north. A notable exception to the exclusion of Dakani poets from standard anthologies is *Naqsh-i Dilpazir: Classical Urdu Poetry*, eds. M.A.R. Barker and Shah Abdus Salam 'with the collaboration of M. Akbaruddin Siddiqi (in the Dakani Selections)', Ithaca, 1977. This is highly uncharacteristic of anthologies produced in Hindustan and Pakistan with which I am familiar. Ironically, while this anthology is quite popular in North American classrooms, the Dakani selections are generally skipped in favour of succeeding eighteenth- and nineteenth-century Dehlavi poetry.
13. *Ab-i Hayat* (The Elixir of Life), 1st published in 1880.
14. Azad, *Ab-i Hayat* (Allahabad, 1980: 88-9). His other biographical remarks concerning Vali include such ruminations as 'the manner of his educations attainments is murky . . . but it is obvious that a poet brings his poetry with him at birth . . .' and 'since there was, in those days education at home, the company of his elders must have afforded him a bit of skill in reading and writing; from his poetry it seems that he had no formal acquaintance with the Arabic language, though his writing suggests a certain proficiency in Persian. . . '.
15. Sadiq (1984: 53). Given that even 'classical' Urdu poetry is generally considered to be an acquired taste, Sadiq's remarks might at first be puzzling. On closer examination, however, the term 'archaic' seems to suggest that it is Dakani diction that is qualitatively alien to the aficionado of eighteenth-century Dehlavi *rekhta*.
16. Since the historical period under discussion predates 1947 and the formation of Pakistan and India as separate nation-states, I use the term 'Indo-Muslim' rather than 'South Asian Muslim'.
17. I have advanced this argument at some length in *Assembly of Rivals* (1992) and 'Urdu in Lucknow, Lucknow in Urdu' (forthcoming).
18. S.R. Faruqi touches on a number of similar points in his explication of the 'Expression of the Indo-Muslim Mind in Urdu Ghazal'. See *The Secret Mirror: Essays on Urdu Poetry* (Delhi, 1981). This essay, brilliant and provocative, is highly recommended though its arguments are ultimately literary rather than historiographic.

19. This general statement is based on close and regular consultation with such scholars as Sayeda Ja'far, Mughni Tabassum, Muhammad Ali Asar and others at Osmania University, Hyderabad (Jan. 1990-March 1991). See also S.R. Faruqi (1981: 28-32) where the term '*piu*' is understood to indicate a feminine narrator. In *ghazal* II, there are other indications of the female narrator, including mention of the '*sakki*' (female companion) who is addressed, and the feminized verb endings in the *qafiya* ('–asi na'), at least as they are transcribed in the Syeda Ja'far edition of Md. Quli Qutb Shah's *Kulliyat.*
20. In this case 'Hindi' does not refer to the contemporary language of much of north India, but rather to the language spoken by Muslims in India, which was known in Persian as 'Hind'. In Urdu literary criticism 'Hindi' indicates indigenous to India, and is synonymous with 'Indic'.
21. Petievich (1990).
22. *Majalla-i Usmaniyya,* Dakani Adab Numbar, 1964, p. 139.
23. Saksena, 48; Garcin de Tassy; Zaidi, 140.
24. Translation mine, original can be found in Zaidi (140) and Insha.
25. Though, as I have elaborated elsewhere (Petievich, 1990, 1993), *rekhti* was always composed and consumed—as far as we know—by men. For a different discussion of *rekhti,* see C.M. Naim, 'Transvestic Words: The *Rekhti* in Urdu', unpublished paper presented to the South Asian Studies Seminar of the University of Pennsylvania, 1992.
26. See the Introduction to Insha's *Divan-i Rekhti,* pp. 394-6 of *Kalam-i Insha* (Allahabad, 1952). '*Rekhti auraton ki zuban men makhsus rang ke ash'ar ho kahte hain. Magar vazih rahe kih sharif auraton ki gharelu zuban se rekhti ki zuban bilkul mukhtalif hoti hai. Ham ne kisi sharif ghar ki auraton ke munh se voh boli hargiz nahin suni jo rekhti men masnu'i taur par boli jati hai.*'
27. This line could also be translated as 'How hard has my heart [had to become], Beloved'.
28. The *virahini* is much older in Indic poetry than just *bhakti* literature. Cf. Descriptions of Shakuntala in Kalidasa's (fourth century AD?) Sanskrit drama *Abhijnana-Shakuntalam* where, in the beginning of Act III, her lovesickness for Dushyanta is described in strikingly similar terms.
29. The reason for saying 'even when the Beloved is understood to be divine' is that love for the divine in mainstream Islam is not meant to be sexual (hetero- or homo-).
30. At one point early in his discussion of the Urdu *ghazal's* beloved, Muhammad Sadiq writes—in an uncontexualized footnote—that 'the reader may substitute: "she" and "her" for "he" and "him"' (p. 631). As far as I know, this routine substitution has never been problematized in Urdu criticism.
31. '*Kahti hain*' can be translated as 'she says' if the person talking is a

female of high regard: the honorific plural would be augmented, in such a case, by what we may call the 'honorific masculine' so that '*kahti hain*' (feminine plural) would become '*kahte hain*'.

32. Nobody, as far as I know, has contested this 'fact' and it is repeated widely in Dakani historiography. For a succinct English description see Eaton (Princeton, 1978); see also B.R. Pray's discussion of the sixteenth-century Punjabi Sufi poet Shah Madho Lal Husain (1539-99) all of which 'is written from the viewpoint and in the voice of women, as is so much South Asian religious poetry . . .' (unpublished Ms, dated November 1989).
33. This female voice was considered appropriate of Sufistic purposes, with the devotee/disciple identifying as the wife of a divine lover, who longed for death from earthly travail and for the promise of satisfaction in the beyond. Cf. Ali Asani, 'Spinning Songs, Yearning Brides, and the Bridegroom Prophet: Muslim Literatures in the South Asian Vernaculars'. Paper presented at the University of British Columbia, 28 February 1992.
34. In the narrative *masnavi* genre love is requited, just as in the Dakani *ghazal*. Thus the *masnavi's* aesthetic stands in sharp contrast to that of the 'classical' *ghazal*, which insists upon a beloved who almost never reciprocates. This lack of reciprocity is crucial to maintaining the *ghazal's* fiction that Man is the *'ashiq* and the God the *mahbub*. Interestingly, the 'Hindu' imagery and terminology employed in much 'classical' *ghazal* poetry around idol-worship (*but-parasti*) does not seem to pose the kind of problem posed by femininity, apparently because it can be justified under the rubric of Sufi heterodoxy.
35. See the *Kulliyat-i Sauda* (Allahabad, 1971) where there are 4,375 *ghazal* verses in Urdu, to 2,100 *qasida* verses. In Persian there are more like 500 verses.
36. The *marsiya* is an elegy celebrating the martyrdom at Karbala in the year AD 680 of the Prophet's grandson, Husain.
37. Again, see Petievich (1990), 'The Feminine Voice in the Urdu Ghazal' (*Indian Horizons*, v. 9, nos. 1-2).
38. Ahmed Ali, *Golden Tradition*, p. 212.
39. See the fulsome discussion of this phenomenon in Barnett (1980).
40. Sadiq, p. 57. Emphasis added.
41. Saksena, pp. 117-20.
42. Ibid. Emphasis added.
43. Sadiq, p. 167.
44. Whereas in that same chapter on the 'Lucknow School' he offers 26 lines of Insha's poetry (including six, five and six, *she'rs* each of three *ghazals*); 12 individual *she'rs* of Jur'at; 15 individual verses of Nasikh; and 34 of Atish). Sadiq, pp. 167-93.

45. Note that I am not arguing that the British targeted Md. Quli—it is not clear that they were even aware of him, for he predates their time as players on the Indian political scene. Rather, I am arguing that modern Urdu critics, schooled in the kind of colonial discourse that had been directed against Wajid Ali Shah to advance British claims on Awadh, seem to have perceived the benefits of turning such discourse against Dakani rivals of Mughal (Dehalvi) culture.
46. See Petievich (1992) and Frances W. Pritchett, *Nets of Awareness: Urdu Poetry and its Critics* (Berkeley, 1994) for fuller studies of these pioneering critics and their relations to British patrons.
47. M. Sadiq, *Muhammad Husain Azad: His Life and Works* (Lahore, 1965), p. 53.
48. Notably the *sarapa* genre is associated with Lucknow, which involves a 'head-to-foot' description of the [females] beloved's physical attributes. For a fuller discussion of critical discourse on Lucknow see Petievich (1992).
49. Lit. 'description form head to foot' a clearly iconographic approach. When applied to a god instead of a human, the description begins at the feet and works upward, and is called '*padadikeshavarnana*'. Many thanks to Nadine Berardi for her expertise on this point.
50. See the discussion of *sharafat*, or nobility, as an ethos in David Lelyveld (1978: 28-30) where, among many other points, he makes clear that the label '*sharif*' (noble) so often attached to the class of Indo-Muslim elites who moved in India's particular 'Islamic culture . . . centred on the Persian language and taking inspiration from courtly styles of Saffavid Iran . . .' suggested almost nothing about religious genealogy and much about social respectability. It could also apply to Hindus who moved in, and identified with, that milieu, but *sharafat* represented an essential opposition to the sensuality and excess of oriental despotism.

REFERENCES

Ahmad, Aziz. 1964. *Studies in Islamic Culture in the Indian Environment*, Oxford: Clarendon.

Asani, Ali. 1992. 'Spinning Songs, Yearning Brides and the Bridegroom Prophet: Muslim Literatures in the South Asian Vernaculars.' Paper presented at the University of British Columbia, 28 February.

Askari, Mirza Muhammad. 1952. *Kalam-i-Insha*. Allahabad: Hindustani Akademi, Uttar Pradesh.

Azad, Muhammad Husain. 1980 [1880]. *Ab-i Hayat* (The Elixir of Life). Allahabad: Ram Narain Lal Beni Madhav.

Barnett, Richard B. 1980. *North India Between Empires: Avadh, The*

Mughals, and the British, 1720-1801. Berkeley: University of California Press.

Eaton, Richard M. 1978. *Sufis of Bijapur, 1300-1700: Social Roles of Sufies in Medieval India.* Princeton, N.J.: Princeton University Press.

Faruqi, S.R. 1987-8. *'Dakani Nahin, Qadim Urdu'* (Not Dakani, Old Urdu). *Shab Khun* (Allahabad), 148, 150.

———. 1981. 'Expression of the Indo-Muslim Mind in Urdu Ghazal', in *The Secret Mirror: Essays on Urdu Poetry.* Delhi: Academic Literature.

Ja'far, Sayeda, ed. 1985. *Kulliyat-i Muhammad Quli Qutb Shah.* Delhi: Anjuman-i Taraqqi-i Urdu.

Jalibi, Jamil. 1986 [1977]. *Tarikh-i Adab-i-Urdu* (History of Urdu Literature). 3 vols. Delhi: Educational Publishing House.

Lelyweld David. 1993. '*Zuban-e Urdu-e Mo'alla* and the Idol of Linguistic Origins'. *Annual of Urdu Studies* 9: 79-89.

———. 1978. *Aligarh's First Generation: Muslim Solidarity in British India.* Princeton, N.J.: Princeton University Press.

Metcalf, Barbara D. 1990. *Perfecting Women: Maulana Ashraf 'Ali Thanawi's Bihishti Zewar.* Berkeley: University of California Press.

Naim, C.M. 1992. 'Transvestic Words: The *Rekhti* in Urdu'. Paper presented to the South Asian Studies Seminar of the University of Pennsylvania.

Naim, C.M. and Carla Petievich, forthcoming. 'Urdu in Lucknow, Lucknow in Urdu', in Violette Graf, ed. [title pending] (Delhi: Manohar).

Pemble, John. 1979. *The Raj, the Indian Mutiny and the Kingdom of Oudh, 1801-1858.* Delhi: Oxford University Press.

Petievich, Carla, forthcoming. 'Heroes, *Virahinis* and Gender-Bending in the Urdu Ghazal', in Sandria B. Freitag, ed., *Culture as Contested Site: The State and Popular Participation in the Indian Subcontinent.* Delhi: Oxford University Press.

———. 1993. Review of Barbara D. Metcalf, *Perfecting Women . . .* in *Middle Eastern Studies Bulletin* 27: 188-9.

———. 1992. *Assembly of Rivals: Delhi, Lucknow and the Urdu Ghazal.* Delhi: Manohar.

———. 1990. 'The Feminine Voice in the Urdu Ghazal'. *Indian Horizons* 3-4, nos. 1-2: 25-41.

Platts, J.T. 1964 [1884]. *A Dictionary of Urdu, Classical Hindi and English.* London: Oxford University Press.

Pritchett, Frances W. 1994. *Nets of Awareness: Urdu Poetry and its Critics.* Berkeley: University of California Press.

Qateel, Hafeez. 1964. 'Dakani men Rekhti' (*Rekhti* in Dakani). *Majalla-i Usmaniyya,* Dakani Adav Numbar.

Sadiq, Muhammad. 1984 [1964]. *A History of Urdu Literature.* Delhi: Oxford University Press.

———. 1965. *Muhammad Husain Azad: His Life and Works*. Lahore: West-Pak Publishing House.

Saksena, Ram Babu. 1940 [1927]. *A History of Urdu Literature.* Allahabad: Ram Narain Lal.

Schimmel, Annemarie. 1975. *Classical Urdu Literature from the Beginning to Iqbal.* Weisbaden: Otto Harrassowitz.

Zaidi, Ali Javad. 1993. *A History of Urdu Literature.* Delhi: Sahitya Akademi.

Technology and the Question of Elite Intervention in Eighteenth-Century North India

IQBAL GHANI KHAN

THE CONVENTIONAL view of the eighteenth century was that it was divided into two halves. The first saw the Mughal decline (and the decline of something so all-pervasive could only result in all-pervasive destruction).[1] And then, according to this view, in the 1750s and 1760s the English East India Company took over the economy of the region and deepened the distress. This is a wholly plausible approach if a critique of British imperialism in India in the latter half of the eighteenth century is our focus. However, to examine the links between technology and culture as well as other micro aspects of the eighteenth century, we shall have to look at very diverse aspects of Mughal decline—the rupturing of agrarian relations, the status of craftsmen, their new organizations and patrons, horse-traders and horse-trading, and the coming of the European mercenaries and the changing weaponry in the indigenous states. An important topic for research would be the manner in which the state builders in Awadh, Rohilkhand, Farrukhabad, Bharatpur, Hyderabad, Bengal, and Mysore equipped their armies.[2] I have been looking at the technical literature in Farsi, English, Urdu, Hindi, and French pertaining to agriculture, military technology, craft production, and town building. I am also looking at the ways in which technical education was imparted to elite youth.[3] This research aims at re-examining Athar Ali's thesis that the decline of the Mughal empire and the destruction that ensued had three causes: Irfan Habib's structural-agrarian crisis, the over-expansion of the empire, and the intellectual and technical barrenness of Mughal elites.[4] It is the last alleged cause that I wish to re-examine in this paper.

Let us first examine how technical the life of an average Mughal mansabdar[5] could be. In fact we even discern much encouragement being extended by the Mughal emperors to nobles trying to become technocrats.[6] Thus we have the *Ain-i Akbari* (compiled *c.* 1600) with its chapters on metal purification, alloying (apparently Abul Fazl knew the techniques for making alloys of varying percentages and constituents),[7] cannon casting, and handgun boring devices; it even included a section on geared wagons that ground grain as they moved. All this was just one indicator of the importance of things technical.[8] Furthermore, the *Ain-i Akbari* reported the introduction in the 1580s of a new syllabus for school-going youth; this consisted, apart from the usual logic, prosody, disputation, and recitation of the Koran, of technical subjects like agriculture, land measurement, medicine, mathematics, algebra, and household management. The last was not a simple subject, because an elite household could often constitute an entire *mohalla* and it involved a variety of managerial as well as practical skills. This syllabus therefore provided the basic grounding for the careers of noblemen as well as military and revenue officers in the Mughal bureaucracy.

After this stage, advanced students of religion and law were trained at another level that allowed specialization in Arabic-based Koranic studies. Interestingly, the allegedly hyper-orthodox Aurangzeb was extremely unhappy about having been trained according to this specialized theological-scholastic syllabus, as shown by his famous outburst against his teacher in 1661 after becoming emperor. This happened when Mulla Saleh was hoping for a reward for having coached him to glory. Aurangzeb responded by criticizing Abdul Saleh for failing to teach him things essential for a Mughal prince. He had not been taught geography to tell him about regional resources, or the peoples and powers at the imperial borders. Nor had he learned about the histories of other peoples, thus leaving him in the dark about the causes for their rise and decline; nothing was imparted on the art of administering men of diverse religio-legal beliefs; nor had he been taught the art of war. He concluded:

> But you taught me to read and write Arabic. Forgetting how many important subjects ought to be embraced in the education of a prince, you acted as if it were chiefly necessary that he should possess great skill in grammar, and such a knowledge as belongs to a doctor of law; and thus did you waste the precious hours of my youth in the dry, unprofitable, and never-ending task of learning words![9]

In fact Aurangzeb was pleased when, at the advent of the eighteenth century, Mulla Nizamuddin Sahalvi of Lucknow began to popularize a syllabus which had only one book on theology and the rest on Greco-Arab rationalism or *falsafa*. It was called the *Dars-i Nizamiyya* (the Syllabus of Nizamuddin) and by the end of the century, it had become very popular all across India. This system of education even proved useful for those who took up academics or law as a career, especially after the coming of the confusing regulation-bound world of colonial India.[10]

In general, therefore, elite youth in Mughal India were destined for more technical roles than was reflected in their *madrasa* syllabi. Apart from the scholastic bases of their knowledge—namely ethics, religion, disputation, and some mathematics, which they had traditionally acquired in the *madrasas*—they now learned science and techniques such as agricultural management as a part of the administrative 'Persian stream' education—especially as ordained by Akbar. However, during the Mughal heyday, as well as later, the only place one could acquire a practical technical education was from master craftsmen employed in the imperial or noble household *karkhaneh*, specialized bonded workshops where goods were made for aristocratic families. Such goods were also made for presentation to a superior officer and thus knowledge of their manufacture was required for entry into the charmed network of gift-givers, so vital for aspirants to high socio-political status.[11] To fabricate these gifts there were experts and a *karkhana* for every craft, and there could be up to fifty-six *karkhaneh* in a large household.[12] The emperors chose to intervene in crafts of their interest, strategic or aesthetic. For example, Akbar personally tested all the matchlocks manufactured in his *karkhana* for accuracy; he also insisted on the dyeing of yarn in different colours of his choice before it was woven, and the results set off a new fashion in textile design.[13] The nobles would follow suit both in the setting up of workshops as well as in taking an interest in output.

The *ustad* and the *ataliq* taught their pupils the martial arts and luxury crafts such as the alloying of coloured metals and the making of scented paper. Basic information on horses, elephants, swords, medicine, architecture, soaps, and hair dyes could also be obtained from the literature and drawings that were produced by and for this class.[14] The details in the technical manuals written for the Mughal elite suggest a much wider role for the written technical word than has so far been assumed.[15]

When the successor states and the entrepreneurial states came into existence, and as long as the old Mughal nobles were in control of these states, we could reasonably expect these elite skills to persist into the eighteenth century. We know from the composition of the ruling class in Awadh, Bengal, and Hyderabad that these states were run by alliances of post-Mughal nobles well into the nineteenth century.[16] Also, elite immigration from Iran and Afghanistan continued, and the immigrants found work in the reorganized political systems that were cobbled together out of the parts of the Mughal empire in the eighteenth century. For example, the founders of two very important northern Indian nawabis of Awadh and Rohilkhand, namely, Saadat Khan and Daud Khan, were first-generation immigrants from Nishapur (Iran) and Afghanistan.[17] The demand for technically competent men could only increase in an environment in which old relations of power were being dismantled, and the ability to perform in actual roles of control would be the deciding factor in one's rise to power.[18] In view of these questions, more serious work needs to be done on the eighteenth century that marks the end of not one but four Asian empires,[19] and the interregnum in which many small state systems came into existence. Northern India's fertile soil and its hard-working people gave the post-Mughal state builders all the inputs they needed for the sustenance of their state—land, water, towns, markets, and skilled manpower.

These political entities were run using all forms of technical knowledge, until they were all appropriated by the needs of British colonialism.[20]

To understand this century, we need to describe the fate of the productive elements that once fed the Mughal empire; how were they redeployed once the monolith ceased to exist? Were there not arenas within which the old talents could be applied? Because clearly the peasantry was still producing a surplus, the artisans were obviously weaving textiles and hammering iron into implements, to keep their families alive. There were also the traders in horses and other goods managing to get past the Marathas and other marauders. Obviously there was a variety of economic and political vacuums within which power could be re-established in accommodation with local potentates.

Furthermore the military-administrative knowledge that informed the Mughal imperial apparatus was not so inflexible that it was incapable of application to smaller state-systems. For example there was the nawabi of Awadh which was trying to pattern itself along Mughal lines.[21] There were even newly-arrived pretenders to political power with their own skills and texts, such as the Afghan immigrants from the mountains, who were settling in Katehr—the fertile submontane plains just below the Kumaon mountains and east of the river Ganga.[22] These were groups in which the technicians were a respected part of the tribal polity and were able controllers of artisanal as well as agricultural labour.[23]

In other words, within the flexibility of the Mughal system, there had been opportunities, avenues and resources for technical intervention—even innovation by the emperor and his elite. Unfortunately, in the changed circumstances of the eighteenth century, with the nobility and bureaucrats at the centre no longer receiving most of the total revenues (67 per cent in *c.* 1600),[24] the emphasis would no longer be mainly on imperial army- or luxury-related innovation but on intervention in mundane areas such as agricultural and craft rehabilitation. They would also be developing locally useful military technology, and in re-establishing state-systems within which producer, production, and revenue could be protected.

Definitions

We take the eighteenth-century elite to be, first, those Irani, Turani, Afghan, indigenous Muslim, Rajput, and Maratha mansabdars who tried to take the emperor in hand and claim territories for themselves as nawabs. In the second category came Rajput, Bhumihar, and Maratha chiefs (clan leaders, rajas, zamindars), now important in the regional states that the post- Mughal elite would establish. The third category was the jagir-holding Kayastha, an official who would translate into proforma the details of government; and in the fourth, the *arriviste* Ruhela and Jat state builders who were not burdened by the trappings of a Mughal past and were therefore most likely to succeed in those times. Serving them all as military experts, and occasionally becoming quasi-lords themselves, were European mercenaries.[25] Clearly we have quite a complex arrangement of groups operating in this region in the middle of the century, and all of them had their own array of technical skills for the acquisition of wealth and power.

Coming thus to the crux of the paper, we need first to define *technology*, and then to understand the difference between *innovation* and *intervention*, because these terms might evoke images of the English country gentlemen inventing steam engines and Spinning Jennies. Technology means not only systematic thinking about practical techniques but also related managerial aspects that facilitate the production of goods for society. For example, technology includes accounting for improving agrarian production via the introduction of new crops, agrarian revenue enhancement techniques by increasing seed yields, better methods of seed storage, and transportation and marketing for agricultural and craft produce. It includes changes in military organization, or even the remodelling of an old canal. This also clarifies the meanings of terms such as *technological innovation* and *elite technical intervention*. Andrew Jamison's recent definition of technical innovation as 'explicit theorizing about technology consequent to industrialization' is well taken. But one who knows the texts produced in the sixth-century in China and in eighth-century India and the Arab world would tend to disagree when he says that this tradition cannot be found before the sixteenth-century writings of Biringuccio (*Pyrotechnia*, 1540), Agricola (*De Re Metallica*,1556), and Ramelli (*Le Diverse et Artificiose Machine*, 1588). The Italian Renaissance was not the first time that one found fascinating details of technical drawings, or the earliest manifestation of men trying to organize and diffuse technical development practices.[26] This process of innovation has been active ever since man began to use tools to feed, clothe, and protect himself in the environment. However, the capability for technological evolution had not been institutionalized; change would come whenever men and women felt that the old tools were not efficient or effective enough to meet the needs of the population and environment. So from wheel to wheelbarrow, to cart, to the domestication of animals—all these changes have been in progress ever since the Stone Age.

While the process was not socialized or systematized till much later, it is a fact that by the ninth century the Abbasids had sponsored the translation into Arabic of the works of Archimedes, Hero, and Ctesiphos, who had been designing mechanical devices ever since 250 BC. Their tradition was revived in the eleventh century when West Asia had technological collectives such as the Sons of Musa or Banu Musa who produced a *Book of Devices* that was the precursor to Al Jazzari's *Kitab al Huyul wa'l Hindsa* (The Book of Ingenious Devices).[27] Elsewhere in Asia, there were the sixth- and seventh-century Chinese technological encyclopaedias that Needham has used in his monumental study, which could have been written even earlier than the Greek sources.[28] The drawings by Al Jazzari and Banu Musa, though somewhat fanciful, served as crude patterns for other useful devices; this was all a part of a slow-paced but interrelated tradition of innovation in which hydrostatic gearing went into making clocks, hand-washing automata, water-driven toys, and furnace bellows. The latter produced changes in smelting procedures, distillation equipment, weavers' looms, and other applications. All these processes underwent change on the basis either of elite demand exercised at the level of luxury demand and quality control, via the nature of elite patronage,[29] or in response to the more broad-based economic demand in general.

The Mughal Background

Until recently, most studies on medieval and early modern Indian elite treated the technical roles of the ruler as an aspect of 'Enlightened Despotism', a part of which were his building activities, the construction of better roads and canals, systems of surplus extraction, and legal devices for ensuring justice. These were the attributes of the good king and were studied in passing and superficially. A change in approach came about when Marxist historians starting with Needham, as well as K.M. Ashraf, D.D. Kosambi, Irfan Habib, Iqtidar Alam Khan, A.J. Qaisar, M.A. Alvi, and A. Rahman, were inspired to study production techniques in a historical context. Interestingly enough, this (the 1950s and 1960s) was also the period when the secular, socialist Indian nation was taking shape and beginning to concretize its ideals especially in the face of a strong right-wing Hindu reaction—which wanted all history to be coloured in terms of 'Glorious Hindu' *v.* 'Dark Muslim' eras. A history of the people, these scholars argued, would be the best way out of this acrimony. And to know the people we would have to know the history of their tools. The study of technology would be for the glory of the working people; and as the subaltern school of historians is doing today, the subject was formulated in a way that the elite was divorced from consideration. Even theories of decline would be built around an alleged elite disinterest in things technical.[30]

It was not until 1992, at the four hundred and fiftieth birth anniversary of Emperor Akbar, that a change in attitude was declared. In a talk entitled 'Akbar and Technology', Irfan Habib demonstrated how close Akbar was to technology and the workmen.[31] He specifically drew our attention to the time Akbar spent in the *karkhana,* and the innovations he had wrought. So effusive was Habib's praise for Akbar that even the inventions once attributed to an advisor like Fathullah Shirazi were restored to Akbar. Two decades ago, we had in our Marxist fervour contended that all inventions that the Mughal chroniclers had reported as being those of the emperor should be taken as a piece of flattery, and we ought to look for their 'actual' creators.[32] In my view, we need to broaden the scope of the history of pre-modern technology to deal with elite technical innovation, invention and intervention, their control over artisan organizations, tools, economic standing, and education.

My studies in this area suggest that elite interest in things technical was aroused, and intervention could occur, whenever one or more of the following factors were in play. First, the use of military-economic resources to control bodies of artisans whom they could secure in their *karkhaneh.* Second, the expectation of increased revenue and military, political and sexual power as well as popularity in general. Third, there was the need for aesthetic pleasure, longevity, and the hope for salvation after death—this last led to the building of masjids and mausoleums surrounded by tanks that cooled the public gardens, and other focal points in their town-planning tradition.[33]

As far as elite scientific as well as technical interest was concerned, it was never lacking. A bio-bibliographical survey has produced a volume with several thousand entries.[34] Then there are the collections in London, Paris, Aligarh, Patna, the hundreds of manuscripts that were carted away from the libraries of the Afghan chief Hafiz Rahmat Khan and the Mysore ruler Tipu Sultan,[35] the books in the Khuda Bakhsh Library, Patna[36] and in the Raza Library, Rampur,[37] to name the prominent few. Hyderabad's Central State Archives and Salar Jung Museum, and the Asiatic Society Collection in Calcutta are also worthy of mention. After the Mughal decline, the courts that attracted scholars also became the repositories for their books. In the 1780s the library in Lucknow had 3,00,000 volumes.[38] But much of this is being lost to moisture, heat, and the looting of palaces that have been going on in India ever since the colonial conquest and to this day.

The history of elite interest in things technical is in fact an early one. In the thirteenth-fourteenth century, royally commissioned chronicles of medieval Indian sultans incorporated technical drawings. For example, there are drawings in Raja Bhoja's illustrated manuscript on technical devices, and there are drawings in the *Tarikh-i Firuz Shahi* that show us how combinations of pulleys enabled the transportation of an immense iron pillar from Meerut to Delhi by Firuz Shah Tughlaq. The figure is collapsed outwards so that the workings of the multiple-pulley combinations may be understood.[39] Later we find Mughal memoirs and gazetteers that specifically emphasize 'inventions of the Emperor'. Babur was proud of his innovators such as the Turkish gun-caster Ustad Quli, who brought into this region new ways of casting cannon. Babur's *Baburnama* shows his fascination with the variety of crafts in India, his keen interest in Indian flora and fauna, crops, and irrigation devices. The next great book to come out of the Mughal court was the *Jawahar ul-'Ulum-i Humayuni* of Mohammad Fazil Samarqandi. This was a massive tome meant to instruct the emperor in all the sciences as well as in some essential techniques. So also was the *Jawahar-nama* of Muhammad bin Asad Rustamdari, in which alloys and their compositions were described and minerals identified.[40]

Akbar's reign, of course, produced the *Ain-i Akbari*. Written around 1595 by Abul Fazl, it contains descriptions as well as illustrations of gun-boring devices, carts fitted with flourmills, fruits, and flowers.[41] Furthermore, the artists who worked in the ateliers of the emperor and his nobles, while illustrating elite chronicles, were encouraged to incorporate detailed studies of craftsmen and their techniques into the scenes showing the emperor. Therefore by example, as well as by the institutional advantage of having at hand places where skilled artisans worked, as well as interest in the process of innovation through trial and error, interest in things technical was kept respectable and desirable among the Indo-Mughal elite, both in the high Mughal era as well as later. In fact paintings and chronicles are crucially important source materials for the historian of pre-modern technology.[42]

In addition to those already mentioned, motivation towards innovation would come from several directions, such as when traders and consumers exerted their influence on the quality and design of textiles. The emperor, or even his noblemen, who also had *karkhaneh* in their establishments, could make demands on the craftsmen to improve the quality of a sword or to change the design or even the 'water' (lit. *aab*, the wavy lines on the blade resulting from repeated folding and beating the steel blade or 'damascening') on a metal surface. When elites wanted to make more intricate the pattern of colours in a woven shawl they could induce subtle changes in the process of production,[43] such as the coming of the treadle in the horizontal loom, or the dyeing of the yarn before weaving to attain a pattern as directed by Emperor Akbar,[44] or his 40-yard-high chandelier (the *akash diya*) which was used to illuminate his camps.[45] Akbar's insistence on accurately bored handguns led to the invention of the *barghu*—a bullock-powered boring machine with geared combinations that enabled 16 gun-barrels to be machined simultaneously.[46] The Persian wheel was modified and made to work inside palaces, in tandem with other Persian wheels to lift water up to the very top of the highest palace chambers in Fatehpur Sikri during Akbar's reign.[47] There were nobles in his reign such as Shah Fathullah Shirazi who, according to some recent historians, designed a portable cannon whose barrel could be dismantled for enhanced mobility.[48]

The *Tuzuk-i Jahangiri* contains instances of the Emperor Jahangir insisting on the softening of a meteorite to have it forged into a dagger for his personal use. The efforts to attain the high temperatures to render malleable a piece of meteoritic metal must surely have forced the metallurgists in the royal armoury to exert themselves in changing the design of the furnace.[49] Their failure to attain the requisite temperature was an oft-occurring drawback in India's technological development—especially in the liquefaction and casting of iron cannon. However there was Moosvi Khan, and other nobles whose innovations on the tempering of swords, the making of soaps, perfumes, masonry targets, and even hair dye were compiled and published in handbooks such as the *Biyaz-i Khushbui*. Similar sources of technical information were the *Dasturs*, the *Farhangs* and the *Majmuat us-Sana'at*.[50] There were also specialized treatises on horses (the *Farsnamas*) and on swords (*Shamsheernamas*—some with misleading titles such as *Sawarin-i Barahin* or The Ride of the Naked). There were, as well, a host of other nobles whose diaries, though difficult to come by, contain bits of technological information. Even if on a better way to make *kababs*, changes in processes and tools were involved, it was thus innovation or at least intervention.[51]

Incidentally another piece of evidence which revises conclusively our image of the allegedly non-technical Mughal nobleman comes from an imperial book of regulations written around 1700. This manual gives a list of such useful knowledge and honourable crafts as would be suitable for a nobleman. According to this list, young nobles ought to be taught iron-working, goldworking, engraving, alchemy, weaving, sewing, carding, dying, pottery making, and cooking.[52] How far this advice was followed is difficult to assess; even comprehending this fact is difficult to correlate with our current misconceptions about what 'noble and manly pastimes' actually were.

Obviously therefore all this was anything but a technically static phase in South Asian civilizational development. The Turkish Sultanate had brought in an 'Urban Revolution' in the thirteenth and fourteenth centuries.[53] The Lodi and the Suri Afghans had demonstrated how easy it was to acquire the throne of Delhi with a disciplined army, as well as ways of linking revenue-collection to productivity. They had put in the roads for trans-continental trade, and had succeeded in driving out the second Mughal emperor in 1540.[54] However the Mughals were restored in 1544, brought all the diverse elite groups together under their tutelage, and centralized the administration to such an unprecedented extent that virtually all orders were personally signed by the emperor and enforced across the subcontinent, with the full force of Mughal military might.[55]

Thus the need of this empire was systematization and organizational change, and this would require technical intervention and technological innovation. The emperor, being so completely in command, would be expected to provide the impetus; and right from Babur and his *Baburnama* we find the Mughal providing the role model for his elite to emulate. And the lessons that we describe were well studied, because these nobles perforce learned agricultural management from the jagirs that were given to them as salary, and their promotions were assessed on their military prowess. Every imperial *farman* appointing a new incumbent over a block of villages required him to establish order in the name of the emperor, repair canals, extend cultivation, settle peasants, enhance artisanal production, and establish towns and markets for commerce. Failure to extend cash cropping meant low returns from the tax collection assignment. Poor knowledge of accountancy meant leakage and less cash to pay the militia each mansabdar was expected to maintain. Providing the requisite clothes, weapons, and horses to their cavaliers was strictly their responsibility too, and so a way of acquiring good and cheap horses from the importers had to be worked out. Irrigation canals drew favourable attention from the emperor as did the construction of bridges, roads, and towns;[56] such enterprises could mean an increase in rank numbers (*zat* and *sawar*). Life was never dull for the Mughal military-cum-bureaucratic nobleman and for his efforts, his class cornered almost 67 per cent of the total revenues of the Mughal empire at its height.[57]

The Eighteenth Century

With the death of Aurangzeb in 1707 there was no longer a great ruler to emulate—nor did the post-Mughal men command immense cash resources to sustain their large households. Nonetheless, the Mughals who had maintained the empire were now beginning to regroup and settle into the territories they felt they would be able to retain in the event of zamindar-led peasant rebellions. For a while they continued to jockey for power in close proximity to the emperor. They even tried to take control of his resources. However when they saw the risks involved and the low returns,[58] they realized that it was safer to use the symbolic authority offered by the emperor to legitimize their new state-systems and to pay cash for it. Despite the attraction the Mughal court held for these ex-Mughal elites, they realized that it was more pragmatic to pay the emperor a nominal tribute, and state formation became their primary and overt objective. It is important to observe that all of these groups were using the technical training they had acquired in the service of the empire. The Ruhelas and the Bangash were the only newcomers; because they had the least to lose, they were the most successful. Some others started off quite well, for example Awadh and Bengal, but the relentless pressure from the East India Company taxed their resources so heavily that they could not survive. Others such as Hyderabad, Bahawalpur, and Bhopal lasted till after Independence, though in a very truncated form. The Afridis and other Afghans at Farrukhabad and Qayamganj did well initially, and since they were on good terms with the emperor, they acquired a number of offices, along with territories in which they encouraged cash cropping, secured trade along the Ganga, and built fortified towns. Their Nawab, Qayam Khan, was an expert at casting cannon and designing footwear.[59]

But for now, we focus on some successful outsiders, the Ruhelas. These Afghans that settled in northern Uttar Pradesh were blessed with good leaders from the outset; they had to be good, because of their fluid political structures in which only the most astute rose to military or tribal commands. These clan leaders were able to outmanoeuvre the rajas and imperial jagirholders in the fertile northern UP and attract skilled cultivators, traders, transporters, and artisans to their areas. In those troubled times, the security of the Ruhela Afghan settlements was all that these skilled cultivators and traders needed. Consequently so well integrated with the countryside were the towns they revived, that the wealth attracted the attention of European travellers, the English East India Company's spies, and writers such as Francklin who referred to this entire region as having been transformed into a garden. Unfortunately this attracted the attention of the Marathas too.

The Ruhelas were so popular as leaders that Katehr began to be referred to as Rohilkhand. Ruh, the mountainous region of south-eastern Afghanistan, was the place of their origin, so they were called Ruhelas, to distinguish them from the more urbane Afghans who had been co-opted into the Mughal nobility in the sixteenth-seventeenth centuries.[60] In fact the reputation for boorishness was used by Bahlol Lodi to gain access to the well-guarded court of a rival who thought they were harmless and let them in. Once inside they imprisoned him and thus helped Bahlol ascend the throne in 1451.[61] One is reminded here of Ibn Khaldun's theory of the *a'sabiyyin*—the uncultured people from the desert coming in to replace the decadent urbanized elite.[62] And this ties into Pierre Bourdieu's theory of symbolic violence. According to this theory, within societies which contain no objectified institutions for sustaining domination, relations of domination can be established and sustained only via strategies which must be continuously renewed, since conditions do not exist for a stable and mediated appropriation of other agents' labour or homage. These would include acts of patronage, and gift-giving so lavish that it cannot be reciprocated, such as substantial loans and other acts of virtue, which Bourdieu calls symbolic violence, the sole objective being to extract and maintain reliable military and agrarian service.[63] Thus we witness the Ruhelas accepting an exceptionally talented non-Afghan, an adopted Jat boy, as their nawab, purely on the basis of his military leadership; we also see imperial commanders being bribed and sent packing by these 'men from the mountains' when these nobles inevitably came to subjugate them.

So the Ruhelas came, they saw, and they settled down. Within fifty years they were the protectors of the peasantry who toiled for them, growing cash crops such as sugar cane and wheat; they were also collectors of revenue, and the sellers of Afghan horses to the armies of the country.[64] Most important of all, they built and developed towns. By 1764, so reputed were the Ruhela as a military force that after the defeat of the allied princely armies by the East India Company at Baksar, Shuja ud-Daulah, the nawab of Awadh, sought refuge in Rohilkhand.[65] An idea of the military reputation of the Ruhelas can be had from the fact that the mere presence of Mir Qasim in Rohilkhand was enough to cause panic in Awadh as well as the Company court. They feared an alliance among Mir Qasim, the Ruhelas, and Ahmad Shah Abdali of Afghanistan.[66]

The fear was well founded because the armies of the Ruhela nawabs were manned by infantry and cavalrymen, all of whom had muskets; each section of ten men had a distinctive colour combination on their pennants. Their cavalrymen and the quality of their horses was their forte. But they had a variety of artillery pieces and were also using rockets (*ban*). Their fortresses could be a group of mud fortifications under the cover of a bamboo grove—thus with double walling, impervious to bombardment. With all these innovative elites taking charge of fertile territories across north India[67] (and south India too—Tipu Sultan, Nizam ul-Mulk, the Pathan nawabs of Bhopal and Arcot), and bringing new lands or long-abandoned lands under cultivation. Thus there were many technical- and production-related areas in which the elite perforce intervened and fostered innovation in an agriculture-dominated economy.

The Ruhelas were just one elite group manifesting technical expertise. There were also Awadhi nobles, the Bangash elite and their Bamtela Rajput *chelas* (local boys adopted and trained by the Afghans for war and tax-collection as well as other sundry favours), the Jat rajas of Bharatpur, Bayana and Wair; the nawabs of Bihar and Bengal, and finally the European mercenaries operating across northern India in the eighteenth century. All were busying themselves with elite education and training, honing their military skills, managing agrarian relations, and establishing safe towns for craftsmen, peasants, traders, bankers, and the families of soldiers, and generally thriving as enterprising post-Mughal men. Let us continue our focus on just one of these groups, the Ruhelas, and look at the process of establishing and managing towns.

Ruhela Towns

The earliest entrepreneur in Ruhela political power was Daud Khan, who came to Mughal India in the first decade of the eighteenth century, and moved about as a mercenary commander for clients of all religions. In the 1720s, conditions around the person of the emperor were chaotic, and Daud Khan made his fortune as a mercenary warlord in the fertile foothills of the Siwaliks. He liked the region so much that he would have settled down in Moradabad or Aonla. Since he was a mercenary, however, he did not survive too long, and was succeeded by his adopted son Ali Mohammad Khan who made his capital at Aonla, about 15 km south-east of Bareilly. This was the earliest example of a new Ruhela town. Whereas earlier the Mughal mansabdars had enjoyed the authority and the resources to establish a new town or village wherever they were posted—according to his letter of appointment, it was one of his duties—in the eighteenth century, such activities were entirely governed by the founder's own resources. To acquire legitimacy, the Ruhelas acquired zamindari rights or became revenue farmers (*ijaradars*) and managing agents at the revenue assignments of important central ministers. Once they had acquired enough control over the peasantry and acquired the services of bands of Ruhela horsemen fleeing from Iran in the wake of Nadir Shah's ethnic cleansing, they set about establishing the final link in the agrarian-military economy, namely, fortified market towns.

The people of northern India were aware that the Muslim town-builders had been around since the thirteenth century and were respected for providing security to venues built for the sale of produce, the purchase of craft goods, and the place where a ruler's power could be expressed in palaces, mosques, temples, or court houses. These towns were not of a particular 'type'; they varied according to the topography and the functions the town was designed to perform, military, political, or commercial.[68]

The Afghans too were known to the Indian people (both rural and urban) ever since the Lodi and Suri rulers had ruled between 1444 and 1544; they had earlier too revived old towns and built new ones at Agra, Sasaram, and Bayana.[69] Afghan kings such as Sher Shah Suri had established a precedent in brick forts, palaces, mosques and mausoleums.[70] The Ruhela Afghans were known for their military prowess and their reliability as soldiers; as well as for their agriculture. Therefore when they began town building, they were signalling their intentions to stay.[71] Thus when Aonla was chosen for a capital, many fellow Ruhelas flocked to it and built houses and cantonments for kinsmen.[72] The newly risen leader Ali Mohammad for another reason urgently needed a capital city too. In an 'open' political system such as that of the Ruhelas, leadership and sovereignty over fellow Ruhelas (especially competing lineage chiefs or *sardars*) would be difficult, until lavish display of control and patronage was institutionalized or objectified by a palace, a fort, a mosque, also by bridges, roads, and markets. As town building became more difficult in the face of the destruction of resources by the Marathas and the coming of the East India Company, an inscription that was most popular on many Afghan structures was:

Naam manzoor hai to faiz ke asbab bana,
Pul bana, chah bana, masjid-o-mihrab bana.

If it were fame that thou desire, build objects of public good.
Build bridges, build wells, build mosques and
build arches (gates).[73]

Soon Aonla had a beautiful masjid and fort, and William Francklin, who visited this region in 1776, after its conquest by Shuja ud-Daulah of Awadh with the help of Company troops, he described it as

> a Pathan town built on a rise from which the country all around is visible. The river Nawab Nadi runs to the S.W. of the city. It is a large town with many buildings . . . many are now in ruins. On a summit is a fort built of brick. It was made some 50 years earlier (*c.* 1730) by Ali Mohammad as was the mosque and other public buildings.[74]

Ali Mohammad had died in 1749 and this territory was now in Shuja's hands. All Ruhela chiefs had been deprived of their authority and revenues.

An interesting aspect of technical intervention, apart from all that went into the choice of the site and the layout, was Ali Mohammad's role in procuring skilled men and materials. When he was unable to get white marble from further south due to disturbed conditions, he ordered the masons to execute all ornamentation in stucco plasterwork, which he then covered with lime. This makes Aonla the precursor of the beautiful ornamental plasterwork of the late-eighteenth-century architecture of Lucknow and Faizabad.[75] Along with the physical construction of a town, it was also necessary to construct a history, and Ali Mohammad wrote histories of Aonla, other Ruhela towns, and aspects of nation-building, in a major work entitled *Hikayat-ul Uruj.*[76] The Ruhela political structure, especially its natural transition towards a confederacy, made town-building a pre-requisite to any claim to leadership by subsidiary chiefs. For example, after the death of Ali Mohammad Khan the Ruhela construction of capital towns received a fillip. His vast territories, which stretched from Amroha in the west to Shahjahanpur in the east, were divided up between his sons and his political allies, especially Hafiz Rahmat Khan and Doondey Khan. As each of these successors established themselves, they developed their own strategic towns. From among Bisauli, Pilibhit, Bareilly, Rampur and Moradabad, the most striking towns were Pilibhit and Bareilly within the jagir of Hafiz Rahmat Khan. In the words of Francklin, Bareilly in 1776 still looked 'large . . . busy and handsome. . . .'[77] Tieffenthaler, the Jesuit cartographer who surveyed this city in 1767, wrote

> Bareilly is a city in the possession of the Rohilla Afghans. Its main street is half a mile long and on it are many shops where merchants sell all manners of goods. The town is 4 miles in circumference. The houses of the rich are made of bricks . . . a river runs along its flank and it has a brick fort. The currency of the Mughal emperor is accepted here.[78]

Ghulam Husain Khan Tabatabai, author of *Saiyar al-Mutā<u>kh</u>k<u>h</u>irīn*, was also a visitor to this region and full of praise for Bareilly and calls it 'the principal city of this region'.[79] Bareilly was also famous for its military supplies, in particular its swords, its bows and arrows made by Afghan artisans, and its horses that came from Afghanistan.[80]

Pilibhit was the new capital that Hafiz Rahmat built in 1764. He chose a site lush with trees and water and built inside it a mosque according to the same design as the Shah Jahani mosque in Delhi. For building confidence and a rapport with his Hindu merchants, bankers, and peasantry, he donated all the building materials for the famous Diwanji ka Mandir that is a landmark in the city today.[81] When he was building a mud wall around his new capital he attracted a large number of migrant peasants fleeing from Maratha raids and famine around Delhi and Agra. The wall was finished but the famine still raged. In a remarkable example of resoluteness and foresight, Hafiz Rahmat ordered the wall to be covered with brickwork. This wall was 4 miles in circumference and the Hafiz thus provided sustenance to a vast body of cultivators and labourers who finished the wall and went on to more projects and finally settled down in and around Pilibhit.[82] Hafiz Rahmat had built the city in a remote part of the province to avoid Maratha raids but soon his markets were bustling and the grain carriers (Banjaras) coming to his towns because in 1764 he had ordered his officers to exempt from transit tax (*rahdari*), all those traders whose goods were bound for Bareilly or Pilibhit.[83]

Ideological intervention too was essential. Hafiz Rahmat was aware of the significance of the moment and in order to encourage national pride he wrote histories and constructed genealogies.[84] And so this Ruhela leader had bound together, via his towns as well as his texts, the most vital components of north Indian state formation: the elite, their history/genealogy and education, and a sketch of the officials, craftsmen, soldiers and peasantry. He was liked by all except for the nawab of Awadh, Shuja ud-Daulah and his East India Company allies. In April 1774, this Hafiz was forced into battle and after desperate attempts at saving his towns and avoiding war, he was killed as he charged a British artillery line.[85] After his death his territories as well as those of his allies were annexed and given over to the favourite *ijaradars* of Shuja ud-Daulah of Awadh. Within twenty years, the countryside that had been cultivated like a garden by the Ruhelas had been so fully plundered that it was nothing more than a wasteland.[86]

The others who inherited territories from Ali Mohammad Khan and built cities for themselves were Doondey Khan, and his sons Faizullah Khan, Mohammad Ali Khan, Sadullah Khan, Abdullah Khan, Mustajab Khan, to name the prominent brothers. Doondey Khan and his son built Bisauli, famous for its fort and the Nawab Doondey's palace. Faizullah Khan settled down in Rampur, which he rebuilt into his capital.

But most remarkable was the establishment of Najibabad by Najib Khan in *c.* 1760. Najib Khan had defected to the Mughal court in *c.* 1750 and rapidly risen to the highest possible rank for a mansabdar (5000 *zat* and *sawar*, the maximum for those outside the immediate family). After 1761 and the intervention of Ahmad Shah Abdali he had been given vast jagirs north-east of Delhi and the title of *Amir ul-Umara Nawab Najib ud-Daulah.* Realizing the fluidity of the situation at the Mughal court, he put down roots in the form of a town that he named Najibabad. Merchants and bankers who had once passed through Punjab along the old Kabul-Lahore-Delhi route now chose to avoid the uncertainties of that disturbed region. Thus Najibabad soon developed into a thriving entrepot where medicinal drugs from the hills, weapons from Lahore, and horses from Afghanistan would stop en route to Delhi, Rajasthan and Central India. To protect his dependents, Najib Khan built a fort about a mile from his beautiful city in which he would seek shelter whenever his town was raided either by the Marathas or by the Sikhs.[87]

Najibadad attracted house builders, traders, bankers, and refugees from the areas disturbed by Maratha raids, and this city survives to this day.[88] Najib Khan also used another technique for urban development: using his knowledge of demography derived from the experience of his nomadic past, he located a fortress between two large villages or *kasbahs* and thus catalysed the three clusters to coalesce into a town. He took up construction of Ghausgarh, equidistant between Thana Bhavan, Jalalabad, and Lohari Hasanpur. Here he settled craftsmen, soldiers, noblemen, and scholars, and laid out gardens and a mosque. Today these three settlements constitute one big town.[89]

So great was the desire to see these towns flourish that these so called 'proud and warlike' Ruhelas would pay large amounts of cash to the Marathas and the nawab of Awadh, and even send emissaries to make peace with the East India Company when they began to covet the potential of this area.[90]

Back in the main polity, Ruhela town builders were busy establishing new *kasbahs* and making them the seats of their individual power. Bisauli was chosen as it was close to Aonla, the capital of Ruhela leader Ali Mohammad Khan, and Doondey Khan's son constructed here one of the finest palaces in the region. It also had a small river, the Sita Nala, on one flank over which a bridge was constructed and mango orchards were planted all around.[91]

Bareilly, as we have seen, was revived by Hafiz Rahmat Khan. Shahjahanpur, founded a hundred years earlier by the Afghan Diler Khan, was flourishing due to its ethnic links with the Ruhelas and its location on the new trade route between Kabul, Moradabad, Bareilly and Lucknow—especially important as this route supplied horses for Awadh's military. Macpherson describes the twin cities of Katra and Shahjahanpur as 'very large with very grand buildings (Shahjahanpur was big enough to be) divided into four magisterial sub-divisions (*faujdaris*)'.[92] Macpherson also describes a small town called Ameerpur built by Amir Khan, the Ruhela adventurer who also revived the old Mughal administrative headquarters of Sambhal, and put in new buildings and court houses until he was finally exiled to Rajasthan where he was pacified with a colonial nawabi in Tonk (Rajasthan).[93]

Like Najib, the other Ruhela chiefs realized that authority would flow much more smoothly if they could acquire legitimacy in the form of a title with rights to collect tax and to maintain order. In the eyes of both peasantry and urban dwellers, the Mughal still stood above all warring factions and was the fount of all that was legitimate. In fact, Ali Mohammad Khan had sought the pardon of the emperor in 1745, and was sent off on a punishment posting as *faujdar* of Sirhind. Two years later he was given the title of *Nawab* and assigned the territories around Bareilly.[94] Soon all of them were able to acquire some form of imperial status even as the empire was breaking up.

Of the new towns that survived the break-up of Ruhela power in 1774, Rampur was the most outstanding, and Faizullah Khan opted to keep this and not any other city when he signed the Treaty of Lal Dang in 1775. Rampur lay in the foothills; it was criss-crossed by numerous river channels which the Ruhelas had linked into a network using their knowledge of hydrology from their mountain homelands. With the annual flood in the Kosi river that flowed past Rampur, their lands were enriched and they grew sugar cane, wheat, tobacco, and rice. The town had markets for grains, horses, swords, vessels, and leatherwares for the Ruhela cavalrymen who resided herein. And to protect the town there was a bamboo wall almost half a mile in breadth that grew around it.[95] This was the only town left to the Ruhelas after their defeat by Col. Champion and Shuja ud-Daulah in April 1774; and afterwards Faizullah Khan was confirmed as a disarmed and pacified nawab.[96] Rampur flourished because this was where the grief-stricken Ruhelas collected after their homes and towns had been looted. In the devastating times for which this century was famous, town building continued under inputs and interventions from the Indo-Afghan elite.

Intervention in town building is also seen amongst the Bangash Pathans of Farrukhabad and Qayamganj. These Afghan groups had come down from Afghanistan *c.* 1700 and helped the Mughals beat back the Marathas, in return for which they had been given vast territories along the Ganga in the central Doab. However, since they had come in at a time when the Mughal emperor still commanded respect, they were becoming more like the old Mughal courtiers than an entrepreneurial Afghan group. They even named their capital Farrukhabad after the Mughal Farrukhsiyar. Nonetheless, the planning and location of this town and its development into a military-cum-trade centre is a lesson in intervention.

For military efficiency they put in twenty bastions for cannons, while for trade there were twelve gates, of which seven had furnished *serais* for traders and travellers. Similarly one may look at the planning that went into the establishment of Qayamganj—a town built in honour of Nawab Qayam Khan Bangash and Mau Rashidabad, a powerful Bangash noble.[97]

These towns and armies could not have been sustained without elite intervention aimed at settling artisans in their capital towns, giving them lands to cultivate and build houses upon.[98] In response, Hafiz Rahmat Khan exempted traders from transit duties.[99] Similarly Chandausi was developed into a major centre for selling the sugar and wheat of Rohilkhand to traders from Delhi and the Doab.[100]

However, after the annexation and exploitation of Ruhela territories, first by the nawab of Awadh (1774) and then by the East India Company (1801), we see how fragile the connections between elite patronage and the economy had been. The Ruhela towns lay in a sort of stupor after the heady rise of twenty years ago. Many observers and even Company officials in Rohilkhand and the other Afghan state of Farrukhabad admit the decay that had set in after the Company's intervention. In total ignorance of the needs of the locality, the Company reintroduced transit duties in 1788; and with the emasculation of the elite and the dismantling of their armies, the famed sword and cutlery industries of Bareilly and Farrukhabad were almost dead by 1803.[101]

Conclusion

These Indo-Afghan towns were not mere stepping stones for the Afghans as they had been for the Mughal mansabdar, en route to higher rank and bigger jagir. Nor were they mere units of revenue assessment, as they became after the Company's tax settlements were fixed. They were nothing less than their *watans*, or homelands away from their original homes. The number of schools, craft workshops, mosques, bridges, wells, mango orchards; the histories and the poetry they wrote about them;[102] and the personal stamp that each founder left by personal involvement in location, investing resources, design, construction, execution, and security—all these are testimonials to the plans these mountain people had for their adopted homeland that we to this day refer to as Rohilkhand.

Insofar as elite intervention is concerned, this example may be reinforced by activities involving military techniques, agricultural incentive mongering, irrigation control,[103] and craft production.

These elite groups were thus stemming the Mughal imperial decline that was aggravated by the Maratha raids for liquid fiscal resources; knowing full well the costs of the alternatives, the Ruhelas would pay them and remain in control of their economic base. Iqbal Husain takes this bleeding to be a fatal wound, but the real affliction was more incisive.[104] When the British entered the military equation with their Subsidiary Alliance in 1773 and Awadh was pulled into a tributary relationship, only then did it become possible to take away the economic basis of Ruhela power; their territories and their cultivators; and this time the decline was terminal.

NOTES

1. See the review article that M. Athar Ali read at the Delhi session of the Indian History Congress in 1992, *Proceedings of the IHC*, 1992, *passim*. For details on the dark century theory see Irfan Habib, *Agrarian System of Mughal India* (London, 1963), 'Conclusion'. Another article on the eighteenth century by Irfan Habib, 'The Colonialization of the Indian

Economy', *Social Scientist*, No. 32, March 1975, focused on post-Diwani Bengal and the economics of tribute extraction in the late eighteenth century. A vast body of political details are found in Z.U. Malik, *The Reign of Muhammad Shah* (Bombay, 1975), and Muzaffar Alam's *The Crisis of the Mughal Empire* (Delhi, 1986). However both focus too early in the eighteenth century to be reflective of the changes in the century and socio-economic relations as a whole. More recent work on the Indo-Afghan Ruhelas, Iqbal Husain's *The Rise and Decline of the Ruhela Chieftaincies in Eighteenth Century India* (Delhi, 1994), and Jos Gommans, *Princes, Paupers, Horse Traders* (Delhi, 1994) fail to throw any new light upon the links between the elite and their technological roles. C.A. Bayly's, *Rulers, Townsmen and Bazaars* (Cambridge, 1983), is one of the few texts that have some defined views on the eighteenth century. Unfortunately, Bayly suffers from a surfeit of issues and theories while Iqbal Husain from the lack of a conclusion. The positive aspect of the books by Bayly, Alam, Wink, Malik et al. is that they have evoked serious responses from Aligarh. For example, Athar Ali, 'The Eighteenth Century—an Interpretation', *Indian Historical Review* (*IHR*), vol. XII; Irfan Habib, 'The Eighteenth Century in India's Economic History', *Proceedings of the Indian History Congress*, Mysore, 1995.

2. Rupa Roy, 'Tipu Sultan and State Formation Techniques in Mysore', Ph.D dissertation in Sociology, Harvard University, 1994. Another dissertation by S.M. Amer, 'Hayder Ali and Tipu Sultan's military modernization techniques', is under preparation under my supervision at Aligarh Muslim University.
3. I.G. Khan, *Agriculture, Warfare and the Crafts: Technical Knowledge and the Elites in Eighteenth-Century North India* (Delhi, forthcoming).
4. Athar Ali, 'The Passing of Empire—the Mughal Case', *Modern Asian Studies*, vol. IX, No. 3 (1975), pp. 385-96. A more comprehensive version is found in Athar Ali, 'The Eighteenth Century—An Interpretation'.
5. A mansabdar was a bureaucrat/military commander working for the Mughal emperor; as salary he was assigned an estate for a temporary tenure, the revenues from which went towards his salary as well as maintaining a militia as per his rank. For details see Athar Ali, *Mughal Nobility under Aurangzeb* (Delhi, rpt., 1997).
6. Note Babur's proximity to Ustad Quli, the Turkish gun-maker. Beveridge, tr., *Baburnama* (Delhi, rpt., 1970), pp. 528-9. See also the rank accorded to Fathullah Shirazi by Akbar in Nawal Kishore, ed., *Ain-i Akbari* (Lucknow, 1882), vol. I, and M.A. Alvi and A. Rahman, *Fathullah Shirazi –an Indian Scientist of the 16th Century* (Delhi). The Afghans had their own technocrats too; see the role of Sher Shah in devising better revenue systems, the development of Sasaram, the Grand Trunk Road across the Gangetic plains, the improvement in sword and metal technology. Abbas Khan Sarwani, *Tarikh-i Akbar Shahi, Waqiat-i Mushtaqi,*

Neamatullah's *Tarikh-i Khan Jahani*, and other such Afghan histories of the sixteenth-eighteenth centuries.

7. For details, see I.G. Khan, 'Metal Technology in Medieval India', in S.K. Bagchi and A.K. Ray, eds., *Technology in Ancient and Medieval India* (Delhi, 1985).
8. I.G. Khan, 'Science and Technology in the Age of Akbar', M.Phil disssertation, AMU, 1980.
9. See the full text of his outburst in Bernier, *Travels in the Mogul Empire*, ed. A. Constable (Delhi, rpt. edn., 1968), pp. 155-6. I am grateful to the late Prof. Athar Ali for drawing my attention to this incident.
10. This scholar was allotted an old haveli owned by a European trading company and thus was established the institution which is known commonly referred to as Firangi Mahal. See details on this 'school' in Francis Robinson's article in Barbara D. Metcalf, ed., *Moral Authority and Control in South Asia* (Berkeley, 1988). See comments on the British in India in 1773, in Ghulam Husain Khan Tabatabai, *Saiyar al-mutākhkhirīn*, ed. Nawal Kishore (Kanpur, 1882), pp. 841-6.
11. On the gift network in elite groups, see Marshall Sahlins, *Islands of History* (Chicago, 1985), *passim.* See also S.P. Blake, 'The Urban Economy in Precolonial North India', *Modern Asian Studies*, vol. XXI, No. 3, 1986, pp. 450-80.
12. See various *dasturs* on Mughal administration, e.g. Yar Mohammad's *Dastur ul-Insha*, pp. 250-3; also Azhar Ali, ed., *Safarnama-i Mukhlis*, p. 135.
13. See Irfan Habib, 'Akbar and Technology', in Irfan Habib, ed., *Akbar and his Age* (Delhi, 1997).
14. See details of this form of documentation in I.G. Khan, 'Changing Patterns of Authority and Control in Eighteenth-Century N. India', in John Neelson, *Gender, Power and Authority in South Asia* (Delhi, 1990). Also I.G. Khan, 'The Social Context of Technical Literature in Mughal India', presented at the Conference on Islam in South Asia, Maison de Sciences des Hommes, Paris, May 1993. The best use of this kind of literature is found in A.J. Qaisar, *Indian Response to European Technology and Culture* (Delhi, 1980). Also his *Building Construction in Mughal India* (Delhi, 1990).
15. For example, the thesis on technological indifference once formulated by Athar Ali in his seminal piece, 'The Passing of Empire—the Mughal Case'.
16. See excellent work on them by Athar Ali, *Mughal Nobility under Aurangzeb, passim*; see also his *The Apparatus of Empire* (Delhi, 1985).
17. See details in Barnett, *North India between Empires*; for the Ruhelas see Iqbal Husain, *The Rise and Decline of the Ruhela Chieftaincies in Eighteenth Century India* (Delhi, 1994), pp. 11-21, *passim.*
18. See details of what was in fact the last imperial military expedition,

against Ali Mohammad Ruhela in 1745 and the Ruhela's reaction in *Safarnama-i Mukhlis*, ed. Azhar Ali (Rampur, 1946), *passim*.

19. The causes delineated in Marshall G.S. Hodgson, *The Venture of Islam*, vol. III, *The Gunpowder Empires and Modern Times* (Chicago, 1974), were suggestions in the right direction and need to be more directly addressed by current researchers.
20. I.G. Khan, *Revenue, Agriculture and Warfare.*
21. For a definitive history of the elite therein, see Barnett, *North India between Empires*; for the earlier period, see Alam, *The Crisis of Empire in North India—Awadh and Punjab.* For studies on early-nineteenth-century Awadh see M.H. Fisher, *A Clash of Cultures: Awadh, the British, and the Mughals* (Riverdale, 1987); on the manner in which indigenous intelligence networks were appropriated by the British, see M.H. Fisher, *Indirect Rule in India: Residents and the Residency System in India, 1764-1858* (Delhi, 1991); and C.A. Bayly, *Empire and Information; Intelligence-gathering and Social Communication in India, 1780-1870* (Cambridge, 1996).
22. This region was a peripheral part of the Mughal *suba* of Delhi; fertile and held by highly respected members of the Mughal court whom the uncouth Afghans were displacing in violation of imperial law. In such instances even the dying Mughal empire struck back as it did against the Ruhelas in a massive campaign in 1745. See details in Anand Ram Mukhlis, *Safarnama-i Mukhlis*, ed. S. Azhar Ali (Rampur, 1946).
23. See the details on the Pathans, in Jean Deloche, ed., *Memoires de Wendel sur les Jats, les Pathans, et les Sikhs* (Pondicherry, 1979), pp. 113-43.
24. Moosvi, *The Economy of the Mughal Empire, c. 1598*, pp. 221-3.
25. Walter Rheinhart or Samroo, Claude Martin, Rene Madec, Gentil, De Boigne, George Thomas, to name a few. For their roles, see Rosie Llewllyn-Jones, *A Very Ingenious Man: Claude Martin in Early Colonial India* (Delhi, 1994).
26. Andrew Jamison, 'Technology's Theorists', *Technology and Culture*, XXX: 3 (July 1989), p. 505.
27. Both these works have been translated and the drawings beautifully reproduced by Donald R. Hill. See his *The Book of Knowledge of Ingenious Mechanical Devices* [an annotated translation of Al Jazzari's work] (Dordrecht: Reidel, 1974).
28. Joseph Needham, *Science and Civilization in China*, vols. I-VII.
29. See drawings and explanations in Needham; also the excellent reproductions in D.R. Hill's translations of the works by the Banu Musa and Al Jazzari. For an idea of the spread of these machines to India, see a remarkable description of a toy in Akbar's court, in Elliot and Dowson, eds., *The History of India as Told by its own Historians* (London, 1867-77), vol. VI, p. 192.

30. M. Athar Ali, 'The Passing of Empire—the Mughal Case', pp. 385-96.
31. Paper read at the Conference 'Akbar and his Age', sponsored by the ICHR, AMU, 9-11 October 1992. Now published as Irfan Habib, ed., *Akbar and his Age* (Delhi, 1997).
32. Compare M.A. Alvi and A. Rahman, *Shah Fat'hullah Shirazi—a Scientist of the 16th Century* (Delhi, 1968).
33. On the town in Islamic civilizations, see special issue of *Environment Design*, vol. 2, Rome, 1989, with the theme, 'The Islamic City as a Garden'.
34. M.A. Alvi, Rahman, Verma, and Ghori et al., *Science and Technology in Medieval India—A Survey of Persian, Arabic and Sanskrit Manuscripts* (Delhi, 1980). See also I.G. Khan, 'The Social Context of Mughal Technical Literature, 1500-1750'. Paper read at the Conference on Persian Sources on India, MSH, Paris, April 1993. Another excellent source is the more general C.A. Storey's *Persian Literature—A Bio-bibliographical Survey*, as well as Ethé's and Rieu's *Catalogue of Persian Manuscripts* in the India Office Library and the British Museum, respectively. See also D.N. Marshall, *The Mughals in India: A Bibliographical Survey*, vol. 1, *Manuscripts* (Bombay, 1963)
35. See Charles Stewart, *Memoirs of Hyder Aly Khan and his son Tipoo Sultan* (in a descriptive catalogue of the oriental library of the late Tipu Sultan), Cambridge, 1809. For the Afghan chief's books there was simply a handlist made by Sprenger, now kept in the India Office Library. Half of these books were lost because they had been dumped in the armoury in Lucknow in 1775.
36. See proceedings of the conferences convened by A.R. Bedar, Director, KBOPL, Patna, on Manuscript Collections on Science and Technology across South Asia, Patna, 1990.
37. I.A. Arshi, *Catalogue of Arabic Manuscripts in the Raza Library*, Rampur. This rich collection is now once again freely accessible to all researchers after a long period of restrictions.
38. Abdul Latif Khan Shustari, *Tuhfat ul-Alam*, pp. 340-50.
39. See drawing in Isami, *Tarikh-i Firoz Shahi*.
40. Edited by Iraj Afshar, Tehran, 1314 H. Solar.
41. Abul Fazl, pp. 22-40.
42. See A.J. Qaisar, *Indian Response to European Technology and Culture* (Delhi, 1980), and A.J. Qaisar, *Building Construction in Mughal India* (Delhi, 1990).
43. In Europe too the German principality of Hesse Kassel had a prince who would insist on better finishing and accuracy in the brass sextants and telescopes his craftsmen made. B.T. Moran, 'German Prince Practitioners: Aspects of the Development of a Courtly Science, Technology and Procedures in the Renaissance', *Technology and Culture*, No. 22, pp. 253-74.

44. *Ain-i Akbari,* ed. Blochmann, I, p. 101; Irfan Habib, 'Akbar and Technology', in Habib, ed., *Akbar and his Age,* cites Persian and Jesuit sources to demonstrate that Akbar was not merely dabbling in the crafts but actually directing a number of changes in military technology, weaving techniques, dying, and architecture.
45. *Ain-i Akbari,* ed. Nawal Kishore, I, p. 27.
46. *Ain-i Akbari,* ed. Blochmann, I, p. 126. Compare description and translation of this passage by Irfan Habib, 'Akbar and Technology' with that in Alvi and Rahman, *Fat'hullah Shirazi.*
47. Geeti Sen, *Paintings from the Akbar Nama,* 1984. Also Irfan Habib, 'Akbar and Technology', pp. 12-15.
48. Alvi and Rahman, *Fat'hullah Shirazi.*
49. See details in Alvi and Rahman, *Jahangir the Naturalist* (Delhi, 1970), *passim.*
50. Jamaluddin Inju, *Farhang-i Jahangiri,* Ms. AMU, Azad Library, is a technical dictionary. Then there are the numerous *Dastur-ul Amals* scattered all over the world in different collections, which tell the reader ways of measuring land, applying tax rates, and sowing different crops; other memoirs focus on the re-excavation of canals and the building of bridges; some have information on military organization as well.
51. See *Biyaz of Nawab Mureed Khan,* SP 318, Bibliotheque Nationale; the *Biyaz of Shah Mirza,* Ms. No. Ethe 412, IOLR; the *Biyaz-i Khushbui,* Ms. 828, IOLR.
52. See *Dastur ul-Amal,* Ms. Or. 1771, IOLR. See also *Khazanat ul-'ilm,* Habibganj Collection 45/11, AMU, as well as *Mukhtasar al-Mufid,* Ms. No. 892, Khuda Bakhsh Oriental Public Library, Patna.
53. Mohammad Habib, 'The Urban Revolution', in M. Habib and K.A. Nizami, eds., *The Comprehensive History of India,* vol. V.
54. Sh. Abdur Rasheed, ed., *Tarikh-i Da'udi,* with English summary by I.H. Siddiqui (Aligarh, 1969); Neamatullah's *Makhzan-i Afaghina* or *History of the Afghans,* tr. by Bernard Dorn (London, 1965).
55. Athar Ali, *The Apparatus of Empire,* Introduction; Ibn Hasan, *The Central Structure of the Mughal Empire*; Irfan Habib, *Agrarian System*; S. Moosvi, *The Economy of the Mughal Empire.*
56. M. Afzal Khan, 'The Mughal Elite, their Building Activities and Cultural Values . . .', *Art and Culture* (Aligarh, 1993), I, pp. 133-41.
57. Moosvi, *Economy of the Mughal Empire,* pp. 221-3.
58. See the politicking that went on even as the allies went after Ali Mohammad Khan, in *Safarnama i Mukhlis,* ed. Azhar Ali (Rampur, 1946).
59. Irvine, 'The Bangash Nawabs of Farrukhabad', *JASB,* vol. 47.
60. Abbas Khan Sarwani, *Tarikh i Sher Shahi,* tr. Ambasthaya, p. 787. He refers to the two as the 'Afghans from Roh' and the 'Afghans from Hind'. On the military identity of the Afghan or the Pathan, see Dirk

Kolff, *Naukar, Rajput and Sepoy: an ethnohistory of the military labour market in Hindustan, 1450-1850* (Cambridge, 1990), pp. 35-40.

61. Neamatullah's *Tarikh-i Afghani*, tr. Dorn (London, 1965), pp. 45-7.
62. Rosenthal, tr., *Muqaddimah* (London: Routledge, 1974). I am grateful to Miriam Cooke of Duke University for this reference.
63. John B. Thompson, *Studies in the Theory of Ideology* (Berkeley, 1984), pp. 55-7. It would be interesting in the light of this theory to look at the severe uncertainty that followed the death of almost every Great Mughal; and then after a war of succession, the total loyalty that the incumbent came to command.
64. Jos Gommans, *Horse-traders, Mercenaries, and Princes: the Formation of the Indo-Afghan Empire in the Eighteenth Century* (Delhi, 1996).
65. Ghulam Husain Khan Tabatabai, *Saiyar al-mutākhkhirīn*, tr. Nota Manus, vol. II, pp. 522-3.
66. *Calendar of Persian Correspondence* (Calcutta, 1911), vol. I, No. 2783. For more contextual information, see Husain, *The Rise and Decline of the Ruhela Chieftaincies*, pp. 120-7, *passim*.
67. The army of Awadh was an exercise in military innovation. Many Mughal soldiers left Delhi and joined the showpiece regiments that attracted even soldiers from Ahmad Shah Abdali's armies because of the good salaries and the uniforms and reliable firearms that the nawabs of Awadh were lavishing on them. See I.G. Khan, 'Revenue, Agriculture and Warfare', Ph.D. dissertation, SOAS, 1990.
68. Gavin Hambly, 'The Urban Centres', in *Cambridge Economic History of India* or *CEHI*, I, pp. 441-51; J.F. Richards, *The Mughal Empire*, New Cambridge History of India or NCHI, vol. I (5) pp. 62-7; H.K. Naqvi, *Urban Centres and Industries in Mughal Hindustan* (London, 1972); S.C. Misra, 'Urban History in India', in Grewal and Banga, eds., *The City in Indian History* (Delhi, 1991), pp. 1-7. On the concept of the Urban Revolution in the thirteenth century, see Mohd. Habib, in *Comprehensive History of India*, vol. V, *passim*.
69. Sh. A. Rashid, ed., *Tarikh-i Daudi* of Abdullah; B. Dorn, tr. Neamatullah's *Tarikh-i Afghani* or *The History of the Afghans* (London, 1965).
70. A.L. Srivastava, *Sher Shah and his Successors* (Agra, 1950), pp. 90-2; Catherine Asher, *Architecture of Mughal India*, New Cambridge History of India (Cambridge, 1992).
71. Ghulam Husain Khan Tabatabai, *Saiyar al-mutākhkhirīn*,, tr. Nota Manus, III.
72. *Tarikh-i Ruhela*, JNU, Persian Ms. Collection, ff. 12-15.
73. In Waliullah, *Tarikh-i Farrukhabad*, this verse is inscribed over the entrance of a mosque in Farrukhabad.
74 William Francklin, *History of the Reign of Shah-Aulum* (London: Cooper and Graham, 1798).
75. See especially the mausoleum of Bahu Begum, the mother of Asaf ud-

Daulah. See also Rosie Llewellyn-Jones, *A Fatal Friendship* (Delhi, 1980), *passim*.

76. Bound up with *Hadiqat-ul Aqalim*, Bibliotheque Nationale, Paris, Ms. No. SP 362A. This set off a series of such personality-projecting texts such as *Amir ut-Tawarikh* for Ameer Khan of Tonk; *Tarikh-i Najibabad* for Najib ud-Daulah, as well the famous *Ausaf-i Asaf* by one Lalji who wrote for Asaf ud-Daulah.
77. Francklin, *Shah-Aulum*, pp. 58-9.
78. Tieffenthaler, *Memoirs* . . ., tr. Bernoulli, vol. I, p. 136.
79. *Siyar*, III, p. 270.
80. Report by Intelligence Officer in Home Misc. 776, IOLR.
81. See drawing by the Daniells in Mildred Archer, *Early Views of India*, (London, 1980), Plate X (56); see discussion in Mustajab Khan, *Gulistan-i Rahmat*, Ms. copy, 106 or tr. C.H. Elliot (London, 1838).
82. Francklin, *Shah-Aulum*, p. 59; Elliot, tr. *Gulistan-i Rahmat*, p. 51; see also Pargana Reports in Urdu, Ms. U27, IOLR.
83. Mustajab Khan, *Gulistan*, pp. 39-40.
84. See his *Khulasat ul-Ansab*, Cambridge Univ., Central Library Ms. Also see Maulana Azad Library, Aligarh Ms. No. AS 146. Also see *Tavarikh-i Hafiz Rehmat Khan* of Muazzam Shah, ed. Roshan Khan (Peshawar, 1969), in which there is no glorification of the Hafiz, but of a sixteenth-century Ruhela hero.
85. *Gulistan-i Rahmat*, IOLR Ms., *passim*.
86. Compare descriptions in Franklin with the later travellers such as Foster, *Journey from Bengal to Britain*, or Twining's *Travels* . . ., or Bishop Heber's *Narrative of a Journey*. See also *Tarikh-i Rampur*, Ms. No. AS 173/39, and *Tarikh-i Farah Bakhsh*, Ms. No. 172, Azad Library, Aligarh.
87. Nuruddin, *Tarikh-i Najeeb ud Daulah*, Ms. 24410, IOLR; Abdus Salam, *Asnad-i Musawwidat Tarikh-i Najibabad*, Ms. Collection of documents and notes in Azad Library, AMU. For an English translation see S.A. Rashid, *The Life and Times of Najib ud Daulah* (Aligarh, n.d.).
88. For a sketch of this town and a description of the trade activity in the diaries of the Daniell brothers, see Mildred Archer, *Early Views of India* (London, 1980). See also observations by Forster, I, pp. 137-49.
89. See details on Ghausgarh in *Asnad*, Ms. in MAL, AMU.
90. On British-Ruhela relations, see Iqbal Husain, pp. 210-12.
91. *Tarikh-i Nawab Doondey Khan*; Macpherson, *Soldiering in India*, pp. 126-7.
92. Macpherson, p. 129.
93. *Ameer ut-Tawarikh*, Ms. AMU, ff. 150-2.
94. Anand Ram, *Safarnama-i Mukhlis*, ed. S. Azhar Ali (Rampur, 1946).
95. *Tarikh-i Farah Bakhsh of Shiv Prasad*; Wendel, *Memoirs sur les Pathans, les Jats et les Sikhs*, ed. Jean Deloche (Paris, 1976); also Francklin, *Shah-Aulum*.

96. See details of this treaty in Aitchison, *Treaties and Sunnuds*, vol. I.
97. Waliullah's *Tarkikh-i Farukhabad*, tr. William Irvine (Fatehgarh, 1887), pp. 32-40.
98. Hasanpur and Moradabad markets were rent-free for craftsmen wishing to sell their goods. Thompson, *Bulandshahr Settlement Report*, (Allahabad, 1871), p. 116.
99. *Gulistan-i Rahmat, passim.*
100. Smith, 'Report on Trade in Turaee [Terai]', *Selections from the Records of Revenue*, see also Barlowe, *Report on the Trade in Oudh*, FDSC, p. 3269, NAI, Delhi.
101. Farrukhabad Magistrate's Report, *Home Misc.* 776, pp. 1205-6, IOLR, 27 Oct. 1814.
102. See history and poetry in praise of Sambhal in *Ameer ut-Tawarikh*, Ms. 192/58, MAL, f. 21. See also *Tarikh-i Rampur*, Ms. No. AS 173/79, MAL, Aligarh; see also titles of local histories such as *Tarikh-i Farah Bakhsh-i Rampur* of Munshi Shiv Prasad, Ms. copy, MAL, AMU; for the other Afghan group see Waliullah's *Tarikh- i Farrukhabad, Nawaban-i Bangash* (Fatehgarh, 1887).
103. Two Afghan engineers, under Bhopal's Diwan Chhotey Khan, built a dam in the 1790s, which produced the famed Lower Lake of Bhopal, 1 km wide at its widest point. This dam, which also serves as a bridge, has survived without major repairs for the last 200 years. Richard B. Barnett, personal communication.
104. Husain, *The Rise and Decline of the Ruhela Chieftaincies*, pp. 168-94. But see his sections on towns and agriculture for a different corpus of evidence.

Amanat's *Indar Sabha* and Nineteenth-Century Constructions of Indian Cultural Identity

AFROZ TAJ

THE FIRST performance of Syed Agha Hasan Amanat's poetic drama *Indar Sabha* (The Court of Indra) in 1854 in Lucknow was a watershed event. Not only did Amanat's play became unprecedentedly popular, imitated almost as widely as it was performed across the country, but *Indar Sabha* founded a whole new genre of Indian drama, and almost single-handedly brought about a revolution in the popular taste; its legacy is apparent well into the twentieth century. This paper speculates on the causes of this phenomenon; a textual and thematic analysis of the play is attempted, with reference to the social and historical context. This analysis suggests that it was precisely Amanat's inspired conflation of Hindu and Indo-Persian Islamic elements—at multiple levels—that appealed to the broadest possible spectrum of Indian audiences. Moreover, it is no coincidence that the play appeared on the eve of the British annexation of Awadh and the Mutiny and its subsequent repression; indeed, there is a direct correlation between the consolidation of British power and the popularity of the play.

The first edition of *Indar Sabha* was published in Kanpur in 1853; the 1870s saw the publication of at least thirty-three editions in many of the major cities of India. The play was produced by the fledgling Parsi Theatre of Bombay in 1864, and we have records of many productions thereafter not only in most of the major cities, and as far away as Singapore and Mandalay.[1] Countless imitations were spawned, named *Indar Sabha,* or with the word '*sabha*' in the title. Inevitably, in 1932 a film version was made in Bombay; it had an amazing seventy-one musical numbers, most of which were taken from Amanat's text.

Some of the play's popularity can be explained by its novelty. *Indar Sabha* was the first literary work for the theatre since the great Sanskrit dramas of more than a thousand years before. Over the centuries Indian theatrical life had become fragmented into a variety of folk, court, and devotional genres, none of which placed emphasis on drama as literary composition. Amanat drew upon these prior forms, but *Indar Sabha* is a radical departure from its antecedents in its emphasis on the literary text.

Moreover, through its propagation in the Parsi Theatre, *Indar Sabha* became the archetype of the modern mode of theatrical production. The fact that it was performed by professional drama companies in public theatre buildings distinguishes *Indar Sabha* from its court and ceremonial predecessors, which were rarely if ever performed outside of the venues for which they were created. *Indar Sabha* also inspired, and continued to participate in, the synthesis of court and folk theatre genres, giving birth to a new theatre of the middle class. The emergence of an audience for Amanat's play in turn reflects the deeper social, political and economic changes occurring in India in the nineteenth century.

What was it about this play, ostensibly a product of the allegedly decadent, escapist literary and cultural environment of Wajid Ali Shah's Lucknow, that captured the attention of theatre audiences? I will argue that the play, with its fantastic hodgepodge of characters, forms, and themes from Indo-Persian and classical Hindu sources, struck a resonant chord in the minds of a nation coming to terms with colonial occupation. The very disunity and diversity of Indian society permeates *Indar Sabha* and, through it, informs the ongoing construction of Indian cultural identity, founded on the image of a glorious, mythical—and pre-colonial—past.

Carla Petievich has analysed, within three centuries of Urdu literature, the construction of this 'mythic past'.[2] Significantly, this construction of Indian cultural history, obsessed as it was with the notion of lost Mughal glory, placed its primary emphasis on the culture of the social and intellectual Muslim and Islamized ruling elites. I would argue that Amanat participated in a transformation of this construction into a broader and more inclusive one. Specifically, *Indar Sabha* carries the mythic past beyond the ruling Islamicate elite to encompass a wider cultural and religious mix, and in so doing, contributes to the emerging notion of a national identity constructed of *complementary* Hindu and Indo-Persian Islamic elements.

We begin by looking closely at the text of *Indar Sabha*, tracing how the peculiar genius of Amanat, stimulated by the extravagant heterogeneous culture of Lucknow, created a work of drama that combined five diverse traditions. These five elements that provide the framework for our analysis are: The Urdu literary tradition, e.g. the *masnavi*, *ghazal*, and *dastan* genres; the north Indian folk theatre tradition (*svang* and *nautanki*); Hindu devotional theatre and dance; classical Sanskrit drama; and Wajid Ali Shah's court theatre.

With the exception of the last, itself a hybrid form, these elements differ from each other in marked ways. First, Urdu literature and classical Sanskrit drama were the province of the relatively well-educated noble or priestly classes, while the secular and religious folk theatre was essentially popular in character. Second, the Urdu and Sanskrit traditions are strongly literature-based, while the folk genres are fundamentally oral. Third, the Urdu tradition, with its Persian and Arabic models, demonstrates the influences of orthodox Islam's proscription of music and stage drama, while the other strands are more closely tied to Hinduism and the Hindu love of the play.

Amanat created a viable hybrid out of the Hindu dramatic forms and the non-dramatic Urdu models; behind his conception was a long tradition of cross-fertilization between indigenous Indian cultures and imported Persian-Islamic forms. Indeed, the 'Islamicization' of Indian culture was simultaneously an 'Indianization' of Islamic culture, that began with the advent of Islam in South Asia, nurtured by generations of poets, saints and scholars, exploded finally came into dramatic flower with *Indar Sabha*.

Our analysis of *Indar Sabha* will treat the following aspects: formal structure and poetics, plot, characters, and links to other genres.[3] The translations of passages from the play are mine.

Dramatis Personae

RAJA INDAR: king of the magical realm of Sangaldeep, identified with the Vedic god Indra.

THE *PARIS* (FAIRIES): female supernatural beings, dancers and singers, named after colours or gemstones:

Sabz Pari, the Green Fairy, heroine of the drama
Pukhraj Pari, the Topaz Fairy
Lal Pari, the Red or Ruby Fairy
Neelam Pari, the Blue or Sapphire Fairy

PRINCE GULFAM: young prince of Akhtarnagar, a city in Hindustan, the only human being in the play.

THE *DEVS*: male supernatural beings, also named after colours, each possessing particular powers and abilities.

Synopsis

Indar, Lord of Sangaldeep, desires to arrange a gathering of the court to watch a concert of dance, poetry, and song. He commands each of his court dancers, the fairies, to present a *mujra* (individual dance with song) before him. Obediently, Pukhraj Pari, Neelam Pari, and Lal Pari dance in succession before him, singing poetry in a variety of modes and styles. Then comes the turn of Sabz Pari (the Green Fairy), but before she can begin, King Indar falls asleep.

The disappointed fairy goes out into a nearby garden, where she meets Kala Dev (the Black Dev). She falls into conversation with him, and describes how on her way to Indar's court, she passed by a beautiful prince, asleep on the terrace of the Lal Mahal (Red Palace) of Akhtarnagar. She tells Kala Dev how she immediately fell in love with the prince heart and soul, and having descended to the terrace, showered him with kisses. Beforc leaving, she had slipped on the prince's finger her emerald-studded ring as a token of her love. Sabz Pari then orders Kala Dev to go and fetch the prince and bring him to Indar's garden. According to her wishes, Kala Dev flies off and soon delivers the still-sleeping prince to Sabz Pari.

Sabz Pari then awakens the prince. When he opens his eyes, he is surprised and disturbed to find himself in a wonderful garden with an unknown woman. Sabz Pari attempts to soothe him, and to charm him with her beauty. She asks him his name, and to what land he belongs. He replies that he is Prince Gulfam of Hindustan, and asks in turn who she is. She reveals that she is Sabz Pari, a dancer in the court of Raja Indar, and moreover, that she is his lover,[4] and has had him abducted. She goes on to express her love for him, but Prince Gulfam is angry at being abducted. He is curious, however, to see Raja Indar's legendary *akhara* (troupe of dancers), and in the end, he promises to love—and make love to—Sabz Pari on the condition that she show him the dances of the fairies in the court. Sabz Pari warns him of the perils of his request, since human beings are forbidden to enter the court of Indar. The prince is not intimidated, and instead, threatens to cut his own throat if she does not comply.

Thus compelled, Sabz Pari brings the prince into the court and conceals him behind a tree. She goes off to resume her performance, but unfortunately, Lal Dev, wandering around the perimeter of the court, discovers Prince Gulfam and, alarmed, bears the news of his presence to Raja Indar. The king is furious and orders Lal Dev to apprehend the intruding human being and bring him before his throne.

Upon questioning the prince, Raja Indar discovers that he has been brought to the court on the orders of Sabz Pari. In a terrible rage, he orders Prince Gulfam to be cast out of the court and imprisoned in a deep well in the Koh-e-Qaf (the Caucasus). Raja Indar then sends for Sabz Pari. She is publicly humiliated, her hair shorn, and her wings clipped. She too is then expelled from the court of Indar.

Sabz Pari, still deeply in love with Gulfam, wanders Fairyland in search of him in the guise of a *jogan*. One day it happens that her old friend Kala Dev hears her mournful singing. Impressed by the beauty of her face and song, the sympathetic Dev goes to Raja Indar with the tale of the most beautiful *jogan* he has ever seen, whose voice is unmatched by any in Fairyland. The king becomes curious and expresses his desire to meet the lovely *jogan* and hear her song. On his order, Kala Dev brings the *jogan* to him.

The *jogan* agrees to sing for the raja, on the condition that if his heart is truly touched, he will grant her anything she asks. Raja Indar agrees, and she begins her song. The song is so filled with sadness and yearning that the king is deeply moved. He offers her *paan* as her reward, which she ignores. After two additional songs, Raja Indar offers her a garland, and a large shawl, both of which she also refuses. Finally, Raja Indar consents to give her whatever she asks. She sings one more song, in which she describes her pain at being separated from Prince Gulfam. Raja Indar then recognizes her, but he is bound by his promise. He sends Lal Dev to deliver Gulfam from the well, and orders that he be reunited with Sabz Pari. When the prince and Sabz Pari are at last in each other's arms, the other Fairies join together in a congratulatory chorus.

Formal Structure and Poetics

The text of *Indar Sabha* takes the form of a series of songs, interspersed with introductory stanzas (*chhands*), and dialogue either in couplets, in the *nautanki*-derived *chaubola* metre, or in *dastan*-style rhyming prose. The play contains 8 songs (*geet*) in a variety of folk genres, 30 *ghazals* or hybrid songs in *ghazal* form, 8 semi-classical romantic songs (*thumri*), 5 *chhands,* and 169 couplets of dialogue. Amanat has provided titles for each song indicating its genre and in many cases its intended *dhun* or *raga.*

The *geet* comprise a collection of the various lighter styles popular in Amanat's Awadh, each representing a particular mood, situation, or season. These include *basant, hori,* and *sawan.* The *basant* is a spring song, concerned primarily with the joy of blossoming youth and, in many examples, the first stirrings of sexual desire. It usually portrays a young woman impatiently getting ready to meet her lover. The *basant's* images are the blooming garden, and the opening, fragrant flower.

The *hori* likewise is a spring song, typically concerning the flirtatious love-play occurring during the Hindu festival of Holi, when people flock into the streets and throw colours on each other in celebration of the arrival of spring and the new year. A *hori* is a very sensuous song, in which the woman disingenuously bewails her compromised modesty after being drenched with coloured water by a mischievous lover. This genre also has Dionysian elements; the Holi festival is a popular excuse for drinking to excess. Many *horis* are in Braj style, which links them to Mathura where Krishna used to dance and flirt with his *gopis.* The following excerpt from a *hori* sung by Lal Pari is representative of both the theme and the language of *Indar Sabha's horis*:

لاج رکھو سے شیام ہماری میں چیری ہوں تمہاری
جرادے سمجھ کر گاری
انترہ
عبیر گلال نہ مو پر ڈارو نہ مارو پچکاری
آدھی دیہنر سب دیکھ پڑے گی ساری بھجو نہ ساری
کہیں گے لوگ متواری

O Shyam [Krishna as beloved], preserve my modesty
I am your disciple.
Beware if you swear at me!
Don't throw *abeer* and *gulal* colours on me!
Don't spray me with the coloured water from your syringe!
[If you do,] half of my body will become visible.
Don't wet my whole sari!
People will think that I'm crazy. . . .[5]

In contrast, the *sawan* concerns the onset of the monsoon, and the intensified longing of a woman for her absent lover. The *sawan* is thus closely identified with the Hindu 'bhakti' tradition, in which the human soul plays the role of the woman, yearning for her absent beloved, God. *Sawan* is the fifth month of the Hindu calendar; its heavy rains are occasions for young women to play outside on swings, enjoying cool relief after the long, hot summer. The following, sung by Lal Pari, is a good example of the *sawan's* style and content:

بن پیا گھٹا نہیں بھاوے
رہ رہ دل روندھو آوے بجری کی چمک ترپاوے ڈراوے

Without my beloved, the monsoon clouds don't please me;
Again and again my heart wants to cry.
The lightning makes me restless and frightens me. . . .[6]

Thumris are semi-classical songs, generally on romantic or Hindu devotional themes. In *Indar Sabha,* the *thumris* are distinguished from *ghazals* chiefly by their preference for Braj or Awadhi Hindi vocabulary over the more Persianized Urdu.

One important feature of classical Sanskrit drama was its incorporation of different dialects to distinguish characters of differing backgrounds and to add linguistic variety. This practice had been continued over the centuries in the *svang–nautanki* tradition, and Amanat availed himself of this tradition in *Indar Sabha.* Thus while the dialogues and *ghazals* of the drama are in Persianized Urdu, many of the *geet* are in Braj Bhasha, a Western Hindi dialect centred on Krishna's birthplace at Mathura or Awadhi Hindi, the dialect found around Lucknow.

Indar Sabha contains thirty songs in *ghazal* form, representative of the Indo-Persian poetic tradition. One of the chief distinguishing characteristics of the *ghazal,* problematic in a dramatic narrative, is that while all of its couplets share a common metre and rhyme, they are not normally related in meaning. In the play, and in general when a *ghazal* is performed as a song, it is customary to repeat some or all of the first couplet as a refrain; this repetition in combination with the consistent rhyme and metre supplies the formal continuity between the thematically unrelated couplets.

Amanat's hybrid songs in *ghazal* form differ from true *ghazals* in that they exhibit greater thematic continuity, use less Persianized Urdu vocabulary, and depend less on traditional *ghazal* images and themes. In *Indar Sabha,* Amanat displays a strong preference for the *ghazal* form; most of the songs in the drama follow the *ghazal* rhyme scheme, although many appear under the headings of *thumri, hori,* etc.

Ghazals, according to custom, concentrate on the complaints of a scorned lover and his appeals to his cruel beloved for mercy. The tone is markedly different from that of folk songs. Whereas folk songs are concerned with specific seasons and weather, and portray the straightforward lives and loves of rural people, the *ghazal* carries us into the sophisticated world of palace intrigues and surreptitious flirtations. The language of the *ghazal* is in general highly elaborate, with multiple layers of symbolism and double meanings. By tradition, the majority of folk songs and *thumris* are sung from the woman's point of view; in them the woman openly declares her love and longing for reunion with her beloved and it is clearly only a matter of time before her desires will be fulfilled. In contrast, the *ghazal*, even when sung by a woman, portrays the frustrated love of a man for an unattainable beloved, a man who despairs of ever winning his beloved's favours. The folk songs are sensual but innocent and direct, while the *ghazals* cloak their sometimes vulgar innuendoes in artificial and hyper-sophisticated language.

The language used in the *ghazals* in *Indar Sabha* follows all of the conventions of Urdu poetry. For example, in accordance with the well-established *ghazal* tradition, the female fairies, when singing *ghazals*, employ the masculine gender for both themselves and for the beloved. The *ghazal* tradition requires this no matter what the gender of the poet/reciter or the beloved may actually be.

Moreover, Amanat's style is characterized by a prodigal employment of all of the devices associated with the Lucknow style of literary Urdu. Foremost among these is *riyaet*, which was Amanat's special forte. *Riyaet* is the device of incorporating a set of related words into a single couplet or stanza, thereby setting up an impressive sequence of semantic correspondences often incidental to the underlying meaning of the poetry. *Riyaet* permeates *Indar Sabha*, and is one of its distinguishing features; typical examples can be found in the introductory songs of the *Paris*, where Amanat exploits the many symbolic connotations of each fairy's respective colour.

Other typical Lucknavite devices used by Amanat are the inclusion of exotic and difficult-to-rhyme *radeef* and *qafiya* combinations, the pursuit of novel metaphors (*takhayyul*), and a marked sensuality.

In addition to the large-scale alternations of poetic voice between the Persian *ghazal* and indigenous folk styles, there are many examples of linguistic variation within pieces and even within couplets, where Amanat's passion for *riyaet* inspires him to employ the richest possible verbal palate, juxtaposing words from regional dialects of Hindi, Persian and

Arabic. The following couplet is a typical example:

بوسہ جو مانگا چشم کا کیا قہر ہو گیا   مجھ پر نہ عین بزم میں آنکھیں نکالیے

When I asked for the kiss of your eye, what a disaster it was!
Please don't glare at me in the midst [eye] of the gathering![7]

A translation of this couplet cannot capture the delightful word play of the original. Three different words meaning 'eye' are used: the poet asks for a kiss from his beloved's Persian *'chashm'*; she responds by glaring, or literally showing him her Hindi *'ankh'*; and this all happens in the Arabic *'a'in'* or central 'eye' of the gathering.

At a higher level of structure, *Indar Sabha* consists of a linked sequence of *mujras.* The *mujra* was the standard format for a concert performance of a courtesan or dancer, consisting of an entrance with introductory stanzas and verses, followed by a set of songs in a variety of styles and genres. In keeping with this format, nearly all of the songs, both instrumental and incidental to the plot, are sung by women. Prince Gulfam is the only male character who has any musical items: two songs and a final duet with Sabz Pari.

The order of performance of the song genres in each fairy's set demonstrates that Amanat compartmentalized the various forms employed; this probably reflects standard contemporary performance practice. Each fairy sings a sequence of songs as given in Table 1.

As Table 1 demonstrates, Amanat consistently saves the pure *ghazals* for last in each character's set. There is a clear progression from the light *thumris,* through the folk songs and hybrids, culminating in a grand finale of *ghazals,* in which Amanat gives his characters the poetic fireworks to dazzle the audience.

Even in the dramatic pieces, Amanat adheres to the Urdu poetic convention of incorporating one of his two pen names, 'Amanat' or 'Ustaad', into the *maqta* (final couplet) of a *ghazal* or song. There is an interesting pattern in Amanat's *maqtas*: he uses the *takhallus* 'Amanat' almost exclusively in the *ghazals,* the exceptions being the three *ghazals* (Prince Gulfam's and the

TABLE 1

Pukhraj Pari	Neelam Pari	Lal Pari	Sabz Pari	*Jogan* in Paristan	*Jogan* before Raja Indar
sher-khwani	*sher-khwani*	*sher-khwani*	*sher-khwani*	—	—
chhand	*chhand* (2)	*chhand*	*chhand*	—	—
thumri	*thumri*	*thumri*	*thumris* (2)	*thumris* (2)	*thumri*
basant		*sawan,*			
basant ghazal,	*hori*	*sawan ghazal,*	—	—	*hori*
hori		*hori*	—		—
ghazals (3)	*ghazals* (3)	*ghazals* (3)	*ghazals* (3)	*ghazals* (2)	*ghazals* (2)

jogan's two), with narrative significance in which the *takhallus* 'Ustad' appears. Otherwise, 'Ustad' is used in the concluding couplet of the *geet, thumris,* and hybrid songs. This pattern evinces a generic distinction in Amanat's mind between the *ghazal* and the folk-style song.

One of the most important features of *Indar Sabha* is the predominant role of music; indeed, the play could be called a music drama, or an Urdu opera. The play combines the *kathak* or story-telling dance genre with the *mahfil,* or music-poetry recital, the devotional dance-plays or *lilas* of Hindu tradition, and the *svang/nautanki* folk theatre form, all of which are traditionally accompanied by music.

The various music-drama paradigms are in themselves linked; *kathak* dance, in which the singer is required to interpret her song simultaneously through dance and gestures, originated in the ancient practice of a solo dancer acting out episodes from Hindu mythology set to music. The name '*kathak*' itself has the connotations of 'story-teller'. Under Mughal, and later Awadhi, patronage, the *kathak* dancers were encouraged to portray romantic scenarios as well as religious episodes.[8] The folk theatre too, with its numerous songs and dances, is derived from older dance-drama genres; incidentally, this legacy is preserved in the modern Indian cinema, where the characters simultaneously sing and dance their way through every film.

The opening sequence of *Indar Sabha* is thus a reproduction of a court *mahfil* or concert. The *mahfil* form has a Hindu devotional subtext, evincing the *mahfil's* descent from ancient Hindu temple dancing, which stems from the identification of the ruler-patron with the invoked deity, a symbolic conflation well established in the Indian synthetic tradition. Performing arts in the Hindu classical tradition had always been associated with devotional contexts, and when the courts of the nawabs and maharajas replaced the Hindu temples as loci of patronage, the conflation of patron with deity was inevitable. It is in the opening songs that the influence of Hindu devotional dance drama is most evident; indeed, many of the opening numbers are folk or semi-classical songs with themes derived from the devotional song and drama genres of Hindu tradition, representing the ambiguous love-devotion relation between the singer-lover and the God-beloved.

Plot Sources

The plot of *Indar Sabha* and many of its devices, borrowed from both the Indo-Persian *dastan/masnavi* tradition and Hindu mythological sources, likewise reveal the play's hybrid character. The *dastan,* similar in structure and theme to the Western chivalric romance, is a lengthy prose chronicle, while the *masnavi,* in contrast, is a shorter tale in poetic form, relating in a more concise fashion the joys and tribulations of the lover and his beloved.

One of the most popular Persian *dastans,* and one of the longest, was the *Dastan-e-Amir Hamzah,* which reached India sometime before the late fifteenth century and probably much earlier.[9] At the heart of this lengthy *dastan* is a long episode in which the hero, Amir Hamzah, is detained in the fairy kingdom in Qaf, the Caucasus, where he fights rebellious *Devs* and resists the advances of the fairy king's daughter, Asman Pari (the Sky Fairy).

There are a number of plot parallels between *Indar Sabha* and the *Dastan of Amir Hamzah.* The human hero in both cases journeys to a supernatural kingdom; the fairy heroine falls in love with the hero at first sight, and then works aggressively to win his love; there is tension between the fairy heroine and the king (in *Amir Hamzah* he is her father) over what should be done with the human hero, with the fairy wanting to keep him as her lover, and the king wanting to remove him from the court. And of course Qaf appears as a location in both stories, although in *Amir Hamzah* the name applies to the entire supernatural world, while in *Indar Sabha* it is simply a remote place of exile and imprisonment.

A second, more immediate source for the plot of *Indar Sabha* is Mir Hasan's *Masnavi Sihr-ul-Bayan,* published in 1785. Amanat borrowed several major plot elements from Mir Hasan's *masnavi.* This concerns a young prince, Benazir, who is, like Gulfam, kidnapped while asleep on a terrace by a love-smitten fairy and transported to Fairyland. Unlike in Amanat's drama, however, the conflict arises when Prince Benazir, allowed out of Fairyland for three hours each evening, falls in love with a human princess. The fairy, on being told by a tale-bearing giant of the prince's betrayal, commands a jinn to cast him into a dry well. In Mir Hasan's tale, it is the human princess' clever friend who disguises herself as a *jogan* and wanders the wilderness in search of news of her friend's lost beloved, playing the lute and singing. A passing prince of the jinnee hears her song and becomes enamoured of her, and it is with his aid that the lovers are eventually reunited and the fairy punished. Like *Indar Sabha, Masnavi Sihr-ul-Bayan* includes a scene in which the *jogan* captivates the king of the supernatural world with her singing and is rewarded with the fulfilment of her request.[10] A comparison of the two texts reveals that Amanat has borrowed the description of the *jogan's* appearance whole cloth from Mir Hasan. Amanat likewise closely follows Mir Hasan in the section where Kala Dev praises the *jogan's* singing to the Raja Indar; Mir Hasan's fairy prince uses similar language to kindle the curiosity of Shah-Jan, the king of Paristan.

If the plot correspondences are not sufficient to convince us that Amanat used the *Masnavi Sihr-ul-Bayan* as a source, we need only to remark that *Indar Sabha* in several places contains direct, acknowledged quotations from Mir Hasan's work. As peculiar as it may seem, Amanat's characters are perfectly capable of saying, in the midst of their lines, '*baqaul-e-Hasan*' (*as Hasan says . . .*) preceded or followed by a quotation from *Masnavi Sihr-ul-Bayan.*[11]

A third source for *Indar Sabha* is Pandit Daya Shankar Naseem's *Gulzar-e-Naseem*, published in 1844, which is one of the most famous *masnavis* in Urdu literature.[12] Raja Indar appears in Naseem's tale, where he plays a role almost identical to that in Amanat's drama. He discovers that the Fairy Bakavali has fallen in love with and married a human prince, and punishes her by turning her partially into stone. She is subsequently reborn in humble surroundings, and after seventeen years of wandering is at last reunited with her prince.

The tale of the love of a supernatural woman for a human man is of course not restricted to the Persian tradition. The romance of Sabz Pari and Prince Gulfam may have its ultimate ancestor in the story of Urvashi. In the *Rig Veda*, there is a hymn-dialogue concerning the Apsara Urvashi and her illicit love for a human king. The *apsaras* were divine beings created to perform in *nataks* or dance dramas before the gods in a vast concert hall presided over by Indra, the prototype of the Indar who appears in Amanat's drama.

The most detailed version of the Urvashi story is given in the *Matsya Purana*, but the story is referred to in Bharata Muni's fifth century treatise on drama, the *Natyashastra*, and Kalidas himself wrote a drama derived from the story of Urvashi, entitled *Vikramorvashi*, 'Urvashi by Valour Won'.

The tale runs as follows. The drama *Lakshmi-Swayambar* is being performed in the theatre of the gods. Urvashi, secretly in love with a human king, is playing the role of Lakshmi, Vishnu's consort, when she falters in her lines by accidentally substituting the name of her mortal beloved for an epithet of Vishnu. The sage Bharata, angered by the disruption of his drama, curses Urvashi, but Indra intervenes and ultimately gives her permission to live in the world with her beloved. Moreover, Urvashi's indiscretion has an unintended good effect, for it is from Urvashi that humans learned the art of dance and drama.

In the tale of Urvashi can be seen several elements of *Indar Sabha*. In both stories, a supernatural dancer's love for a human is discovered in the middle of a performance, and the offending dancer is cast out of the assembly into exile. Moreover, in both cases, Indra is presiding over the performance, and it is he who decrees the *apsara's* punishment.

Indian dramatic theory essentially begins with the *Natya-shastra,* whose author Bharata is identified with the sage responsible for presenting plays before the gods. Much in this nearly two-thousand-year-old work has been carried down, often in corrupted form, to the folk and religious theatre of Amanat's time and our own. The Sanskrit dramas were thus the ultimate ancestors of all Indian theatre, and Amanat was certainly an heir to this tradition.

The theme of the rejected and outcast lover links *Indar Sabha* with the tradition of 'realistic' folk tales of star-crossed love. Kathryn Hansen has pointed out that one of the most popular themes in the folk theatre was the conflict between love and the social order;[13] this theme is certainly present in *Indar Sabha,* with an added supernatural dimension. In Amanat's play, the social order is represented by Indar and his court, which, although the epitome of wealth and generosity, has no place for love, especially the love between a human and a *Pari.*

The disruptive effect of love between different castes is contextualized by the clear social hierarchy in *Indar Sabha,* with Raja Indar at the top, the fairies below him, humans below them, and the subservient *Devs* at the bottom; Raja Indar specifically censures Sabz Pari's love as being beneath her.[14] Sabz Pari is well aware of her own position in this hierarchy, and of her superiority to the human Prince Gulfam. She repeatedly reminds him of his good fortune in being loved by a superior supernatural being like herself.[15]

In this connection, there are several interesting thematic parallels between the story of Sabz Pari and Gulfam and Indo-Persian folk tales such as *Laila-Majnoon* and *Shirin-Farhad,* which were popular subjects for the *svang-nautanki.* In all the three tales, love causes a disruption of the prescribed order by bringing an outsider into the forbidden society of his beloved. When his intrusion is discovered, the society takes drastic action, and one of the lovers is forced to become a renunciant, a wanderer in the wilderness, a *jogi* or *fakir.* In the cases of Majnoon and Farhad, it is the man who is ejected into the wilderness; in *Indar Sabha* of course it is Sabz Pari who is exiled to wander the world singing.

Amanat's incorporation of this theme from the folk theatre

tradition accounts for much of the success of the play. In contrast both to Indian devotional theatre, with stories derived from Hindu mythology and the *Ramayana* and *Mahabharata*, and to the elaborate fantasy of the Persian *dastans*, the love-society or intercaste conflicts of *Indar Sabha* and *Laila-Majnoon* had universal relevance and immediate appeal to contemporary audiences. It is certainly no accident that this theme continues to dominate modern Indian cinema.

Characters

While it has been demonstrated that the plot of *Indar Sabha* has roots in Islamic-Persian and Hindu sources, it is Amanat's characters which most vividly demonstrate the blending of the two traditions. Abdul Halim Sharar, chronicler of the last days of Awadh, describes the extent of the mixture of Hindu and Persian elements in *Indar Sabha* as follows.

> The greatest achievement of *Indar Sabha* is that there is no better example of the intermixture of Hindu and Muslim style, interest, and taste. . . . In the play, a Hindu deity is seen in the guise of a Muslim ruler. The hero, Prince Gulfam, is precisely a prince of Lucknow. . . . The fairies are the apsaras of Hindu mythology, but in the costumes of the fairies of Koh-e-Qaf in Persia. . . . And for a human to fall in love with a fairy is essentially a Persian or Arabic concept. But the notion of the fairies dancing before the assembled court of Lord Indar is completely Hindu. Sabz Pari assumes the guise of a Hindu jogan, with the requisite Hindu musical instrument on her shoulder, in order to search for Prince Gulfam, imprisoned in a well in the Persian Caucasus.[16]

Raja Indar is identified with Indra of the *Rig Veda*, a warrior god, thundering across the sky in his war-chariot, wielding lightning-bolts as weapons. As the storm god, Indra was associated with the monsoon, and rain in general. These affinities with Zeus, Odin, and Jupiter, combined with his ancient title *devaraja* make it likely that he was once the chief or king god in the Indo-Aryan pantheon. In *Indar Sabha*, written centuries after he had ceded his primacy to the trinity Brahma, Vishnu, and Shiva, Indra still retains this royal air.

By the time the *Mahabharata* and the *Natyashastra* were

composed, Indra had acquired his retinue of *apsaras*, whose duties had come to include the temptation of mortal men away from meditation and austerities. In the *Mahabharata*, the warrior Arjun is taken to heaven to see the court of Indra, where he is permitted to sit on the god's throne to view the dancing of thousands of *apsaras* and to hear the singing of the divine musicians.

Clearly the leisure-loving Indra of the mid-nineteenth century has become somewhat diminished over his Vedic and Epic predecessors. Yet certain similarities remain. Even many centuries before *Indar Sabha*, Indra had come to symbolize the ideal Indian monarch, presiding over a golden age in which luxury is tempered by generosity, and opulence is adorned with cultural achievements. Furthermore, he retains his association with the performing arts. For example, the Nepali *Indrayatra* (Indra Pilgrimage) was by the seventeenth century the occasion for the production of plays based on the Sanskrit epics.[17]

Amanat's work was by no means the first in Indian literature to use characters from Hindu mythology in a Persian setting. It has been mentioned how Pandit Daya Shankar Naseem introduced the character of King Indar and his musical court into his Persian-style romance. Perhaps their earliest manifestation in Indo-Persian literature was in the prose *qissā* (romance) *Mehr Afroz-o-Dilbar,* thought to have been written in the late seventeenth or early eighteenth century. In this *qissa,* Raja Indar and his fairies appear overhead to witness the wedding of the lovers Mehr Afroz and Dilbar.[18]

Amanat drew upon this tradition, and worked it into what can be seen as an extended allegory of Wajid Ali Shah's Lucknow. In *Indar Sabha,* Indar of course represents Wajid Ali Shah, who himself maintained a 'Paristan' of dancers, and whose *takhallus* (pen name) was 'Akhtar', which appears in the name of Prince Gulfam's home town of Akhtarnagar. There is even an apocryphal story that Wajid Ali Shah played King Indar in the premier of the play. And given the traditional symbolic function of Indar the benevolent ruler, it is probable the Wajid Ali Shah consciously patterned himself on his divine counterpart. Indeed, in contemporary sources, his court is often compared to that of the mythical Indra. For example, Suroor's *Fasana-e-Ibrat* describes a typical evening at the palace:

The lovely *jalse-walian* [singers and dancers], as beautiful as fairies, were [Wajid Ali Shah's] carefree and intimate companions. Some were holding jars of red wine, others had carven, gilded, *baid-mushq* [fragrant willow wood] goblets, still others wielded ornate *gulab-paash* [rose water censers]. . . . Here eating, drinking, music, singing and dancing were going on. It looked like the fairies were from the *akhara* of Raja Indar.[19]

Raja Indar's relative impotence is an important symbolic aspect of his character. In contrast to the Vedic thunder god, the Indar of *Indar Sabha* is essentially passive. We get only one hint of his potential, when he discovers Gulfam and flies into a rage. But in the end, he is powerless to enforce his will, and is overcome by the singing of a simple *jogan.* In this sense too, Amanat's Indar is a fair picture of Wajid Ali Shah. Despite his wealth and power, Wajid Ali Shah could not stave off the loss of his kingdom. Indeed, his real influence extended no further than the decorated walls of his Paristan. The eclipsed god is thus a powerful metaphor for the doomed king.

Amanat further used the varied supernatural and fabulous characterizations in the play allegorically, to portray and comment on the epicurean excess of the kingdom of Awadh, which was facing imminent annexation by the British.

The fate of Delhi could not have been lost on Amanat, or any writer of his generation. It was a matter of historical record that the blind folly of pleasure-loving emperors such as Mohammad Shah 'Rangila' had combined with incessant internecine strife to render the former capital vulnerable to invasion and destruction. The British had taken advantage of Delhi's incapacitation to consolidate their power there, and would, following the Mutiny, make it their new capital.

The writing was on the wall for all Awadh to read. Is it then mere coincidence that the main theme of Amanat's play is the intrusion of an outsider into the hermetic fantasy of Raja Indar? He, surfeit with song and lulled by luxury, falls asleep and loses his dearest possession, Sabz Pari to a human prince. His anger at the interruption of his peaceful existence and his attempt to banish the offenders is unsuccessful, precisely because of his addiction to the fine arts. Sabz Pari, well aware of this weakness, exploits it to force the king to meet her demands.

Sabz Pari's portrayal in *Indar Sabha* has certain unusual aspects. Sabz Pari is neither the wilful fairy princess nor the virtuous beloved of *Amir Hamzah* and *Sihr-ul-Bayan*, nor is she the heroine's resourceful friend who wanders the world as a *jogan* singing as in *Sihr-ul-Bayan*. Her closest analog is the Fairy Bakavali in *Gulzar-e-Naseem*, who also undergoes terrible punishment for loving a human.

In one sense Sabz Pari is an amalgamation of all of these characters. She is the aggressive lover like her fairy counterparts, but she is also the patient renunciant, and the faithful beloved. In terms of character and role, however, Sabz Pari is clearly patterned after the courtesan-queens of Lucknow. Wajid Ali Shah would often marry a dancer-courtesan with whom he had become enamoured, and who, if she produced a child, could be promoted to *mahal* or queen status. Many of the king's wives, however, found it inconvenient to forsake their courtesan ways and engaged in liaisons with other notables, much complicating the intrigues of the zenana.[20]

It should not be forgotten that the Lucknow courtesan was in some important ways very different from that of the modern conception of the prostitute. She was a complex, sophisticated woman who had been carefully educated in the highly specialized arts of singing, dancing, and other, more intimate forms of entertainment, and who was capable of developing intense love for one of her client nawabs even while obliged by virtue of her position to entertain others. We can thus easily imagine that at one of Wajid Ali Shah's concert gatherings, a fairy who had just completed her performance would go out into the garden for some fresh air—and a tryst with a lover.

The courtesans were free from the restrictions of purdah and family-enforced morality, allowing them to play a much more active role in their lives and loves than their more respectable sisters. The royal courtesans were even more fortunate in having the resources of the court at their disposal. They were thus strong women, who could actively pursue the richest and most powerful nawabs as clients and lovers.

Sabz Pari's character is thus modelled on the courtesan culture of Wajid Ali Shah's zenana. She is an aggressive, passionate woman, educated in poetry, music and dance, who is bound to entertain the king but by no means bound to love him. Her pent-up emotions find an outlet in her love for the prince, and she pursues him with a fervor that is explicitly masculine in nature.

Sabz Pari's love for Gulfam is the love of a high-class courtesan for a client nawab, and as such it is infused with an explicit sexuality not found in the delicate relations of regular lovers. Sabz Pari's tale of how she fell in love with the prince is surprisingly sensual,[21] and as she seduces the prince, it is clear that she is a practised lover who will not at any cost let her quarry escape. Her aggressiveness and explicit references to the *wasl* or sexual union must have been titillating for the audiences of *Indar Sabha.*

Although Sabz Pari's love begins as infatuation and lust, subsequent circumstances force it to deepen into something else. The discovery of her love, and the resulting disgrace, is the crisis which begins Sabz Pari's transformation. As she dons the garb of a *jogan,* we begin to see the spiritual aspects of her love for Prince Gulfam. The overlapping of erotic and divine love is well established in both Hindu and Islamic Sufi traditions, in which the devotee occasionally even takes on the role of a courtesan, God being an un-possessable yet all-providing customer. Sabz Pari is the dramatic embodiment of this conflation.[22]

Despite the literary precedents and Wajid Ali Shah's experiments, it seems odd that Amanat, a devout Muslim, would have his heroine turn into a Hindu *jogan.* There is, however, a deeper meaning to be found in the theme of the lover becoming a *jogan* as it appears not only in *Indar Sabha,* but in so many of the *masnavis* and folk tales of the eighteenth and nineteenth centuries. Annemarie Schimmel has remarked that Islam won many Hindu converts in India through the activities of Sufi mystics who began travelling around the subcontinent as early as the eleventh century.[23] These mystics, called *shaikhs* or *pirs,* to some extent adopted the lifestyles and habits of the Hindu *jogi/jogan* of the *bhakti* tradition, and espoused the philosophy—not incompatible with Hindu beliefs—that everything in the universe is an emanation and manifestation of God. These mystics had an enormous impact on the shaping of Indo-Islamic culture; Amir Khusrau, the fourteenth-century poet-musician-composer, was a passionate disciple of the Sufi Pir Nizamuddin Auliya (d. 1325), while Akbar was a follower of Shaikh Salim Chishti.

The shrines of the greatest of these *pirs* are visited to this day by Hindu and Muslim pilgrims, and most evenings their tombs are the scene of a concert of devotional songs or *qawwali*. The *qawwali* tradition, said to have originated with Amir Khusro, owes a large debt to the Hindu devotional song, and shares with it the image of the devotee as the lover and God as the beloved. It is this image that became a powerful symbolic bridge between the nearly irreconcilable worlds of Hinduism and Islam.

There is thus a deep, internal logic driving the seemingly haphazard mixing of Hindu and Muslim elements in the transformation of the female lover into a *jogan* in *Indar Sabha*. The *jogan*, outwardly a purely Hindu character, dramatically represents the point of contact between Hinduism and Islam, and the passionate love of God which lies at the heart of both faiths.

It is in this context that Sabz Pari's love must prove itself, and her exile and wandering as a *jogan* is a test. If her love were truly superficial and physical, she would lament the loss of her pride of place in Indar's court, and her loss of its luxury. But on the contrary, she willingly becomes the renunciant, and sings only of the pain of separation from her beloved. As a result, by the end of the drama, Sabz Pari's love has matured to the point that she herself is able to make King Indar understand the nature of true love in her *jogan* songs at his court.

Prince Gulfam is described by Amanat in the commentary on the *Indar Sabha* as wearing a heavy embroidered long coat, glitter and stars pasted on his face, and adorned with plenty of jewellery. He is only thirteen or fourteen years old. His name means that his aspect is like a flower, and he has a character to match. He is passive and effeminate, which makes him a good counterpart to the aggressive Sabz Pari, but as the hero of the story, he is rather disappointing. He has no outstanding virtues, and upon waking in the strange garden, he demonstrates first cowardice and then venality.[24]

Like Raja Indar, the prince is essentially impotent. In this regard, he is quite different from his ancestors in the *Masnavi Sihr-ul-Bayan, Gulzar-e-Naseem,* and the *Dastan-e-Amir Hamzah.* In the earlier tales, the hero prince is an active protagonist who never ceases struggling against the supernatural powers of the *Devs* and *Paris.* Gulfam, in contrast, is powerless to resist Sabz Pari, and to effect his own deliverance, and it is up to Sabz Pari to win his release from prison.

Sabz Pari herself treats him more like a delicate girl than a hero prince. In the final reunion scene, when Lal Dev hauls Gulfam back from Qaf, she expresses concern that his delicate wrist has been bruised by the roughness of the *Dev,* and worries about the effects of the imprisonment on his frail health.[25]

With very little imagination we can see in Prince Gulfam the portrait of a typical young nawab of Wajid Ali Shah's Lucknow. Spoiled by luxury, these nawabs had willingly surrendered the administration of their country to outsiders long before the actual annexation of Awadh. With so many courtesans and prostitutes to choose from, there was no arena in which to develop or exercise the strength of character shown by the heroes of stories like *Laila-Majnoon* or *Shirin-Farhad.*

The *Paris* and the *Devs* are derived most immediately from Persian sources. Frances Pritchett's definitions of these beings in her glossary to *Amir Hamzah* can, with some commentary, be equally applied to their counterparts in Amanat's play:

PARI: 'Fairy.' The dominant race of Qaf-dwellers. Creatures of fire, invisible to ordinary human eyes, they have the power of flight, and many other powers as well. They seem to be about the size of humans, and are often extremely beautiful; they can visit the World at will.

DEV: A species of immensely huge, powerful, strong demons, mostly violent and brutal; they are invisible to ordinary human eyes, and can fly. They live in Qaf, and are kept in subjugation by Shahpal [King of the Fairies]. . . .[26]

I hardly need mention that the idea of singing and dancing fairies came to Amanat most directly from the Paristan of Wajid Ali Shah, who had in turn borrowed the concept of fairies as seductive women from Persian folklore. And in Wajid Ali Shah's

Masnavi Darya-e-Ta'shuq we also find fairies named after colours: Lal Pari, Neelam Pari, Sabz Pari.

Yet *Indar Sabha's* fairies are ultimately derived from the *apsaras* of Hindu mythology, directly created by Brahma to interpret the divine dance dramas of the *Natya Veda*. Amanat's fairies possess the dramatic and dancing talents of the *apsaras*, and in this they differ from their Persian prototypes. One characteristic of the mythological *apsaras* is particularly relevant; when the gods feared that a human, through sincere and protracted meditation, was in danger of acquiring too much spiritual power, they would send an *apsara* down to distract him from his contemplation, and it is perhaps this tradition that gave birth to the *masnavi* writers' fairy seductresses.

The costumes and make-up of the *Devs*, as described in Amanat's notes to the play, emphasize their ugliness, and correspond to Western and Indian images of devils. Amanat's *Devs* wear red or black skin-tight costumes, with faces painted in horrifying grimaces. Their mouths are broad, their teeth are large, their noses are flat, and they have horns. They wield a *gurz* (mace or club).

The two *Devs* have clearly defined symbolic functions, embodying extraordinary powers, and representing elemental forces. Yet, like machines, they have no wills of their own even though they are the dynamic forces in the plot, and through them the dramatic conflicts are created and resolved. The Black Dev, for example, has the power of strength, and the power to transport people instantly through the air. As the confidant and helper of Sabz Pari, he is a positive character, but he is also in the role of the pander or the pimp.

His counterpart, the Red Dev, is the agent of conflict in the plot; it is he who informs Indar of Gulfam's presence. His colour, with its connotations of flame and blood, is well suited to his function in the story. He perhaps represents the negative forces of tale-bearing, sycophancy, palace intrigue, and officiousness.

A deeper symbolism may be imputed to the *Devs* in Amanat's play. When *Indar Sābha* was written, Awadh's autonomy had long been falling slowly prey to the insinuations of the British.[27] The last kings of Awadh inherited a crown that was largely nominal;

while the Resident, his staff, the East India Company and the British army essentially controlled the administration of capital and countryside, the kings were left more and more to their own devices, such as were available to them in the luxurious confines of the palaces. The Lucknow court was thus the scene of constant intrigue and tension between the scheming British agents and the native elite. Is it too far-fetched to interpret the tale-bearing, trouble-making Red Dev as an embodiment of British attempts to disrupt Wajid Ali Shah's reign, and the helpful but irresponsible Black Dev as a fanciful portrait of a native courtier?

Links to other Genres

Given the critical analysis of Amanat's drama, we can now review the diversity of elements which Amanat combined to create his *Indar Sabha*.

Amanat was first and foremost an Urdu poet, who wrote *Indar Sabha* as a diversion from his work in more serious genres. It is not surprising therefore, that his play is first an Indo-Persian *masnavi* in its basic dramatic shape. The plot is certainly taken directly from the *masnavi* and *dastan* traditions, the *Pari* and *Dev* characters are derived from the Urdu-Persian *dastan*, and much of the language, especially in the dialogues, has a strong *masnavi* flavour.

Amanat has filled in this *masnavi* outline with songs derived from several different traditions, the two chief genres being the *ghazal* of the Lucknow *mujra* and the folk song in the Hindu devotional style. The *ghazals* are clearly recognizable as belonging to the mid-nineteenth-century Lucknow tradition, with their stylized Urdu, their predilection for sensual and meretricious themes, and their delight in elaborate word play. Taken as a group, the songs in *Indar Sabha* define a spectrum with the Lucknavite Urdu literary tradition at one end and the Braj, Awadhi, and Hindu devotional genres at the other. It is the delight in musical settings of poetry which provides the unifying element, firmly linking the *ghazal*, religious and regional folk song genres.

Indar Sabha is on one level a work of Urdu literature. But when it came to the theatrical aspects of his work, there was nothing whatsoever in Urdu literature that Amanat could draw upon. He was thus forced to look for other sources of inspiration.

In creating a spectacle for the stage, Amanat's most immediate models were Wajid Ali Shah's court entertainments, which were essentially an amalgamation of traditional Indian music and dance genres like the *Ras Lila* with tales inspired by the Persian *masnavi* and *dastan.* The last king of Awadh, Wajid Ali Shah (r. 1847-56), was himself a trained poet and musician. He is known to have written at least three long *masnavi,* which he staged for performance, and to have composed both the words and music to many *ghazals* and *thumris*; certain *ragas* are still associated with his name.

Wajid Ali Shah's birthday was special occasion, celebrated every year with a court musical function at which the king always dressed up as a *jogi,* or Hindu ascetic. His mother had begun this custom in an attempt to ward off evil influences predicted by soothsayers at his birth, and Wajid Ali Shah continued this tradition throughout his life. After his accession to the throne, his wives would join in and wear the clothes of *jogans* (female ascetics), and eventually, the royal dancers and other members of the court used also to dress as *jogans* or *jogis.* In 1853, one year before *Indar Sabha* was first performed, Wajid Ali Shah supplemented his birthday celebration with a public fair. It is unlikely that the king himself appeared in public dressed as a *jogi,* but Sharar reports that young and old alike used to don ochre robes in honour of this festival.[28]

Well before his accession, Wajid Ali Shah had developed an interest in the *lila* devotional play genre. There were two major manifestations of this genre: the *Ram Lila* and the *Ras Lila.* In the *Ram Lila,* dancers act out episodes from the *Ramayana* or from Tulsidas's seventeenth-century *Ramcharitmanas.* The *Ram Lila* included the recitation of passages from Tulsidas's text, songs, dances, and the acting out of episodes. The *Ram Lila* genre was closely tied to the kingdom of Awadh, whose very name derives from the ancient holy town Ayodhya, traditionally the birthplace of Ram.

The *Ras Lila* arose in the Braj region in western Uttar Pradesh, between Agra and Aligarh. Mathura in Braj is the traditional birthplace of Krishna and the site of his revelries with the *gopis.* The *Ras Lila,* which may have originated as early as the sixteenth century, consists of circle dances by boys or women representing the *gopis,* and the enactment of comic episodes from Krishna's life. Both the *Ram Lila* and the *Ras Lila* forms were well known in Awadh.

It is easy to see what appealed to Wajid Ali Shah in the *Ras Lila.* The scenes of *gopis* dancing around Krishna, and Krishna's love dialogues with his consort Radha, provided ample opportunity for music and dance, as well as fertile ground for love poetry, in both its elevated and carnal forms. Wajid Ali Shah, a self-proclaimed womanizer and romantic, identified in many ways with the flirtatious Krishna. Moreover, Krishna is perhaps the most musical of the Hindu deities, wooing his conquests by playing on his flute.

The king staged dance dramas of this type regularly, calling them *rahas dhari,* or simply *rahas,* and through a succession of innovations, he transformed this simple folk dance into an elaborate theatrical presentation. Although unlike Wajid Ali Shah's plays, Amanat's drama contains no *Ras* dance *per se,* it does contain folk songs and dances evoking the Braj tradition, where the singer calls to Shyam, her 'dark beloved' or refers to him as *sanvla,* 'the dark one', terms which are traditional epithets of Krishna. Thus, indirectly, the *Ras Lila* tradition is carried on in *Indar Sabha.*

In conjunction with his passion for the *Ras Lila* form, Wajid Ali Shah drew extensively on folk theatre genres in his palace presentations; his *masnavi* stagings in particular gave broad scope to the incorporation of folk forms. In the early 1850s, just prior to the premiere of *Indar Sabha,* Wajid Ali Shah prepared his three *masnavis* for theatrical presentation. These productions required up to forty days to perform, and included numerous dances, and solo and choral songs.

Wajid Ali Shah initiated a process of change in the popular theatre which *Indar Sabha* accelerated. Although the *masnavi* and *rahas* dramas were performed primarily for the king's enjoyment, many other people, nawabs and commoners alike, may have had the opportunity to witness them. Suroor writes in his *Fasana-e-Ibrat* that 'the *rahas* became extremely famous, providing amusement and education to hundreds of courtiers and servants. These *rahas* used to be grand occasions, with huge crowds enjoying the show in performances continuing day and night.'[29]

Wajid Ali Shah's influence on *Indar Sabha* and its successors had three chief components. The first was the introduction of Indo-Islamic, and especially Indo-Persian, styles and characters into essentially Hindu performing art forms. The king's passion for the conflation of Hindu and Muslim elements in his presentations is well illustrated by the character list of his first *Tale of Radha and Kanhaya*. In the tale appear not only the Hindu Krishna and his consort Radha, but Persian *Devs, Paris,* and an *Ifrit,* as well as a Hindu *jogan* and the obligatory milkmaid devotees of Krishna. The Persian and Islamic fashion in vogue at the court of Lucknow could not help but stimulate Amanat, himself a devout Shia, and thence continued to propagate throughout the folk theatre of north India.[30] The 'Persianization' of India's drama culture was subsequently reinforced and propagated in the Parsi drama companies of Bombay throughout the latter half of the nineteenth century.

The second contribution of Wajid Ali Shah to the Lucknow theatrical matrix was an infusion of classical musical elements into a theatre dominated by folk music. The king's tastes in music were substantially more refined than the folk theatre was able to provide; by employing classical musicians and pedagogues, he was able to ensure that his fairies would sing according to his elevated standards. In particular, Wajid Ali Shah delighted in the genres of *ghazal* and *thumri,* and helped bring these semi-classical forms to their modern prominence. As a result, even the folk-derived musical dramas presented at the royal court were strongly coloured by classical practice, as was the public play *Indar Sabha.*

Wajid Ali Shah's third contribution was the accelerated adoption of a wider variety of poetic forms and metres by the popular theatre. In the early nineteenth century, the scripts of the folk theatre were primarily in the *doha-chaubola* metre. The Lucknow court theatre stimulated not only the professional Urdu theatre from its inception, but the north Indian folk theatre as well, to borrow and incorporate Hindi poetic forms such as the *basant, sawan, hori,* and *thumri,* as well as Urdu-Persian forms like the *ghazal,* the *masnavi,* and the *qawwali.*

Amanat's models must also have included the folk theatre, but an analysis of the impact of the folk theatre on *Indar Sabha* is complicated by the fact that we have almost no texts of *svang* or *nautanki* that predate the published text of *Indar Sabha.* Indeed, in some ways, Amanat's text reveals more about the folk theatre of that time than vice versa. However we know that *Indar Sabha* and the *svang* tradition had in common the use of the *chaubola* and *chhand* metres for narration and dialogue.[31] Furthermore, the performance practice of *Indar Sabha* bore many resemblances to contemporary stagings of *svang* and *nautanki*: the play relied heavily on music, song and dance, it was originally performed in a tent or in a public place, the curtain and other theatrical accessories were absent, the musicians were on or near the stage, and the actors did not leave the stage when their characters 'exited' but rather stood in the background or sat off to one side.[32]

Several elements of Amanat's drama are also found in the folk theatre and perhaps borrowed from it: the mythical or fantastic background, the conflict between lovers and their society, the appearance of one of the characters as a renunciant, and the frank references to sex. On the other hand, as Kathryn Hansen has pointed out, *Indar Sabha* was directly responsible for the marked enrichment of the popular theatre form, helping to transplant courtly styles into the popular milieu.[33] This exchange itself demonstrates how closely *Indar Sabha* was tied to the north Indian folk theatre tradition.

Indar Sabha owes something to Lucknow's Shia Islamic traditions as well. The nawabs of the kingdom of Awadh had been nursed on the dramatic spectacle and poetry of the *majlis,* a ceremony commemorating the massacre of the Prophet Muhammad's grandson Husain and his family at Karbala, which included singing and recitation of poetic laments, and even some dramatizations.[34] They thus bore none of orthodox Islam's abhorrence of the theatrical arts, and instead, were avid patrons of music, song and dance. Amanat himself was Shia, and it was precisely the Shi'ite Muharram practices that paved the way for the general acceptance of a dramatic tradition founded by Muslims and in which Muslims could actively participate.

In Amanat's day the Sanskrit dramatic tradition, which had fallen slowly into obscurity over the centuries, was undergoing something of a revival at the hands of Sir William Jones at Fort William College. The tastes of the nawabs of Awadh had never run in this direction, but it is not unlikely that Amanat was familiar to some extent with the *Natyashastra* of Bharata and the classical dramas.

The Sanskrit tradition, as the ultimate progenitor of Indian theatre, is manifested in *Indar Sabha* in certain ways. First, the story of Urvashi and its clear parallels with the tale of Sabz Pari forms an identifiable link between Amanat, the *Natyashastra* and the works of Kalidas. Second, if we look carefully, we can detect a marked family resemblance between the first Urdu drama and its Sanskrit ancestors. Sanskrit theatre had many offspring: folk theatre, medieval religious theatre, and the later *kathak* dance styles, all of which share a common emphasis on music and dance as the primary media of dramatic expression, and all of which contributed to *Indar Sabha* and its linkage with the older tradition.

Moreover, there are undeniable affinities of spirit between the tale of Sabz Pari and the erotic 'harem dramas' classified as a unique genre by the Sanskrit dramatic theorists. This genre, *kaishiki*, was concerned with love and love's intrigues, and relied on songs, dances, costumes and make-up to produce its titillating effects.

Not only in the *kaishiki* genre, but in Sanskrit drama in general, courtesans were entirely legitimate heroines. Indeed, love stories like the *Mrchhakatika* show a marked preference for a courtesan heroine; we can conjecture that this was because it was not considered respectful or in good taste to chronicle the amorous adventures of, for example, an innocent girl like Shakuntala or the archetypal ideal wife and help meet Sita. Moreover, since the actresses usually were themselves courtesans, and since the drama required them to dance and sing, it enhanced the dramatic illusion to present them as courtesans on stage.

There are additional points of contact between *Indar Sabha* and Sanskrit drama. For example, Bharata describes a device called *patakasthanaka*, or 'banner-post', which refers to dramatic foreshadowing, and which is used by Kalidas to great effect in the opening scenes of *Shakuntala.*

Amanat too shows his skill at foreshadowing. In a direct parallel with the technique described by Bharata, Amanat's characters' in the opening sequence speak on two levels; hidden in the lyrics are references to future dramatic events of which even the speakers are unaware. The fairies' opening songs establish the themes of the story, sensual attraction, the frustration of love, and the hope of union with the beloved—but in an abstract way. It is one of Amanat's finer touches that Sabz Pari's set of songs is outwardly indistinguishable from those of the fairies that have preceded her, but is laced with hidden meanings and references to her real situation. To Raja Indar and to the *sabha,* she is simply following custom and the precedent of the other fairies. But in reality she is expressing her innermost personal emotions. Amanat uses this fore-shadowing to create real dramatic tension when he has Sabz Pari sing her love songs before Raja Indar while unbeknownst to the king, Prince Gulfam is present in the court. The dramatic tension in Sabz Pari's songs is heightened by their outward semblance to the paradigm set by the other three fairies. This technique of dramatic irony, in which the characters' lines and actions have hidden meanings, echoes the device described by Bharata Muni.

Indar Sabha shares other features with classical Sanskrit drama. Sanskrit drama is characterized by its emphasis on the musical and poetic exploration of the characters' mental states, through the dual media of *ras* (essence, literally 'juice') and *bau* (expression of emotion). The plot, which is the main focus of both Western drama and Indian folk drama, is subordinated to the analysis of emotion. The performance of an Indian *raga* or a soliloquy in Sanskrit drama are equally attempts to get to the heart of a specific, well-defined internal state. *Indar Sabha* is in this respect closely linked in spirit to classical Sanskrit drama. The primary emphasis is placed on the interpretation of the characters' emotional states through discrete songs linked by dramatic dialogue. All of the dramatist's tools are employed toward this end: gestures, dance movements, facial expressions, poetry, music, etc.

Likewise, Bharata describes the practice of having characters colour-coded according to dramatic function and prevailing emotion. Not only are the *Paris* similarly colour-coded in their apparel, but it can hardly be coincidence that in the *Natyashastra* the colour of love, particularly that of supernatural beings, is green.

Amanat seems to have been familiar with both the general tradition and to some extent with the particulars of classical Sanskrit dramatic practice. And just as the works of Racine and Shakespeare can be traced ultimately to Aristotle and Sophocles, so are the family resemblances between Amanat and his Sanskrit predecessors unmistakable.

Conclusion

What then accounted for *Indar Sabha's* extraordinary popularity? Most immediately, it was perhaps Amanat's success in pitching his drama to win both royal attention as well as public approval. The intermingling and synthesis of Hindu and Muslim cultural elements was well calculated to make the drama appeal to the mixed population of Lucknow as well as to the diverse tastes of the monarch. Likewise, the ostentatious display of wealth and luxury was both a tribute to the court of Awadh, and an awe-inspiring pageant for the public at large. Moreover, in contrast to the labyrinthine poetic romances of Amanat's predecessors and, for that matter, of Wajid Ali Shah himself, *Indar Sabha's* story is folk-tale like in its simplicity: the lovers meet, are parted, and reunited by virtue of perseverance through hardship and separation. Elaboration is provided not by plot complications, but rather by interpolated musical numbers which do not distract the viewer from the central story. The simplicity of the plot gave the drama much of its popular appeal, while the host of musical numbers provided something for everyone, nawab and peasant alike.

Yet I submit that there was a deeper factor in the popularity of the play. In the decades of decline preceding its ultimate fall,

Awadh possessed enormous symbolic value as the last major ostensibly independent native kingdom in north India. Unlike many of its neighbours, Awadh had neither sold out to British enticements, nor, despite occasional military defeats and territorial losses, surrendered to British military power. Furthermore, Awadh had not suffered from the depredations of invaders that had devastated Delhi and north-western India during the late eighteenth and early nineteenth centuries. For these reasons, Awadh was seen by many as the last bastion of Mughal, or Indo-Islamic, culture, as well as a refuge from foreign enemies, and a shining beacon of defiance in a darkening world.

The 'last bastion' image was reinforced by the fact that the wealth, safety, and relative stability of the Lucknow court had served as a powerful draw for many noble families, poets and other artists who found Delhi and elsewhere in India less and less hospitable.[35] Their migration to Awadh had infused it with new importance as a cultural rival to the declining former capital.

Indar Sabha premiered in 1854, and a short two years later, in 1856, the worst fears of the people of Awadh were realized. The surreptitious manoeuvering of the British and their deliberate attempts to malign the last Nawab, Wajid Ali Shah, and to discredit his administration, finally culminated in the order for annexation. The British army presented Awadh's last king with a contract providing for a generous pension and the freedom to remain in Lucknow, which Wajid Ali Shah refused to sign but was in no position to contest. Deeply distraught, the king departed from Awadh for Calcutta, where he would spend the rest of his days in exile.

Cultural constructs such as the image of Awadh are not only abstract paradigms; they can have a direct impact on historical events. Many in the British administration, recognizing this, had advised against annexation, and deplored it when it took place. They were soon vindicated. Historians suggest that it was this final insult that precipitated the Mutiny which was to wrack British India less than a year later. A large percentage of the troops serving the British had been recruited from Awadh, and it was their cultural allegiance, combined with the general perception that Awadh, more even than Delhi, was the lone limb remaining on the tree of Mughal glory, which made the insult so intolerable.

The subsequent rumour that the British cartridges were greased with impure animal fat was only the catalyst for the mutineers, already enraged by the annexation of Awadh.[36]

With the suppression of the Mutiny, and the deposition and exile of Wajid Ali Shah and Bahadur Shah Zafar, India bid farewell to the centuries of Islamic rule during which not only the Mughal emperors and the nawabs of Awadh, but many other Muslim and Hindu rulers had enriched culture through their patronage of indigenous arts. The British Raj, in contrast, held a general disdain for Indian culture, or attempted to disparage the population it ruled.

The wide dispersion of *Indar Sabha* was a major element of the fallout from the annexation of Awadh and, as such, its impact on the subsequent construction of Indian cultural identity was far-reaching. For the Indian public of the late nineteenth century, it was as if the 'mythic past' of the Mughals, the luxury of the court of Lucknow, and the two-thousand-year history of Hindu and Muslim cultural achievement had been encapsulated in Amanat's *Indar Sabha.* Its lasting popularity is evidence of the power it had over the collective imagination to evoke memories of what had been.

The eclipse of the Islamic dynasties was succeeded by the dawn of a new era in Indian culture, in which the evils of British hegemony inspired in India a new awareness of indigenous cultural achievements. It was in this atmosphere too that the seeds of *Indar Sabha,* transplanted to more hospitable soil, began to grow and flourish. Kathryn Hansen has remarked that it was the evocation of the vanished Islamic court atmosphere that motivated the popularity of *Indar Sabha.*[37] I would argue that it was more precisely the evocation of the richness and diversity of Indian culture, with its interpolations and conflations of Hindu and Muslim elements, that truly explains the play's success.

The downfall of the Islamic kings and their extravagant courts also coincided with the emergence of the modern middle class, and a shift in the loci of power from the ancient political and administrative centres of Delhi and Lucknow to the new cosmopolitan economic centres of Bombay and Calcutta. Even though the British later shifted their administrative capital to Delhi, Bombay continued its rapid rise as a centre of commercial and economic power, and, with the drying up of the reservoirs of royal patronage, Bombay also assumed new importance as a cultural centre. It was there that the fledgling Parsi Theatre companies were able to exploit the popular appeal of *Indar Sabha* to resurrect, if only for a few fantastic hours, the spirit of India's past glory.

NOTES

1. Ibrahim Yusuf, *Indar Sabha aur Indar Sabhaen* (Lucknow, 1980), Appendices 1 and 2, pp. 307-12.
2. Carla Petievich, 'From Golkunda to Lucknow: Transitions in Urdu Poetry', presented to the workshop, 'New Perspectives on Early Modern India', University of Virginia, October 1994, a revised version of which is published in this volume as 'Making "Manly" Poetry: The Construction of Urdu's "Golden Age"'.
3. In this analysis, I have had recourse primarily to the editions of *Indar Sabha* prepared by the following editors: Syed Masood Hasan Rizvi Adeeb, Massih-uz-Zama, Viqar Azeem, Ibrahim Yusuf (Lucknow, 1980), and Malik Hasan Akhtar (Lahore, 1990).
4. Sabz Pari uses the word *'aashiq'* which usually refers to a male lover, and thus Amanat underscores the fact that she is the active party in this relationship.
5. Amanat, *Indar Sabha*, ed. Malik Hasan Akhtar (Lahore, 1990), p. 97.
6. Ibid., p. 95.
7. Ibid., p. 88.
8. Abdul Halim Sharar, *Lucknow: The Last Phase of an Oriental Culture,* (London, 1975), pp. 141-2, and Amir Hasan, *Vanishing Culture of Lucknow* (Delhi, 1990), p. 85.
9. Frances Pritchett, *The Romance Tradition in Urdu: Adventures from the Dastan of Amir Hamzah* (New York, 1991). The dissemination of the *dastan* in India is difficult to chronicle because it was transmitted orally by professional story-tellers. Incidentally, the continuing popularity of this work is attested by my mother, Anwar Bano Rizvi, herself an accomplished poet, who enjoyed reading from *Amir Hamzah* all her life.
10. Mir Hasan, *Sihr-ul-Bayan* (Delhi, 1990).
11. Akhtar Amanat, ed., pp. 112 and 114.
12. Pandit Daya Shankar Naseem, *Masnavi Gulzar-e-Naseem,* ed. Rashid Hasan Khan (Delhi, rpt. 1992).
13. Kathryn Hansen, *Grounds for play: the nautanki theatre of North India* (Berkeley, 1992), pp. 144ff.

14. Akhtar Amanat, ed., p. 114.
15. Ibid., p. 105.
16. My translation of Abdul Halim Sharar, *Taqreez Diwan Fasghat* (Lucknow, 1925), pp. 493-5.
17. Hansen, op. cit., p. 74.
18. Mohammad Hasan, *Thought patterns of XIX century literature of North India* (Karachi, 1990), p. 16.
19. My translation of Mirza Rajab Ali Beg Suroor, *Fasana-e-Ibrat,* ed. Syed Masood Hasan Rizvi Adeeb (Lucknow, 1957).
20. Michael Edwardes, *The Orchid House: Splendours and Miseries of the Kingdom of Oudh, 1827-1857* (London, 1960), p. 161.
21. Akhtar Amanat, ed., p. 101.
22. For an interesting study of how this is manifested in south Indian poetry, see, *When God is a Customer: Telegu Courtesan Songs by Ksetrayya and Others,* eds. and trans. A.K. Ramanujan, Velcheru Narayana Rao and David Shulman (Berkeley, 1994).
23. Annemarie Schimmel, *Pain and Grace: a study of two mystical writers of eighteenth century Muslim India* (Leiden, 1976), pp. 4-5.
24. Akhtar Amanat, ed., p. 103.
25. Ibid., p. 126.
26. Pritchett, pp. 260-3.
27. For a detailed discussion of Awadh between the Mughal and British empires, including an analysis of how the political, social, and administrative control mechanisms changed hands, see Richard B. Barnett, *North India Between Empires: Awadh, the Mughals, and the British 1720-1801* (Berkeley, 1980).
28. Sharar, 1975, p. 65. For a vivid description of this annual event, see Mirza Rajab Ali Beg Suroor, *Fasana-e-Ibrat,* ed. Syed Masood Hasan Rizvi Adeeb, 1957, p. 103.
29. My translation of Mirza Rajab Ali Beg Suroor, *Fasana-e-Ibrat,* ed. Syed Masood Hasan Rizvi Adeeb (Lucknow, 1957), p. 103.
30. Hansen, p. 79.
31. Hansen, pp. 220ff.
32. Masih-uz-Zama, *Amanat ki Indar Sabha Muqadma,* pp. 27-8.
33. Hansen, p. 79.
34. J.R.I. Cole, *Roots of North Indian Shi'ism in Iran and Iraq: Religion and State in Awadh, 1722-1859* (Berkeley, 1988), pp. 101-19, and Sharar, pp. 215-17.
35. Sharar, 1975, p. 78, and Muhammad Sadiq, *A History of Urdu Literature,* (Delhi, 1984), pp. 165-7.
36. Edwardes, pp. 178ff.
37. Hansen, pp. 78-9.

Contributors

CATHERINE B. ASHER teaches art history at the University of Minnesota. Author of the volume, *Architecture of Mughal India* in the New Cambridge History of India series, she has also published numerous articles on medieval and early modern painting and architecture.

RICHARD B. BARNETT has taught at the University of Virginia since 1974. His first book is *North India Between Empires: Awadh, the Mughals, and the British*; he has written articles on early modern environmental history, politics, and gender.

SUSHIL CHAUDHURY is a senior member of the history department at Calcutta University. Author of *From Prosperity to Decline: Eighteenth Century Bengal,* he is widely cited for his many articles on the economic and political history of eastern India.

DAVID L. CURLEY teaches history at Western Washington University, and is the author of several papers on eighteenth-century Bengal, temple patronage, Vedic sacrifice, the merchant community, and literary activity.

DANIEL J. EHNBOM is director of the Center for South Asian Studies at the University of Virginia, where he teaches art history. A specialist on pre-Mughal and early Mughal painting and architecture, he has published widely-cited catalogues of personal collections and exhibits, and numerous articles.

STEWART N. GORDON specializes in Maratha history and recently completed the New Cambridge History of India volume, *The Marathas.* His collected articles have been published under the title, *Marathas, Marauders and State Formation in Eighteenth-Century India.* He is past president of Independent Scholars of South Asia, and past vice-president of the American Institute of Indian Studies.

EDWARD S. HAYNES is in the history department at Winthrop Uni-ver-sity. He has co-authored and authored several articles on land use in north India, as well as early modern Rajasthan, for major journals.

IQBAL HUSAIN is Reader Emeritus of the Centre for Advanced Study in History at Aligarh Muslim University, and the author of *The Rise and Decline of the Ruhela Chieftaincies in Eighteenth Century India* in addition to many articles on early modern north India.

IQBAL GHANI KHAN teaches history at Aligarh Muslim University in India. He has published numerous articles on technology in Mughal and early modern India, and is completing a monograph on technology in eighteenth-century Rohilkhand.

CARLA PETIEVICH teaches non-European literatures and South Asian and Islamic history at Montclair State University in New Jersey. She has written *Assembly of Rivals: Delhi, Lucknow and the Urdu Ghazal* and several articles on Urdu literature and Indo-Muslim cultural history.

AFROZ TAJ teaches Hindi and Urdu at Duke, North Carolina, and North Carolina State Universities. He has written numerous papers on literature, drama, and the media, and performs publicly as an artiste.